Where Is America Going?

Where Is America Going?

Marxism, MAGA & The Coming Revolution

by Caleb Maupin

CONTENTS

1. The Root of the Problem 1

*Where Do Profits Come From? – The Problem of
Overproduction – The Falling Rate of Profits – Where
Did The Computer Revolution Come From? – A Long-
Term Economic Crisis – How Can This Crisis Be Solved?
– Ensuring Economic Growth – A Government of Action*

2. Bonapartism & Fascism in the 21st Century 39

*The Road to 2008 – Napoleon's Nephew, The First Bonapartist
– Bonapartism in the United States – Bonapartism Case Study:
Nazi Germany – There is no "fascist ideology" or aesthetic – The
Nazis in Power – Bonapartism Case Study: Roosevelt's America
– Roosevelt's Worldview – The Difference Between Roosevelt-ism
and Nazism – Fascist Economics in the 21st Century – Bringing
Depopulation Home – The Distortion of Marxism – Re-
inventing Anti-Racism – The Proposed High Tech Dark Ages*

3. Counter Gangs and Revolutionaries 146

*The Society of December 10th – The Crisis of Marxism
– The Sorelian Critique of Marxist Organizing – The
Fascist Weltanschauung – Counter Gangs in Kenya and
Ireland – Fourth Generation Warfare – Brzezinski and the
Late Cold War – Alexander Parvus and the Bolsheviks –
Defeating the Kornilov Reaction – The New People's Study
Society – The Long March to Power – Top and Bottom*

*Organizing – Counter-gangs in America – 2008-2011: The
Left Failed – Black Lives Matter & Antifa – The Proud Boys
– BreadTube and Twitch-Streamer Leftism – Peterson-ism –
The Netflix Cult Obsession – A Country Without Ideology?*

4. The Coming Triumph of Illiberalism 250
*Philosophical Irrationalism – Where is Julius Caesar?
– The Last "Yankee and Cowboy War" – The New
Battleground – The Communist Party and the Anti-
Monopoly Coalition – The New Communist Movement
– The Boston Trap – The Great Retreat – The Bolivarian
Coalitions – Defending American Values – "Country Joe
and the Fish" – "Out of the Movement, to the Masses!"*

Appendix #1: Timeline 1978-1981 342

**Appendix 2: Three Socialist Movements and The Global
Crisis We Now Face** 359

Bibliography 402

1. The Root of the Problem

Where Do Profits Come From? – The Problem of Overproduction – The Falling Rate of Profits – Where Did The Computer Revolution Come From? – A Long-Term Economic Crisis – How Can This Crisis Be Solved? – Ensuring Economic Growth – A Government of Action

Let's for a moment imagine self-driving cars. We have been told this great technological achievement is not very far in the future. Soon driving may be a thing of the past and artificial intelligence, computer sensors, and other innovations may be applied in a way that makes automobile transportation completely automated.

In a rational society this would be a cause for a celebration. The amount of human labor that goes into driving could be expended elsewhere. We could move to a higher level of material abundance with one form of human labor no longer necessary. However, we do not live in a rational society. We live in a society governed by money and profits. In our highly irrational market-centered economy, self-driving cars would be a complete nightmare. It is a nightmare that is already hanging over us. As Andrew Yang, a New York businessman and a candidate in the 2020 Democratic Party primaries, told the *New York Times*: "All you need is self-driving cars to destabilize society... we're going to have a million truck drivers out of work who are 94 percent male, with an average level of education of high school or one year of college... We have five to 10 years before truckers lose their jobs and all hell breaks loose."

In the high-tech 21st century for-profit American economy, human beings live by selling their labor power to a boss. If someone is unable to sell their labor power they are rendered unemployed, and it becomes very difficult for them to feed, house and clothe themselves.

In a rational society, self-driving cars would be a good thing. However, in a profit-centered economy, they would lead to mass poverty and suffering.

Even in the good old days of the 1950s when the US economy was booming, you still had lots of hungry stomachs in Appalachia, the rural south and impoverished urban centers. Despite its once big prosperous middle class, America has always had an underclass of those who often populate the prisons and the lower ranks of the military. Among this permanent underclass there has always been a significant overrepresentation of African-Americans, Chicanos, and people of color, in addition to whites. The existence of the permanent layer of impoverished workers is something that US media has aimed to cover up. It is a strong argument against the image the US elite seek to present of a land of unending prosperity.

However, these are not normal times in America. The conditions that have always been present for some are now expanding to the bulk of the population. Sixty percent of American workers are living paycheck to paycheck. Food banks are overwhelmed with demand. The percentage of children living in households deemed to be "food insecure" by the US Department of Agriculture has risen. The suicide rate and the rate of deaths from alcohol poisoning and drug overdoses are rising.

The infrastructure of the United States, from power plants to water treatment facilitates, to roads and bridges, is falling apart. The life expectancy of Americans has decreased to the lowest point in 25 years.

Though the economic crisis is the basis, there is a wider cultural and spiritual crisis that has unfolded. There is a political crisis as the elite battle each other and seek to resolve the crisis with heavy handed force.

The root of this crisis can be found in economics, and this book will put forward primarily economic solutions. The economic foundations of our society must be reinvented so that all the human creativity, labor energy, and natural resources found in the vast territory of the country can be unleashed to once again create huge amounts of growth.

Where Do Profits Come From?

We don't live in a society where houses are built because people need shelter. We don't live in a society where food is grown, processed and packaged because people need to eat. We live in a society where the guiding force of production is profit. Houses are built so that landlords and banks can make money selling or renting them. Food is produced so agribusiness corporations and big box stores can make profits from sales.

Apple makes iPhones, Kraft makes cheese, and every other major corporation is operated on the basis of maximizing profit for its shareholders. Profit is in command of production. The banks, the major media, the means of transportation, the oil wells, all the major players in our economy operate so that those who own them can get a return on their investment. This is the definition of capitalism.

Currently there is a great deal of confusion about capitalism. Capitalism is not a term for "having money." Money existed in ancient Rome, Greece, and Medieval Europe. China was printing paper money before Marco Polo ever visited this thriving civilization. Capitalism is not synonymous with money, and many non-capitalist societies have money.

Capitalism is not synonymous with inequality either. There was inequality in feudalism. There was inequality in the slave civilizations of ancient Egypt, Greece and Rome. There is inequality in the socialist, non-capitalist societies that exist around the world today.

Capitalism, as Mao Zedong, the founder of the Chinese revolution defined it, is "profits in command." Friedrich Engels defined it saying "under capitalism, the means of production only function as preliminary transformation into capital." Karl Marx wrote about "the anarchy of production."

Capitalism is the economic system we live under in the United States, and it is defined as production organized to make profit for private owners.

As William Z. Foster, leader of the Great Steel Strike of 1919 in the USA explained: "The basic contradiction of capitalism, the source of all its weakness and of its final dissolution, is found in the fact that this system does not carry on production for the benefit of society as a whole but for the profit of a relatively small owning class. The great industries by which society must live are owned by private individuals who ruthlessly exploit the masses who work in these industries. Under capitalism production is regulated not by the needs of the masses but by whether or not the capitalist class can make a profit by such production; commodities are not produced primarily for use, but for profit."

So, in a capitalist economy where production is organized for the profit of private owners, how are these profits created? Where do profits come from? The truth is that profits can only come from human labor.

Imagine you had a capitalist who manufactured pens. The cost of the materials to go into the pens shall be represented by A. The cost of shipping the pens shall be represented as B. The labor cost of the employees he hires shall be represented by C. The final cost of the pen, which is paid by the consumer who purchases it shall be represented as D.

$$A + B + C = D$$

The cost of the pen is the combined total of the materials, shipping and labor costs.

But, there is a problem. How can the capitalist who sets this up make a profit, a return on his investment?

The owner cannot change how much the materials cost. A must remain untouched. The owner cannot change how much the shipping costs. B must remain untouched.

The profits that the capitalist makes can only be extracted from C. It is the value put into the pen by the labor costs from which the capitalist can extract his profits.

So, in order to ensure that profit is made from each pen, our equation must be corrected:

$$A + B + C1 + C2 = D$$

C1 represents what the worker is actually paid in wages. C2 represents the "surplus value" that is extracted by the employer as profit.

The Problem of Overproduction

This is how production is done under capitalism, and capitalism has always had a built-in problem. The cause of the boom bust cycle, in which the market goes up and down, is this.

$$C1 < D$$

The final cost of the pen is always significantly higher than the wages paid to the worker to produce it. If this is extrapolated throughout the entire economy, we see the problem that the wages paid out to workers who produce products is never enough to purchase the products they produce.

This is called the problem of *overproduction*. The worker can never buy back what he produces. The market inevitably always has more products than it can sell. Karl Marx wrote about this problem of "overproduction" in capitalism. John Maynard Keynes, another economist, spoke of "underconsumption."

The result of overproduction is what economists call *glut*. This is a situation where the market has so many goods, that prices drop, businesses close down, workers lose their jobs, and the economy experiences a downturn.

The problem of overproduction and glut is a problem that only exists in capitalism. In previous societies, people were homeless because there was not enough housing, and people were hungry because there was a shortage of food. But only under capitalism are people hungry because there is too much food. Only under capitalism are people homeless because there is too much housing.

Capitalism creates a problem which is deeply irrational, a problem of poverty amid plenty, or poverty created by abundance. The more wealth is created, the poorer people get.

This is expressed by a famous dialogue labeled "The Coal Miner's Riddle" that takes place between a father and son.

Son: Father, why is it so cold? Can we turn on the stove to keep warm?
Father: No, we don't have any coal to heat the stove.
Son: Father, why don't we have any coal to heat the stove and keep warm?
Father: Because I cannot afford it.
Son: Why can't you buy any coal?
Father: Because I lost my job at the coal mine. I was laid off. I am now unemployed.
Son: Why did you lose your job at the coal mine?
Father: Because there is too much coal.

Production for profit will always have this built in problem of overproduction. In the US state of Missouri there is a cave where 1.4 billion pounds of cheese has been buried. Why does the US government purchase so much cheese, simply to bury it in a cave? Because this keeps the price of cheese and other dairy products from dropping. It is just one artificial mechanism among many created to deal with overproduction. The governments of the world have developed all kinds of mechanisms to attempt to abet the economic turbulence created by overproduction.

The US Federal Reserve bank, the various corporate subsidies that are distributed, the military industrial complex, the food stamps programs, the huge amounts of government spending on various projects, are all necessary to keep the capitalist economy churning along, despite the fact that the amount of wages paid out will never be enough to purchase the products.

Karl Marx wrote of this problem in 1848 when he published *The Communist Manifesto*. "It is enough to mention the commercial crises that by their periodical return put the existence of the entire bourgeois society on its trial, each time more threateningly. In these crises, a great part not only of the existing products, but also of the previously created productive forces, are periodically destroyed. In these crises, there breaks out an epidemic that, in all earlier epochs, would have seemed an absurdity — the epidemic of overproduction. Society suddenly finds itself put back into a state of

momentary barbarism; it appears as if a famine, a
universal war of devastation, had cut off the supply of
every means of subsistence; industry and commerce
seem to be destroyed; and why?" he wrote. "Because
there is too much civilization, too much means of
subsistence, too much industry, too much commerce.
The productive forces at the disposal of society no
longer tend to further the development of the conditions
of bourgeois property; on the contrary, they have
become too powerful for these conditions, by which
they are fettered, and so soon as they overcome these
fetters, they bring disorder into the whole of bourgeois
society, endanger the existence of bourgeois property.
The conditions of bourgeois society are too narrow to
comprise the wealth created by them."

Marx's close collaborator, Friedrich Engels, explained
it this way: "As a matter of fact, since 1825, when the
first general crisis broke out, the whole industrial and
commercial world, production and exchange among
all civilized peoples and their more or less barbaric
hangers-on, are thrown out of joint about once every 10
years. Commerce is at a stand-still, the markets are
glutted, products accumulate, as multitudinous as they
are unsaleable, hard cash disappears, credit vanishes,
factories are closed, the mass of the workers are in want
of the means of subsistence, because they have produced
too much of the means of subsistence; bankruptcy
follows upon bankruptcy, execution upon execution.
The stagnation lasts for years; productive forces and

products are wasted and destroyed wholesale, until the accumulated mass of commodities finally filters off, more or less depreciated in value, until production and exchange gradually begin to move again. Little by little, the pace quickens. It becomes a trot. The industrial trot breaks into a canter, the canter in turn grows into the headlong gallop of a perfect steeplechase of industry, commercial credit, and speculation, which finally, after breakneck leaps, ends where it began — in the ditch of a crisis. And so over and over again."

Explaining the roots of this problem, Engels wrote "Money, the means of circulation, becomes a hindrance to circulation. All the laws of production and circulation of commodities are turned upside down. The economic collision has reached its apogee. *The mode of production is in rebellion against the mode of exchange...* The whole mechanism of the capitalist mode of production breaks down under the pressure of the productive forces, its own creations. It is no longer able to turn all this mass of means of production into capital. They lie fallow, and for that very reason the industrial reserve army must also lie fallow. Means of production, means of subsistence, available laborers, all the elements of production and of general wealth, are present in abundance. But "abundance becomes the source of distress and want" (Fourier), because it is the very thing that prevents the transformation of the means of production and subsistence into capital. For in capitalistic society, the means of production can only function when they have undergone a preliminary transformation into capital, into the means of exploiting human labor-power. The necessity of this transformation into capital of the means of production and subsistence stands like a ghost between these and the workers. It alone prevents the coming together of the material and personal levers of production; it alone forbids the means of production to function, the workers to work and live."

William Z. Foster explained it this way: "naturally a worker getting a wage of three to five dollars a day cannot buy back the ten to twenty or more dollars' worth of commodities he has produced. This gap between his producing and buying powers widens by the constant increase in the workers' productive capacity through machinery and the speed-up and also by the lowering of their standards of living… The capitalists waste huge masses of these stolen commodities through luxurious living, by the creation of hordes of parasitic occupations, by immense military establishments and wars. They seek to dispose of them by export trade. But the surpluses are not exhausted by these means. There is an inevitable tendency to glut the market with unsaleable commodities. Even though, as now, the millions of producers, who make up the bulk of the population, may actually starve and die for want of the barest necessities of life, the market suffers from over-production."

The Falling Rate of Profits

However, the constantly existing problem of overproduction gets worse in certain periods.

The capitalist wants to sell as many products as possible, and at the same time, he wants to pay as little in wages as he can. The capitalist is competing with other capitalists, and he is motivated to make the highest amount of profit by selling the most products.

One of the main ways a capitalist can increase the amount of profit he makes by selling products is to reduce labor costs. Replacing workers with machines makes it cheaper to produce products. The less and less workers that are hired, the more profits the capitalist can make.

But this also presents a new problem. Let's revisit our equation.

$$A + B + C = D$$

$$A + B + C1 + C2 = D$$

In our equation C represents the value put into the product by the labor of the worker. As we can see, the profit of the capitalist is extracted by cutting into this value. The wages the worker receives are C1 and the capitalist profits are represented by C2.

As the capitalist reduces labor costs by replacing workers with machines, he cuts into his own profits. The cost of the machines that replace workers are unchanging. He can only make profits from human labor.

As the percentage of D, the final cost of the product that is input by C, human labor, goes down, C2 must also go down. The more efficient production becomes, the amount of profit that the capitalist can make on each product decreases.

Because the capitalist is making less and less profits per item he produces, with his rate of profit decreasing, he is incentivized to produce more and more to make up for the losses. The already existing problem of overproduction becomes compounded by this problem which is called *The Tendency of the Rate of Profit to Fall* or *The Falling Rate of Profit*.

With workers being paid less and less as their place at the assembly line decreases, their ability to buy products decreases. With the capitalist seeing the rate of profit he makes on each product going down, his drive to produce and sell more and more products in order to maintain his profits increases.

This all leads to a situation where the market is glutted with products that cannot be sold. The worker cannot afford to buy them, and the capitalist is driven to produce more and more than ever because the amount of profit he makes on each item has decreased.

In his book *The Future is Up To Us,* Nelson Peery asked the question: what does robotics demand? "The robots demand that their production be given away because there is no value to their production. What makes revolution absolutely inevitable is that we have a society based upon the creation of value and production that is increasingly more valueless. What is value? Value is the exchange relationship between things. This cup is worth so many tape recorders or this pair of shoes is worth so many marbles. It is the relationship between things. Thus, if one robot is producing cups and another robot is producing tape recorders how do you equate them? If a human being makes a cup and a human being makes a tape recorder you can equate their relationship by how much labor time went into making the cup and how much labor time went into making the tape recorder. You can establish how many cups are worth by how many tape recorders. But if a robot makes them how do you then establish a value relationship between them? I don't think you can. Robots can make cars, but they can't buy them. Since production is increasingly carried on without human labor, without creating value, such production cannot be distributed with money. Money expresses value. Expended labor time is the basis of exchange and it is represented by money. If the worker doesn't work anymore and the robot creates the commodities how is it possible to sell them? You cannot sell them, and if you don't sell them how are you going to distribute them?"

In his book *High Tech, Low Pay*, the Marxist writer Sam Marcy observed the same problem: "Profit does not come from machinery itself. It is the labor of a worker… Workers produce a greater value than they receive back in wages, and it is the unpaid portion of their labor that produces surplus value. But a robot is not a worker. A robot is fixed or constant capital, which does not produce profit. Only unpaid human labor produces profit."

Marcy goes on to explain: "...the individual capitalists are driven to substitute labor-saving machinery for workers because it gives them a competitive advantage. For a certain period, the capitalist who is able to utilize the new technology and lower the unit cost of his product can actually enjoy a greater profit because the market reflects a generalized cost still based on the old technology. Eventually, however, the new technology itself becomes generalized and the rate of profit falls. The advantage to a higher composition of constant capital is always temporary. Moreover, it spurs on destructive competition, in which much equipment that could still be socially useful is made prematurely obsolete. In order to compensate for the falling rate of profit, the owners are forced to increase the volume of profit. This can only be done by further increasing production.... Much of the economic literature deals with the displacement of jobs as the result of the introduction of high technology, but it does not deal with the decline in the rate of profit from the long-range point of view. Technology is a double-edged weapon. Furthermore, automation does not solve the problem of the capitalist contradiction that leads to economic crisis. On the contrary, it exacerbates it precisely because of the decline in the rate of profit. High technology does not produce high profits. It increases the productivity of labor, but decreases the proportion of labor used in production in relation to the amount of fixed capital."

Where Did The Computer Revolution Come From?

If you can understand that human labor creates all value, and how in a capitalist economy this leads to the problem of overproduction which is then compounded by the tendency of the falling rate of profit, you can understand the crisis we are in as a civilization.

In 2014 many American moviegoers were entertained by a film called *The Imitation Game*. This was a historical drama portraying a true story about how a brilliant mathematician named Alan Turing was utilized by the British government during the Second World War to create an elaborate decoding machine. This decoding machine laid the basis for much of what has been described as the computer revolution.

The film focused on Turing being unrecognized for his genius and tragically committing suicide after being forced to take medication intended to cure his homosexuality. Many have noted that the symbol of one of the biggest computer corporations of today, may actually have been some kind of demented inside joke about the fact that Turing committed suicide by eating an apple he dipped in cyanide.

During the Cold War, the United States and the Soviet Union invested in advancing computer technology. In 1970 Zbigniew Brzezinski, a Cold War strategist based at Columbia University composed a book entitled *Between Two Ages: America Role in the Technetronic Era.* In the book, he argued that the "New Left" of anti-war and civil rights protesters in the United States did not pose a danger of overthrowing western capitalism. He pointed out that the various Communist groups had no real base among the population, and that the rise in protests was not so much a revolutionary movement as it was a response to changes in the culture brought on by information technology. With more access to information people in the United States and across the world were questioning old customs and habits. The way people interacted with authority and tradition was being renegotiated and many young people felt stifled by "Cold War conformity" and wanted more social liberalism.

Cold War Strategist Zbigniew Brzezinski developed the strategy of putting the United States at the center of the information revolution.

Brzezinski argued that rather than fighting the New Left as the Nixon administration had done, the United States should embrace this wave of liberalism and rebellion wrought by the information technology. He argued that putting the United States at the center of the information technological revolution could "Americanize" the world. The wave of cultural confusion and anti-authoritarianism that information technology created could be utilized to sow dissent and destabilize the Soviet Union and the Communist countries. With control of media, art, and culture, the United States could push its system of free market capitalism and its values of radical individualism to a position of dominance in the world.

Brzezinski went on to establish the Trilateral Commission, a think tank he directed along with Henry Kissinger. This strategy of using information technology to secure US dominance became highly respected and accepted among the Council on Foreign Relations and the US intelligence apparatus. The so-called "Deep State" began engaging in covert activities to ensure that the United States came out ahead in the computer revolution. Corporations like IBM, Apple, Microsoft and eventually Google, Facebook, Twitter and Amazon were created due to covert, and now admitted, support from the intelligence agencies. Money from the US Central Intelligence Agency, the National Security Agency, the Department of Treasury, and other shadowy and unseen wings of the US government provided loans and other forms of assistance to create what is now called Silicon Valley. California became the center of the Computer Revolution.

The Soviet Union had its fair share of successes when it came to computer technology. The country launched the first spacecraft, the Sputnik satellite, and launched the first man into outer space. In 1957 Soviet engineer Leonid Ivanovich Kupriyanovich patented the first mobile phone. However, the Soviet Union had begun its process of rapid industrialization in 1928, and prior to that it had been a non-industrialized agrarian society. The USSR simply did not have anywhere near the resources the United States had in order to invest in the computer revolution.

While western countries freely adopted Soviet technology and inventions like LED lights, the NATO countries created the *Coordinating Committee for Multilateral Export Controls*. The *New York Times* described the treaty as "organized to ensure that strategic technology, such as computers, machine tools and microelectronics items that could be used for weapons and other military applications, did not fall into the hands of the Soviet Union." The Soviet Union went as far as manufacturing its own home computer system in 1985, the Elektronika BK-0010. Regardless, the technology embargoes and lack of resources enabled the United States to sit at the center of the global technology revolution.

Ironically, this victory for western capitalism was not generated by the market. If Brzezinski had not reoriented the deep state, and the intelligence apparatus had not poured its resources and efforts into creating massive computer corporations, the market would never have enabled the US to win the technology war. The very methods that western capitalism used to "win" over Communism involved strategic central planning, not market chaos.

A Long-Term Economic Crisis

But regardless, we now live amid a huge leap in technology. Years ago thousands of people worked in factories that produced books called book binderies. Now a single book with a press of a button can be produced by a single person. Short order cooks are becoming a thing of the past, along with assembly line workers of all kinds. Computers can trade stocks more effectively than humans can. Artificial intelligence and other breakthroughs are rendering human beings more and more irrelevant in the process of production.

However, it is still from the wages paid out to workers that consumers derive their purchasing power. Furthermore, it is still only human labor that can generate profits for the capitalist. The built-in laws of capitalism have exploded into a long term crisis of overproduction and falling profits. The huge monopolies that dominate the global market in the 21st century have gotten so good at producing goods that the world is now facing the greatest crisis of poverty amid plenty yet to be seen. The technological leaps have created a deep, systemic crisis of capitalism.

Marxist writer Fred Goldstein explained in 2013: "Capitalist overproduction always causes these recessions. Production under capitalism expands very rapidly so long as there are markets. This is because of the laws of capitalist competition. The capitalists are in a permanent race to out-produce each other, to outsell each other and to capture the markets from each other as each wants to gain the most profit. This competition drives the system. But they fight each other by racing to lower wages, increase production and use technology to get rid of workers. So while production expands at a rapid pace under capitalism during a boom period, the income of the masses grows at a snail's pace, very, very gradually, or actually declines. Soon, the bosses find that they cannot sell their goods at a profit. So they shut down businesses and cut back workers' hours; the crisis of unemployment begins. This is the law of capitalism. It cannot operate in any other way. This is the profit system at work. This is called the boom-and-bust cycle. We say that capitalism is at a dead end because the traditional boom-and-bust cycle is over. There is no boom. It was the boom, or greatly increased production, that put workers back to work during past recoveries. But once the system loses the ability to bounce back and move forward and upward in production and services, a permanent crisis sets in for the workers and the oppressed."

He went on: "They have created a technological machine that is so productive and a low-wage workforce that is so impoverished, that as soon as they increase production at a rapid rate, the system fails. People cannot buy the commodities produced. Inventories back up and no hiring goes on at all or else layoffs take place. Capitalist productivity is strangling capitalist production."

The capitalism of today, which is leading toward a more and more intense economic and social crisis, is not the capitalism of mere factory owners and wage workers. It is what Lenin called *Imperialism: The Highest Stage of Capitalism*. It is the rule of the world by trusts, cartels and syndicates, huge monopolies based in Wall Street and London. The Silicon Valley tech giants were preceded by the super major oil corporations and their respective houses of finance as the dominant axis within this global apparatus. As Lenin explained, the imperialist stage of capitalism is defined by financiers holding back and preventing economic development around the world in order to ensure their monopoly, carving out spheres of influence, and captive markets in the colonized world.

The globalist nature of 21st Century capitalism recalls the words of British Fascist Oswald Mosley who bemoaned this emerging setup in the post-war years. The racist demagogue told his English audience in the early 1960s: "Everyone one of us in this hall was old enough to see before the war, every one of you knows what happened. How the financial forces in the thirties went into these backward countries, into India within the Empire, into Hong Kong, into Japan, into China, and exploited these peoples to produce cheap sweated goods which ruined the great industries of Britain and of Europe; which put Lancashire out of business in the cotton trade, Yorkshire out of business in the woolen trade, and these poor devils were exploited for a wage of a few shillings a week, for what purpose? To enable the city of London and Wall Street New York to make fatter profits. That is why it was done. That was the whole purpose… and all these countries have been exploited, thrown and tossed aside by finance and now becoming the victims of communism, so finance seeks fresh fields of exploitation. So, where do they turn when the old people are exhausted, when many a poor laborer has died of consumption and of other horrible diseases in their sweatshops, when they've exhausted fields of exploitation, where do they turn now? New pastures, new forests, fresh virgin lands… and these poor devils are going to be sweated and exploited in Africa, like the other poor devils in China, India and Japan, a great new field for sweatshops to be opened up, so that these new industries we are creating in Britain today can be destroyed as the old industries were. Simplified, rationalized machinery with a few white surveyors and the masses of cheap colored labor torn off the land and taken into the sweatshops to work and labor and cough their guts out with tuberculosis. Is that worthy of Britain? Is that the future of Europe? And is this competition to be organized within our European brotherhood? Bringing these sweat fields in Africa into our European civilization so that the financial power in one European country can be used against the financial power in another? All the great financial power of the world now shifted from the city of London to Wall Street New York who shall be able on the mass of money of wealth and of power it brings to it again and again to exert its influence in politics, until as you see today, it is childish nonsense to say that British government rules Britain. It's nothing to do with the British government or the British people. The government of the world is the financial government, the power of money and of money alone."

During the 20th Century, the western capitalist home countries were kept stable by a layer of well-paid industrial workers who were loyal to their bosses. This "aristocracy of labor" was made up of working class people who saw their living standards increase along with the ascendency of the big corporations. This bought their loyalty and made them supportive of wars and defenders of the status quo.

However, in the 21st Century, the "aristocracy of labor" is being systematically destroyed. The once-prosperous industrial cities have been reduced to ghost towns dotted with empty foreclosed homes. America's once booming suburbs have become centers of opioid addiction, human trafficking, bitter decaying elderly people, and hopeless angry youth.

As the productive economy comes to a halt amid a long-term crisis of overproduction, the primary methods of profiteering among the already rich have become what some describe as "destructive accumulation." Prisons for profit, military contracting, an epidemic of addiction caused by doctors being pushed to over-prescribe dangerous pain-killers. The public education system is being auctioned off to the highest bidder with "school choice" charter schools where private corporations make money from maintaining the youth. Municipalities in 27 different US states have become so indebted and bankrupt that they began un-paving roads, replacing paved roads with gravel dirt roads, saving money from the cost of maintaining them.

The physical economy of the United States lays in ruin. The system has become cannibalistic to keep profits flowing when very little value is being created. This state of affairs cannot continue indefinitely without some kind of big dramatic fallout or correction.

We should be reminded of how Karl Marx described how crises of overproduction are resolved: "And how does the bourgeoisie get over these crises? On the one hand by enforced destruction of a mass of productive forces; on the other, by the conquest of new markets, and by the more thorough exploitation of the old ones.

That is to say, by paving the way for more extensive and more destructive crises, and by diminishing the means whereby crises are prevented."

How Can This Crisis Be Solved?

The resolution of the long term economic crisis facing western capitalist countries can be found in abolishing the system of production for profit. To put it simply, a government of action that fights for working families must mobilize the population to enforce rational planning and control over the means of production. The economy must be reinvented in order to function according to a central plan rather than merely the short-term gain of private owners.

An economy where production is no longer dictated to profit, but rather on the basis of an overall plan is called *socialism*. Much like the word "capitalism" this term has also been subjected to a huge amount of confusion and misunderstanding.

All capitalist economies have somewhat of a state sector. Capitalist societies have roads paved by the government. The US constitution mandates the creation of a postal service that is publicly owned, and not accountable to any individual owner. From the time of Adam Smith, even most ardent free marketeers understood that some level of public works and state facilitation was necessary for the market to function. It is only since the 1970s and the rise of Neoliberal economic delusions that anyone has been as confused as to see the Post Office, the US military or the private Federal Reserve Bank as "socialism."

Socialism is not synonymous with government or state ownership. In Post-WW2 Britain almost every major industry was nationalized. This was done so they could be rebuilt at the expense of the taxpayer in order to facilitate the restoration and functioning of British imperialism, and the economic dominance of British bankers on the global stage. Saudi Arabia maintains a heavily state controlled economy, but though the government is heavily involved the economy functions to maximize profits for the ruling family and its various cronies. Singapore also has a heavily state-run economy, but it is run to generate profits for the ruling families.

Socialism is also not synonymous with taxation or "redistribution of wealth." This goes on, to some degree or other, in all capitalist societies. Societies that maintain a bigger welfare state may have higher tax rates than societies that maintain a more libertarian approach, but neither is "more socialist" or "more capitalist" than the other. The Norwegian welfare states that currently face dramatic confusion from the inflow of refugees, and their alliance with the NATO anti-Russia crusade, are not "socialist" countries.

Capitalism is production for profit, and socialism is an economy where profits are not in command. Socialism emerged in the 20th century as country after country broke free from the domination of western imperialism and seized control of its industries and natural resources. Socialism in the 20th Century involved popular governments that emerged in explosive revolutionary upsurges mobilizing the population to industrialize, electrify and modernize deeply impoverished countries.

Ensuring Economic Growth

The notion that "socialism does not work" should seem laughable to anyone familiar with basic economic history. The Russian empire was an impoverished "prison house of nations" with massive illiteracy, a low life expectancy, and primitive agrarian economy when the Bolsheviks took power in 1917. By 1936 it was a fully industrialized superpower that produced more steel than any other country on earth, and had the biggest hydro-electrical facility ever constructed at that time, the Great Dnieper Dam.

The Five Year Economic Plan launched under the leadership of Joseph Stalin in 1928 transformed the lives of many millions of people. A huge modern educational system was created. Illiteracy was wiped out. Modern universities sprung up. Great achievements in athletics and the arts were carried out. The entire planet was in awe of the explosion of economic growth that socialist central planning was achieving in a once impoverished country. Writing for *The Nation* in 1931, Louis Fischer wrote: "The Soviet frontier is like a charmed circle which the world economic crisis cannot cross. While banks crash, while production falls and trade languishes abroad, the Soviet Union continues in an orgy of construction and national development. The scale and speed of its progress are unprecedented." American Radio personality Frazier Hunt, writing for *The New York American* in 1931, emphasized how dramatic the Soviet Union's explosion of economic growth really was. He said, "Japan, westernizing and industrializing itself 50 years ago, was doing child's play compared to what the Soviet Union is doing today… Already, almost overnight, the USSR has become an industrial country."

The problems of the Soviet Union set in after the initial wave of industrialization, and during the 1970s and 80s the country was unable to adjust its socialist economic model due to changing circumstances. The inability to adjust led to the political crisis that saw the Soviet Union's demise. China, on the other hand, was able to rapidly adjust its socialist economic system, and starting in 1978 with the "reform and opening up" China began speeding forward with five year economic plans, state run banks and industries, and a Marxist-Leninist party in command of the economy.

In a report from the World Bank published on April 1, 2022 Manuela V. Ferro, World Bank Vice President for East Asia and Pacific is quoted as saying: "China's poverty reduction story is a story of persistent growth through economic transformation." The report adds "Over the past 40 years, the number of people in China with incomes below $1.90 per day — the International

China's rapid growth is largely a result of its state-run economy organized to serve the purpose of building socialism with Chinese characteristics.

Poverty Line as defined by the World Bank to track global extreme poverty — has fallen by close to 800 million. With this, China has contributed close to three-quarters of the global reduction in the number of people living in extreme poverty. At China's current national poverty line, the number of poor fell by 770 million over the same period."

Likewise, the World Economic Forum published an article on September 11th, 2018 entitled "The Story of Vietnam's Economic Miracle." The article observed "a mere 30 years ago the country was one of the poorest in the world." The article went on: "Today, Vietnam is one of the stars of the emerging markets universe. Its economic growth of 6-7% rivals China, and its exports are worth as much as the total value of its GDP."

Observing the source of Vietnam's strength, the World Economic Forum noted: "Vietnam has invested heavily in human and physical capital, predominantly through public investments… Vietnam invested a lot in its human capital and infrastructure. Facing a rapidly growing population - it stands at 95 million today, half of whom are under 35, and up from 60 million in 1986 — Vietnam made large public investments in primary education. This was necessary as a growing population also means a growing need for jobs. But Vietnam also invested heavily in infrastructure, ensuring cheap mass access to the internet. The Fourth Industrial Revolution is knocking on Southeast Asia's door, and having a sound IT infrastructure in place is essential preparation. Those investments paid off. Armed with the necessary infrastructure and with market-friendly policies in place, Vietnam became a hub for foreign investment and manufacturing in Southeast Asia… Since 2010, Vietnam's GDP growth has been at least 5% per year, and in 2017 it peaked at 6.8%. With such rapid economic growth, the country grew from one of the poorest countries in the world to a comfortably middle-income one. Whereas its GDP per capita was barely $230 in 1985, it was more than ten times that in 2017 ($2,343). Corrected for purchasing power, it stands even higher, at over $6,000."

There is certainly a role for private enterprise in a socialist economy. But profits and markets are not in control, a popular government is. The private enterprises are not free to function according to market logic, but guided and controlled by state subsidies and oversight.

The socialist economy of Nicaragua under the leadership of the Sandinistas had astounding successes. Between 2005-2014, poverty in Nicaragua has decreased by 30% according to the Wall Street Journal. GDP rose by 36% between 2007 and 2016. The shining success of the government that rules under the slogan "Christianity, Socialism and Solidarity" has been its micro-entrepreneurship program which subsidizes low-income Nicaraguans to start individual businesses or worker cooperatives.

The socialist government of Evo Morales in Bolivia oversaw similar explosions of growth, with the highest GDP expansion in South America for many years. A 2019 article from *The Nation* observed: "During the Morales era, the economy has grown at twice the rate of the Latin American average, inflation has been stable, the government has amassed substantial savings, and an enterprising and optimistic indigenous middle class has emerged."

The article described the policies through which the popular anti-imperialist government enabled this growth: "Morales passed a law seizing tens of thousands of square miles of land deemed unproductive or illegally held, and redistributed it to landless peasants. He placed the natural gas, oil, telecommunications and electricity industries under state control. And he continually raised the minimum wage, which has tripled since he entered office. Morales also dramatically increased social spending. He poured money into building roads, schools, and hospitals, an expansion of infrastructure that was particularly transformative in the countryside. And he established modest but deeply popular cash transfer programs: a universal non-contributory pension system for Bolivians over the age of 60; assistance to households with elementary school–aged children who can demonstrate their children are attending school; and funds for pregnant women or mothers with children under the age of 2 without health insurance."

The living conditions of Cubans are far superior to those of Haitians, Dominicans, or Jamaicans in terms of access to healthcare, education and employment. The Communist Party of Cuba presides over a socialist economy and has constructed what Ban Ki Moon calls the greatest medical school in the world.

Socialism in Libya built the world's largest irrigation system, the Great Man-Made River. Under Gaddafi's leadership Libya had the highest life expectancy on the African continent, and experienced huge amounts of economic growth.

Socialism constructed the massive Aswan Dam, the biggest hydroelectric power plant in the Middle East, which fully electrified Egypt. Ba'ath Socialism brought running water, electricity and literacy to Syria.

When the chaos of the market, the anarchy of production is overcome, economic growth is no longer restrained. With socialist central planning human creativity and the drive to expand are no longer held back. The problems inherent in production organized for profit are overcome.

A Government of Action

The solution to the crisis in the United States can best be summarized with the slogan "We Need A Government of Action to Fight for Working Families." The state must step in and control the centers of economic power, forcing production to move ahead and wealth to increase. The invisible hand must be pushed aside, and a state that enacts the popular will must assert itself over the means of production.

If a government came to power in Washington DC and carried out the following four steps, the US economy would regenerate rapidly:

- **A Mass Mobilization to Rebuild The Country.** A government of action would hire millions of unemployed or under-employed people and put them to work rebuilding the country. This would mean a mobilization by the state to build new hospitals, power plants, water treatment facilities, schools, universities, high-tech research facilities, and a high speed railway.

- **Public Ownership of Natural Resources.** A government of action would institute public control over natural resources. The wealth generated from America's oil, natural gas, coal, and timber would go into the public budget rather than into the pockets of private owners. This would ensure that the state had enough resources to fund its efforts, stimulate the economy, oversee growth and lift the burden of taxation from the population.

- **Centralization and Public Control of Banking & Credit.** A government of action would centralize credit and banking in the hands of the state, lending money strategically at a state, federal and local level. Credit would be assigned based on enacting an overall economic vision and ensuring long-term growth rather than simply the profits of private lenders. The massive debt that hangs over the US economy as a curse must be canceled and the "debt industry" forcibly broken up by the state.

- **An Economic Bill of Rights.** A government of action could then implement an economic bill of rights, ensuring the population the right to jobs, housing, education, and healthcare. The population would be maintained for the good of the country overall. People would be seen as assets to the society, capable of creating wealth and making the country stronger. Thus, it would be in society's interest to make sure the population is healthy, well-educated, and fully utilized for the good of the country overall.

These actions would result in a rise in wages and the near elimination of unemployment. Small businesses would flourish. Regions that are struggling and stagnating would become renewed and filled with prosperity and hope.

These four steps are within the reach of the US government. Governments across the planet have carried out similar endeavors. However, these four steps erode the property rights of wealthy corporations. The right of private bankers to lend money at interest would be eradicated. The oil and natural gas wells, the coal mines, and other resources that are the private corporations property would be seized by the public. The state would become the primary employer, with an industrial and construction army being mobilized to regenerate the economy. Taxes would decrease. Private property and personal property would still exist on a massive scale. Inequality of income would certainly remain a reality.

None of these steps would be the "socialist nightmare" envisioned by right-wingers, in fact they would be the opposite. These steps would result in "making America great again" more effectively than anything Trump has so far put forward. A wall along the border, protectionism in the form of tariffs and renegotiated trade deals, renewed emphasis on national sovereignty against globalism, would all be almost meaningless compared to these four dramatic steps.

In order to enact these four steps a government would need to have massive public support, and this support could not come in the form of silent approval. A well-organized and awakened public would have to back the efforts of popular leaders to enact these policies.

Though it seems far off, the conditions in the United States for such a "Government of Action" to emerge are ripening. Divisions among the elite are intensifying and conditions are worsening for the broad masses. The remainder of this book will focus on how a "Government of Action" could emerge as the crisis, rooted in the built-in flaws of capitalism, becomes more intense.

2. Bonapartism & Fascism in the 21st Century

The Road to 2008 – Napoleon's Nephew, The First Bonapartist – Bonapartism in the United States – Bonapartism Case Study: Nazi Germany – There is no "fascist ideology" or aesthetic – The Nazis in Power – Bonapartism Case Study: Roosevelt's America – Roosevelt's Worldview – The Difference Between Rooseveltism and Nazism – Fascist Economics in the 21st Century – Bringing Depopulation Home – The Distortion of Marxism – Re-inventing Anti-Racism – The Proposed High Tech Dark Ages

The deep crisis of overproduction and falling rates of profit which has gripped the global economic apparatus centered around Wall Street and London has forced the ruling class to strain itself and scramble for new methods of stabilizing society. So far, these methods have largely been unsuccessful and the crisis continues.

The Road to 2008

When the 2008 financial crash hit the United States, it became very apparent that the old methods of managing both the economy and the public were no longer sufficient. All the smartest economists had been unable to prevent a dramatic Wall Street crash. Since 2008, the US has been spinning from political crisis to political crisis, with unrest continuing to break out among the population, as all the smartest managers of the masses have been unable to restore domestic tranquility.

Alan Greenspan, a committed follower and personal protege of Ayn Rand, had been running the US Federal Reserve since the 1980s. He had pushed deregulation of lending in accordance with his overall free market, libertarian perspective. However, as the 21st Century rolled around, Greenspan escalated his deregulatory push for non-ideological reasons. The reality was that the spending power of the US public was decreasing.

The good paying industrial jobs had been eliminated by technology and off-shoring. Technology was replacing human labor at the assembly line. The problem of overproduction was becoming a daily reality in the aftermath of the 90s "dot com boom." A US public that had seen its living standards go down, while the rate of household debt went up, couldn't afford to keep purchasing things.

After the September 11th terrorist attacks, President George W. Bush urged Americans, who wanted to help the country, to "go out and shop." His call was echoed by all the top CEOs and major media outlets. Alan Greenspan pushed for deregulation of credit card lending practices to make sure this spending could be facilitated. Greenspan also pushed the deregulation of mortgage lenders, in order to ensure that Americans could keep buying homes and to encourage Americans to take out second mortgages on homes they already owned in order to deal with living expenses.

The result was a wave of home foreclosures across the Midwest, California, and much of the country. Soon 'the housing bubble burst" and the rest is history. The US economy has largely never recovered. The lost jobs have never returned. The family owned home is becoming a thing of the past. The once prosperous

US President George W. Bush's unilateral invasion of Iraq drove up oil prices, making lots of profits for Wall Street, but also strengthening anti-imperialist forces in Russia, Iran, Libya and Venezuela.

suburbs of the American heartland are financially devastated. The next generation languishes in a life of low wage, short term service sector jobs, and household debt continues rising.

The economic crisis was compounded by the fact that internationally the forces of resistance to western capitalism had significantly rebounded during the first years of the 21st Century. George W. Bush's invasion of Iraq had driven a major oil producing state off the market and the oil prices had shot up to the highest in history. This wasn't just good for Chevron, BP, Shell and Exxon-Mobile. It was also good for Russia, Iran, and Venezuela.

Russia's president Vladimir Putin had restructured Russia's economy to be centered around state controlled oil and gas. The wave of state revenue that came from Bush's oil price hike enabled Putin to rebuild Russia's industrial base.

In the Republic of Venezuela, President Hugo Chavez used oil revenue to launch a continent wide anti-imperialist movement called Bolivarian Socialism. Soon Bolivia, Nicaragua, and Ecuador were onboard with a leftist mass movement that swept the hemisphere. A new brand of politics that mixed Marxism with Christianity and indigenous pride and heritage was reinventing the region, and China was pouring in as the foreign investor to help the process along.

The hardliners of Iran who took to heart the anti-capitalist and anti-imperialist goals of the Islamic

WHERE IS AMERICA GOING?

Revolution were brought back into power after Bush named Iran as one of the "Axis of Evil." In 2006, Hezbollah, the Iran-aligned Shia revolutionary movement of Lebanon, became the heroes of the entire Muslim world after inflicting a humiliating defeat to Israeli invaders. The Muslim allies of the USA, such as the Muslim Brotherhood and even some among the Saudi camp, had not appreciated Bush referring to the War on Terror as a "crusade." The anti-Islamic rhetoric of Bush's supporters in the American religious right alienated them further.

In light of the domestic economy crashing and the international forces of anti-imperialism riding high, Bush and the Neoconservatives were suddenly out of a job. Barack Hussein Obama swept into office in the hopes of restarting the US economy, improving US relations with Middle Eastern proxy fighters, as well as NATO allies. Obama was met with swift opposition from the Tea Party and other forces that wanted a more deregulated economic setup.

The dramatic battle that has been unfolding among the elite in the United States represents a process called "bonapartism" by scientific socialists. In hopes of resolving the crisis and stabilizing society, sections of the capitalist class are battling against each other for control of the state and the ability to use the state to take strong economic measures that cut into the profits of their rivals.

Napoleon's Nephew, The First Bonapartist

In 1851, Karl Marx was living in Paris and closely observing the political turmoil that resulted from a crisis of capitalism. Workers were on strike, unemployed and hungry people were rioting, and the military was in the streets attempting to prevent a total explosion of unrest. In June, Paris was shaken by a working class uprising. Marx wrote: "On the side of the Paris proletariat stood none but itself. More than three thousand insurgents were butchered after the victory, and fifteen thousand were deported without trial. With this defeat the proletariat passes into the background on the revolutionary stage. It attempts to press forward again on every occasion, as soon as the movement appears to make a fresh start, but with ever decreasing expenditure of strength and always slighter results."

Among the rich and powerful, two factions emerged. The factory owners wanted a heavy handed crackdown on the unrest. They sought to bring back the monarchy, restore the sanctity of religion, and get the broad masses of French workers to be less "uppity" by reinstating much of the traditional authoritarianism that had existed under feudalism, before the revolution. This conservative faction was called "the party of order." It was old money, aristocrats, and conservative military figures.

However, the more powerful finance capitalists had a different plan. They sought to harness some of the unrest in the streets and the nostalgia for the French

Revolution among the population, in order to bring in a government that would use the state to stabilize the economy and get growth going again. In opposition to the Party of Order, they formed the Society of December 10th. They tapped Louis Bonaparte, the nephew of French Emperor Napoleon Bonaparte. Declaring himself the new Emperor, Louis seized power with the backing of the military crowning himself Napoleon III.

Decades before, Napoleon Bonaparte had declared himself military dictator in November of 1799, bringing to an end the ten year period of political confusion and turmoil that came in the aftermath of the French Revolution. Napoleon had stabilized the country, using heavy handed military rule to enact reforms that lined up with the progressive sentiments of the enlightenment. The first Napoleon had called himself "the revolution in boots" and proceeded to march his "empire" across Europe.

In 1851, the hope on the part of France's finance capitalists was that Louis would do just as his uncle had done a generation earlier, and bring stability to the country by tapping into the ideals of the revolution and mobilizing the population. In his book *Market Elections*, Vince Copeland explains this tendency that Marx first described in 1852. Copeland writes: "The phenomenon —of calling upon one class against another and seeming to rise above class while serving the status quo —has been called *bonapartism* after Napoleon Bonaparte and his nephew Louis Bonaparte. The first Bonaparte was so all-powerful and seemed to concentrate all the political power so much in his own person that the feudal kings of Europe literally pushed one another aside to kiss his hands. This was before they ganged up with the British bourgeoisie to defeat him in 1815. Actually, Napoleon's tremendous political power flowed from the fact that with military means he could save the new bourgeoisie bankers from the political overthrow of the feudal aristocracy, while at the same time using the same means, he held down the revolutionary masses who were willing to fight feudalism —and the bankers —to the end. His power flowed from the fact that he employed huge armies of newly freed peasants to join with the serfs of old feudal Europe to overthrow their feudal masters in other countries, thus securing his own reputation as the ever-victorious general." Marx wrote of the two Napoleons "Hegel remarks somewhere that all great, world-historical facts and personages occur, as it were, twice. He has forgotten to add: the first time as tragedy, the second as farce."

Louis Bonaparte was a demagogue who engaged in all kinds of political stunts to gain popularity. He raffled off bars of gold and paid for impoverished French people to move to California during the 1849 Gold Rush. This charade was illegal under French law, but Bonaparte considered himself to be above the law and had sections of the military and mobs of desperately poor *lumpen proletarians* who marched behind him.

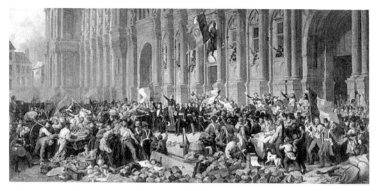

In the aftermath of the 1848 working class uprising in France, Louis Bonaparte began positioning himself to establish a military dictatorship to stabilize society.

Louis Bonaparte's political movement that openly flaunted the law was tolerated because it offered an alternative to the revolutionary socialist radicalism that was widespread among the population.

Louis Bonaparte's seizure of power in 1851 was necessitated by the fact that the widespread discussions and debates that resulted from having elections and competing political parties put the rule of the rich and powerful in danger. To bring order to society and stop the threat of working class uprisings, the capitalists needed to abolish the democratic institutions they themselves had created when overthrowing feudalism. Marx wrote: "What the bourgeoisie did not grasp, however, was the logical conclusion that its own parliamentary regime, its political rule in general, was now also bound to meet with the general verdict of condemnation as being socialist. As long as the rule of the bourgeois class had not been completely organized, as long as it had not acquired its pure political expression, the antagonism of the other classes likewise could not appear in its pure form, and where it did appear could not take the dangerous turn that transforms every struggle against the state power into a struggle against capital. If in every stirring of life in society it saw "tranquility" imperiled, how could it want to maintain at the head of society a regime of unrest, its own regime, the parliamentary regime, this regime that, according to the expression of one of its spokesmen, lives in struggle and by struggle? The parliamentary regime lives by discussion, how shall it forbid discussion? Every interest, every social institution, is here transformed into general ideas, debated as ideas; how shall any interest, any institution, sustain itself above thought and impose itself as an article of faith? The struggle of the orators on the platform evokes the struggle of the scribblers of the press; the debating club in parliament is necessarily supplemented by debating clubs in the salons and the bistros; the representatives, who constantly appeal to public opinion, give public opinion the right to speak its real mind in petitions. The parliamentary regime leaves everything to the decision of majorities; how shall the great majorities outside parliament not want to decide? When you play the fiddle at the top of the state, what else is to be expected but that those down below dance? Thus by now stigmatizing as "socialistic" what it had previously extolled as "liberal," the bourgeoisie confesses that its own interests dictate that it should be delivered from the danger of its own rule; that to restore tranquility in the country its bourgeois parliament must, first of all, be given its quietus; that to preserve its social power intact its political power must be broken; that the individual bourgeois can continue to exploit the other classes and to enjoy undisturbed property, family, religion, and order only on condition that their class be condemned along with the other classes to like political nullity; that in order to save its purse it must forfeit the crown, and the sword that is to safeguard it must at the same time be hung over its own head as a sword of Damocles."

Ironically, the very capitalist newspapers that had called for suppression of socialists and working class agitators, now screamed in outrage as Louis Bonaparte crushed their freedom of speech. Marx wrote on this irony as well: "the extra parliamentary mass of the bourgeoisie, on the other hand, by its servility toward the President, by its vilification of parliament, by its brutal maltreatment of its own press, invited Bonaparte to suppress and annihilate its speaking and writing section, its politicians and its literati, its platform and its press, so it would then be able to pursue its private affairs with full confidence in the protection of a strong and unrestricted government. It declared unequivocally that it longed to get rid of its own political rule in order to get rid of the troubles and dangers of ruling. And this extra parliamentary bourgeoisie, which had already rebelled against the purely parliamentary and literary struggle for the rule of its own class, and had betrayed the leaders of this struggle, now dares after the event to indict the proletariat for not having risen in a bloody struggle, a life-and-death struggle on its behalf!"

In order to stay in power, Louis Bonaparte's faction among the rich and powerful of France had to build up a base of support among the wider population. It entered an alliance with the small farmers, the labor unions, and various left-wing agitators who kept the spirit of the French Revolution alive. Small farmers constituted the biggest base of support for the new regime. Marx wrote: "And yet the state power is not suspended in the air. Bonaparte represented a class, and the most numerous class of French society at that, the small-holding peasants... The small-holding peasants form an enormous mass whose members live in similar conditions but without entering into manifold relations with each other. Their mode of production isolates them from one another instead of bringing them into mutual intercourse. The isolation is furthered by France's poor means of communication and the poverty of the peasants... They are therefore incapable of asserting their class interest in their own name, whether through a parliament or a convention. They cannot represent themselves, they must be represented. Their representative must at the same time appear as their master, as an authority over them, an unlimited governmental power which protects them from the other classes and sends them rain and sunshine from above. The political influence of the small-holding peasants, therefore, finds its final expression in the executive power which subordinates society to itself."

Louis Bonaparte formed an army of desperately poor people, criminals, intellectuals, and marginal elements of society called "The Society of December 10th." They poured into the streets to cheer him on as the French Army divisions that had previously occupied North Africa marched into Paris and arrested his political rivals on December 1st and 2nd of 1851. Over 300 people were killed in the political violence that followed in the next few days. First Bonaparte arrested the members of parliament from the "Party of Order" who opposed him, as well as others who spoke out publicly against his coup. Thousands of people were deported to prisons in France's colonial territories in Africa and South America. Many wealthy people had their property confiscated. The famous writer Victor Hugo was forced to flee the country. When the dust cleared on December 20th, Louis Bonaparte held a national referendum asking the public to vote on whether or not he should remain in power, and he won with over 7 million people casting their ballots in support of him. Once secured in power, Bonaparte declared the Second French Empire saying "Some people say the Empire is at war. I say the Empire is at peace... We have immense unplowed territories to cultivate; roads to open; ports to dig; rivers to be made navigable; canals to finish; a railway network to complete… We have ruins to repair, false gods to tear down, truths which we need to make triumph. This is how I see the Empire."

Marx observed the new authoritarian regime's springing up under the auspices of nostalgia for the French Revolution writing: "The Constitution, the National Assembly, the dynastic parties, the blue and the red republicans, the heroes of Africa, the thunder from the platform, the sheet lightning of the daily press, the entire literature, the political names and the intellectual reputations, the civil law and penal code, the liberté, égalité, fraternité and the second of May 1852—all have vanished like a phantasmagoria before the spell of a man whom even his enemies do not make out to be a magician. Universal suffrage seems to have survived only for a moment, in order that with its own hand it may make its last will and testament before the eyes of all the world and declare in the name of the people itself: Everything that exists has this much worth, that it will perish."

With his dictatorial power Louis Bonaparte worked to resolve the crisis of overproduction that had gripped the French economy and caused so much unrest. He created government-run factories and "national workshops" to hire unemployed people, and he used taxpayer money to create free hospitals for poor people to get medical care. He had the government build railways to stimulate the industries. He enacted a

12-hour workday to improve conditions for factory workers and increase employment.

Those who had opposed these reforms, most especially the conservative "Party of Order" had been forced to flee the country, if not arrested, imprisoned or outright killed during the coup. The monarchy had been the rallying point of many conservatives, so Bonaparte specifically worked to make sure the old King Louis-Phillipe's family could never be restored to power. The deposed royal family was banned from owning any property and all inheritance members of the monarchist family received was confiscated by the state.

Freedom of the press was gotten rid of, and newspapers were forced to have everything they wrote approved by government censors. The Ministry of Education reviewed university courses and vetted professors to make sure what they taught fit the goals of the government. Professors deemed to be monarchists or sympathetic to the Party of the Order, were fired. Marx wrote about the irony of the very bourgeois figures who brutally repressed the June proletarian uprising, now facing heavy handed government repression from Louis Bonaparte: "During the June days all classes and parties had united in the party of Order against the proletarian class as the party of anarchy, of socialism, of communism. They had "saved" society from "the enemies of society." They had given out the watchwords of the old society, "property, family, religion, order," to their army as passwords and had proclaimed to the counterrevolutionary crusaders: "In this sign thou shalt conquer!" From that moment, as soon as one of the numerous parties which gathered under this sign against the June insurgents seeks to hold the revolutionary battlefield in its own class interest, it goes down before the cry: "property, family, religion, order." Society is saved just as often as the circle of its rulers contracts, as a more exclusive interest is maintained against a wider one. Every demand of the simplest bourgeois financial reform, of the most ordinary liberalism, of the most formal republicanism, of the most shallow democracy, is simultaneously castigated as an "attempt on society" and stigmatized as "socialism." And finally the high priests of "religion and order" themselves are driven with kicks from their Pythian tripods, hauled out of their beds in the darkness of night, put in prison vans, thrown into dungeons or sent into exile; their temple is razed to the ground, their mouths are sealed, their pens broken, their law torn to pieces in the name of religion, of property, of the family, of order. Bourgeois fanatics for order are shot down on their balconies by mobs of drunken soldiers, their domestic sanctuaries profaned, their houses bombarded for amusement – in the name of property, of the family, of religion, and of order."

What happened in 1851 was not a revolution by any means. It was a power struggle among the capitalists to determine how the government would act in order to deal with an economic crisis. An economic crisis of overproduction had resulted in a political crisis among the French capitalists. This political crisis had resulted in the western liberal French society collapsing into authoritarianism and illiberalism in order to bring back stability. As Marx observed: "The bourgeoisie apotheosized the sword; the sword rules it. It destroyed the revolutionary press; its own press is destroyed. It placed popular meetings under police surveillance; its salons are placed under police supervision. It disbanded the democratic National Guard, its own National Guard is disbanded. It imposed a state of siege; a state of siege is imposed upon it. It supplanted the juries by military commissions; its juries are supplanted by military commissions. It subjected public education to the sway of the priests; the priests subject it to their own education. It jailed people without trial, it is being jailed without trial. It suppressed every stirring in society by means of state power; every stirring in its society is suppressed by means of state power. Out of enthusiasm for its moneybags it rebelled against its own politicians and literary men; its politicians and literary men are swept aside, but its moneybag is being plundered now that its mouth has been gagged and its pen broken.... France therefore seems to have escaped the despotism of a class only to fall back under the despotism of an individual, and what is more, under the authority of an individual without authority. The struggle seems to be settled in such a way that all classes, equally powerless and equally mute, fall on their knees before the rifle butt."

Under Louis Bonaparte the bankers and farmers won out. The factory owners lost, but so did the revolutionary working class movement. "Bonaparte would like to appear as the patriarchal benefactor of all classes. But he cannot give to one without taking from another," Marx observed. All kinds of economic reform programs were introduced in the hopes of stabilizing capitalism, pleasing one group of society, and preventing instability.

The French economy got better for a time as a result of massive government intervention, but it did not last. Marx noted: "Driven by the contradictory demands of his situation, and being at the same time, like a juggler, under the necessity of keeping the public gaze on himself, as Napoleon's successor, by springing constant surprises – that is to say, under the necessity of arranging a coup d'état in miniature every day – Bonaparte throws the whole bourgeois economy into confusion, violates everything that seemed inviolable to the Revolution of 1848, makes some tolerant of revolution and makes others lust for it, and produces anarchy in the name of order, while at the same time stripping the entire state machinery of its halo, profaning it and making it at once loathsome and ridiculous."

As Louis Bonaparte stayed in power, the French government had to spend more and more money to keep the economy rolling. The problem of overproduction, the root of the crisis, persisted. Finally in 1870 France went to war with Prussia, and lost. The results of the Franco-Prussian War were the eventual collapse of the French government, and the temporary establishment of a Communist Government in the capital city, the Paris Commune of 1871.

Marx, living in Paris during 1851 and 1852, observed the struggles in the streets, the protests, the strikes, and coup d'état first hand. His groundbreaking pamphlet quoted above is called *The Eighteenth Brumaire of Louis Bonaparte*. He stated that the purpose of his pamphlet was to - "demonstrate how the class struggle in France created circumstances and relationships that made it possible for a grotesque mediocrity to play a hero's part."

The concept of "Bonapartism" is a widely misunderstood or overlooked piece of analysis that Marx put forth. Essentially, the crisis of capitalism drives the capitalists to turn against the liberal principles they came to power espousing. During the overthrow of feudalism, capitalists had screamed about "Liberty, Egalite, Fraternity" and "Life, Liberty and the Pursuit of Happiness." They had composed documents extolling "The Rights of Man." However, in a capitalist crisis, these principles had to be abandoned in order to restore order. Not only did Louis Bonaparte violate the freedom of the press and freedom of speech that French society had once boasted off, but he imposed on the property rights of capitalists. He nationalized industries, he used the massive state bureaucracy, and he mobilized peasants, workers and lumpen mobs to get his way and try to stabilize a naturally unstable system.

Bonapartism in the United States

A long-term crisis of overproduction, such as the one currently gripping the western financial order, results in dramatic divisions and fights among the capitalist class. These fights are resolved with one faction seizing control of the state and suppressing others, while enacting economic policies to resolve the crisis.

Bonapartism is not foreign to the United States. Throughout US history there have been many examples of heavy handed state repression being used to implement economic reforms and offset an economic crisis.

Abraham Lincoln was a bonapartist. He used the federal government to crush an uprising of slaveholders. In order to win the war he engaged in all kinds of strong-arm authoritarian tactics, executing slave traders who violated the Emancipation Proclamation, reforming the US currency with Greenbacks, and holding an election in 1864 in which southern states were not able to participate. Like Louis Bonaparte, Lincoln formed a coalition of radicals and rabble rousers. Religious fanatics who opposed slavery, small farmers called Free Soilers, poets like Walt Whitman, intellectuals like Emerson and Thoreau, labor unionists and others were Lincoln's "Society of December 10th." To win the US civil war, Lincoln made Harriet Tubman the first woman ever to lead U.S. soldiers into battle, giving her and other former slaves weapons to raid plantations along the Combahee River in South Carolina. Lincoln allowed German immigrant and Communist, August Willich, to rise to the rank of Brigadier General in the US Army. He commissioned Joseph Weydemeyer to lead the Ohio 9th Infantry Regiment, an openly Communist division of the Union Army that carried the Red Flag as its emblem.

A generation later, Woodrow Wilson functioned as a bit of Bonapartist in the United States as well. Wilson took power presenting himself as a highly educated professor who could use his expertise to stabilize the country amid rising labor unrest and economic crisis. Wilson associated himself with the Progressive

Abraham Lincoln made Harriet Tubman the first woman to lead US soldiers into battle. She led a band of former slaves to raid plantations along the Combahee River in South Carolina.

Movement and promised reforms to make life better for working people and make US society more rational and modern.

Wilson faced opposition from the urban political machines of major US cities. In New York City, Chicago, and Philadelphia, many Roman Catholic immigrants were gaining political influence within the Democratic Party and city governments. Police, Fireman and other urban public servants tended to be Irish or Italian, and Roman Catholic. Meanwhile, small farmers and others living in rural areas of the Midwest and south remained loyal to the Republican Party that had emerged with Lincoln.

In order to gain the upper hand within his own party, and over the Republicans, Woodrow Wilson arranged for Hollywood to create the first full length movie in history. Director G.W. Griffith created *The Birth of a Nation*, a propaganda film retelling the history of the US Civil War, demonizing Lincoln and presenting the Ku Klux Klan as heroes who protected whites from misguided attempts to give Black people equal rights. Quotes from Wilson's writings on US history appeared in the film as captions. Audiences were so fired up with hatred from watching the film Wilson helped create that on several occasions they went and lynched Black people after the screening had concluded.

Shortly after the release of *The Birth of a Nation*, the Ku Klux Klan was re-established in a mass rally in Stone Mountain, Georgia. The KKK became a mass right-wing political movement that mobilized small farmers to oppose Roman Catholics, Jews, and the Republican Party. The Klan functioned as Wilson's shock troops to retake control of the Democratic Party from the urban political machines and win the rural areas of the midwest away from the Republicans.

Shortly after launching the KKK, Wilson was re-elected as President in 1916. Wilson's campaign slogan was *He Kept Us Out of War*, and he was re-elected promising to keep the US out of the First World War that was raging across Europe. However, after he was re-inaugurated, the RMS Lusitania, a UK-registered ocean liner, was sunk and the press reported that Germany had attempted to recruit Mexico to attack the United States with the infamous and probably forged "Zimmerman Telegram."

Wilson then led the United States to declare war on Germany and enter the conflict on the side of the British and French. When the US entered the First World War, Wilson established a near full-scale military dictatorship. The Socialist Party and the Industrial Workers of the World were crushed by the Department of Justice. Mass rounding up and deporting of immigrants who were accused of being Communists took place with the infamous "Palmer Raids." Hundreds of people were sent to Federal Prison for speaking against the war. J. Edgar Hoover rose up the ranks of the Justice Department working against Communists and labor unionists, eventually establishing the Federal Bureau of

Investigation. Just before Wilson left office in 1921, the Ku Klux Klan and the Republican Party successfully passed Prohibition, outlawing alcoholic beverages.

Wilson used authoritarian tactics to stabilize the US economy amid a crisis. Lincoln and Wilson were both wildly popular, presenting themselves as champions of the people. They both crushed many rich and powerful people in the process of stabilizing the economy, though they protected others whom they aligned with. Wilson, like Louis Bonaparte, was eventually forced to go to war as his methods of stabilizing the economy became exhausted.

Let's recall what Marx wrote about how capitalism resolves the crisis of overproduction: "And how does the bourgeoisie get over these crises? On the one hand by enforced destruction of a mass of productive forces; on the other, by the conquest of new markets, and by the more thorough exploitation of the old ones. That is to say, by paving the way for more extensive and more destructive crises, and by diminishing the means whereby crises are prevented."

What better means of carrying out "destruction of a mass of productive forces" than war? War also can lead to "conquest of new markets." And who can better enforce the "more thorough exploitation" of the existing economy than a strong-armed tyrant? Bonapartism is part of the natural breakdown of the capitalist economy, in the long term crisis of overproduction, which arises naturally from its drive for technological innovation and maximizing profits. The political turmoil facing the United States since 2008 makes perfect sense when this understanding is provided.

It is also worth noting that Bonapartists are generally widely hated by the capitalist class, despite their activities being necessary to save the economy. After Lincoln's assassination the US government eventually removed federal troops from the South and enabled the Jim Crow Segregation system to emerge. US history was taught for generations from the southern perspective, and films like *Gone With The Wind* repeated the narrative first put forward in *The Birth of a Nation*, where Lincoln was portrayed as tyrannical.

The bonapartism of Wilson was similarly decried after serving its temporary purpose. By 1924, the Ku Klux Klan had so much power within the Democratic Party that many among the ruling elite were threatened by it. To rally support among the population, the KKK began engaging in much more pseudo-populist rhetoric and targeting figures among the elite in addition to its usual scapegoats, Blacks, Jews, and Catholics. A resolution condemning the KKK by name could not be passed at the Democrat Party's 1924 national convention. Historian Linda Gordon describes the convention this way: "The Democrats were divided, not only among candidates for the nomination, but most intensely between pro and anti-Klan factions. The Democratic Convention became known as "the Klanbake" signifying both the intensity of animosities among delegates on the floor and the record breaking heat outside… The Ku Klux Klan was the protagonist in this drama. It was outraged because the New York delegation had the temerity to nominate New York Governor Al Smith, a Catholic, for the Presidential ticket. Before the convention he appeared to be the strongest candidate but he was anathema to the Klan. Not only a Catholic, not only an opponent of prohibition, he aggressively denounced the Klan's candidate William Gibbs McAdoo, former Secretary of the Treasury. A darling of evangelicals because he was an uncompromising prohibitionist, McAdoo even supported the ban on alcohol at the convention. He commanded the loyalty of many working class and populist voters because earlier in his career he had supported workmen's compensation for workplace

In 1924 the Democratic Party was held hostage by the Ku Klux Klan. The national convention went on for 13 days as delegates could not agree on a nominee.

accidents, unemployment insurance, the eight-hour work day, and a minimum wage."

Just across the river from the 1924 Democratic Convention in Manhattan, the KKK had a rally to support McAdoo with 20,000 people attending. They not only burned crosses, but also effigies of Al Smith. As delegates left the convention hall in Madison Square Garden each night they could see burning crosses across the river in New Jersey. Violence on the floor of the convention broke out on several occasions, and a resolution condemning the Ku Klux Klan narrowly failed to pass. The convention went on for 16 days and was the longest major party convention in US history. Though Ku Klux Klan candidate McAdoo had clearly won the overwhelming majority of the popular vote in the Democratic Primary, the Democratic Party machine was able to block him. However, the Klan was able to prevent Al Smith, the favored establishment candidate from getting the nomination. Ultimately, the Democrats nominated John W. Davis, a somewhat bland candidate who lost to Republican Calvin Coolidge in the General Election. Only after 106 different ballots were cast could the Democratic Party finally agree on a nominee for President.

The 1924 convention, full of chaos and widely reported on by the press, clearly indicated that the Ku Klux Klan was a threat to the political establishment. Many of the rich and powerful people shifted their support to rival wings of the Democratic Party. In the 1920s, the US economy was stabilizing amid the "roaring twenties" and there was no longer a need for an army of brownshirts in white sheets to keep order. A public relations war and a campaign of prosecutions from the US Department of Justice soon reduced the KKK's size and influence. Linda Gordon writes: "By 1927 Klan membership had shrunk from several million to about 350,000... Scandals exposing the leader's crimes, hypocrisy and misbehavior hit both local and national newspapers... In Indiana, Klan member Governor Ed Jackson was indicted for bribery, the officers of the state's major Klan bank were indicted for embezzlement and grand larceny and a Klan minister was accused of crimes "so sensational that persons who heard the sordid details loath to believe they were true"... the FBI prosecuted Klan leader Edward Clark for violating Prohibition and the Mann Act (which criminalized taking an unmarried woman across state lines for "immoral" purposes)." In 1928, Al Smith was able to win the Democratic nomination without much ruckus, though he lost in the General election.

Abraham Lincoln was deemed necessary amid the crisis and Civil War of the 1860s, but afterwards he was assassinated, his policies reversed, and reconstruction was betrayed. In 1877, Jim Crow Segregation was implemented across the South as federal troops were withdrawn. From then on Lincoln was diminished by historians and *Gone With The Wind* became the standard establishment interpretation of US history.

Likewise, while the KKK had functioned as shock troops to give Wilson the power to enact certain reforms and take the US into the First World War, afterwards it was widely condemned and stripped of political power. The Klan has been a fringe political current ever since.

Once the capitalist economy is growing again, bonapartist leaders and the mass movements they create are tossed aside by the ruling class. While they are necessary in a crisis, their very existence is a threat to capitalist power. Marx explained why in *The Communist Manifesto*: "Altogether collisions between the classes of the old society further, in many ways, the course of development of the proletariat. The bourgeoisie finds itself involved in a constant battle. At first with the aristocracy; later on, with those portions of the bourgeoisie itself, whose interests have become antagonistic to the progress of industry; at all times with the bourgeoisie of foreign countries. In all these battles, it sees itself compelled to appeal to the proletariat, to ask for help, and thus, to drag it into the political arena. The bourgeoisie itself, therefore, supplies the proletariat with its own elements of political and general education, in other words, it furnishes the proletariat with weapons for fighting the bourgeoisie."

Empowering working class people and bringing them into politics, which is necessary for bonapartists, lays the seeds for a potentially overthrowing capitalism.

Bonapartism Case Study: Nazi Germany

The prolonged capitalist crisis of the 1930s brought in a new wave of bonapartist leaders in the western capitalist countries, who took dramatic moves to liquidate the crisis. The ground-breaking work of political economy *Fascism and Social Revolution* written by R. Palm Dutt in 1934, described how the response of the capitalist governments of the world to the great depression was to unleash destruction. He wrote: "The distinctive modern stage of capitalist policy for the destruction of wealth and of the productive forces is marked by three outstanding characteristics. The first is the gigantic scale of destruction, conducted over entire principal world areas of production, and calculated in relation to world stocks. The second is the direct government organization and subsiding of such destruction and restriction of production by all the leading imperialist governments. The third is the extension of destruction, not only to the destruction of existing stocks of commodities, but to the destruction of the productive forces, the ploughing up of crops and sown areas, the artificial limitation of production, the dismantling of machinery, as well as holding unused the labor power of millions of workers. The examples of this process throughout the capitalist world are too familiar to require repetition. The burning of millions of bags of coffee or tons of grain, in the midst of mass starvation and poverty, have horrified the world. But all this has not been accidental or exceptional happening through the action of individuals, but on the contrary directly organized by all the capitalist governments of the world, and in the forefront by the most "progressive" governments, by the Roosevelt Government in the United States, by Social Democratic governments, etc."

During a capitalist crisis, the capitalists often mobilize mass destruction of productive forces in the hopes of stabilizing the economy. Bonapartism that focuses on restarting the economy with destruction is called fascism, and this definition of fascism as a particular form of bonapartist maneuvering is key to understanding political developments in our time. The most clear historical example of fascism is Nazi Germany.

Much has been written about the Nazis and their horrendous crimes, as well as the timeline of their rise to power. However, almost all of the books one finds on the shelves of Barnes & Noble focus on Hitler's personality, the aesthetics of the Nazi Party and its propaganda, or other trivial matters that do not get to the essence of what took place. In order to really understand the nature of Nazism, one must understand its economic roots. The economic nature of fascism is best explored in *Hitler's Banker,* a biography of Hitler's economist and primary financial backer Hjalmar Schacht written by John Weitz. R. Palm Dutt's book *Fascism and Social Revolution* and *Dialectical Economics* by Lyn Marcus provide similar analysis.

Let's look at the rise of Hitler and the trajectory toward the Second World War from a historical materialist lens. Following the First World War, Germany had a Marxist uprising. The German Kaiser, Wilhelm II, and king of Prussia, ordered the navy to make a final suicide mission after peace had been declared on land, and the sailors refused. In response to the ensuing revolt within the military, strikes took place across Germany and workers councils declared themselves to be the new governing bodies. Humiliated by defeat and losing control of his own military, the Kaiser abdicated and handed power over to the deputies from the Social-Democratic Party, the Independent Social-Democratic Party and their allies who ran the labor unions. The Social Democrats convened an election for delegates who were sent to the city of Weimar where they composed a new constitution for a democratic republic.

The most thorough analysis of fascism and its economic roots ever published is the 1934 book "Fascism and Social Revolution" by British Communist leader R. Palm Dutt.

Even though the majority of those elected to write the Weimar Constitution called themselves Marxists, the new constitution they composed was a liberal democratic one. Karl Kautsky, Friedrich Ebert, and other social-democratic leaders argued that socialism had to be achieved through the democratic process and could not be imposed by revolutionaries amid the crisis. The Social-Democratic leaders feared civil war and further invasion by the allied powers, and they shared the western powers' hostility to the recently victorious Bolsheviks in Russia.

Some German revolutionaries and labor activists wanted to see full socialism. The province of Bavaria refused to accept the Weimar Constitution and declared the "Bavarian Soviet Republic" as a briefly existing Marxist regime. Rosa Luxemburg and Karl Liebknecht led an uprising in Berlin with their "Spartakusbund," but it was put down. The events of 1918 and 1919 in Germany had the effect of greatly demoralizing the Marxist movement, and causing many German workers to look elsewhere for leadership. Hitler's rise a decade later was rooted in this epic betrayal and inability to accept victory on the part of the German socialists. The "big moment" had come. The military had risen up against the Kaiser, the largest Marxist party in the world had taken the helm of power, and the result was more of the same. The words of Marxist agitators in Germany were cursed from there forward by the utter disappointment of the masses and the failure of the revolutionaries to deliver on their promises when it seemed the revolution had triumphed.

The Social-Democrats not only failed to create socialism in Germany, but they employed right-wing soldiers organized into militias called the *Freikorps* to suppress those that refused to accept the Weimar Republic and wanted socialism. Throughout the 1920s the *Freikorps* became semi-permanent associations of anti-communist veterans who kept firearms and were used to put down strikes and protests.

Germany was stripped of its colonies by the Versailles treaty at the end of the First World War and barred from having its own military. The German government was obligated to pay reparations to the countries that had been victorious in the war. Throughout the 1920s, the Weimar Republic in Germany was unable to bring stability as unemployment and inflation made life miserable for German workers. The Social-Democratic Party accepted war guilt, and recognized the Versailles Treaty as legitimate, however the German Communist Party did not.

The Communists said that the First World War had been created by big monopolies and capitalists, and making German workers pay reparations to France and Germany was absurd. The Social-Democrats acceptance of "war guilt" and their insistence on full compliance with the national humiliation of Germany discredited them even further than their inability to take power in 1919.

The German Communist Party organized protests among the unemployed, demanding jobs and food. Often these protests escalated to armed revolts, and the German Communist Party formed its own militia, the Red Front Fighters League. Marxist uprisings became more frequent, in most cases it was the Social-Democratic Party's leaders who mobilized to crush uprisings led by the Communist Party.

Some German Communists argued that because Germany had been stripped of its colonies following the war, and the working class was being forced to pay reparations to the British and French along with the capitalists, that the Communist Party should position itself differently. The group labeled "National Bolsheviks" argued that Germany should be viewed as an oppressed nation by the Communist International, and much like in China, the Communists should strategically position themselves as leaders of a block of different classes fighting to liberate the nation from imperialism. However, the Communist International rejected this idea, arguing that despite being stripped of its colonies and having its domestic economy suppressed, Germany was still an imperialist nation. The focus of the German Communists was on "class against class" and portraying the social democrats as "social fascists" and "class traitors" who collaborated with the employers against the workers movement.

Increasingly, the Marxist movement in Germany divided into two wings. The Social Democrats became the party of industrial unions, representing the German factory workers who were still employed amid the economic downturn. The Social Democrats passed legislation forcing various German corporations to allow a representative of the labor union to have a seat on the board of directors, arguing that this, not the struggle for political power, represented moving toward socialism. With a representative of the reformist union on the board of a profit-centered corporation, "democracy was being introduced into the workplace" and the workers were "starting to control the means of production."

The German Communist Party, on the other hand, became the party of the desperately poor and unemployed. The Communist led "Bread Riots' ' where hungry people smashed store windows and took food to distribute among the working class. Increasingly the German Communist became adventurist and obsessed with violence, and unlike the social democrats who became reformist and focused on the more comfortable industrial workers, the German Communists became the party of the lumpenproletariat, associating itself with organized crime and other plagues on the life of the desperately poor whom they organized.

With continued instability in the heart of Europe, the British and Americans very much feared the results of the German Communist Party taking power. If the newly former Soviet Union was to combine its strength with Germany, Communism would very quickly spread across the European mainland. The result would be the British and the Americans would be locked out of Europe's heartland, and lose control of the world. This geopolitical scenario had long been openly feared by British and American strategists, even before Communism became a factor. The British had long engaged in intelligence intrigue to destabilize the European mainland and prevent it from unifying against them.

As instability continued in Germany, British and American intelligence began offering covert support to various anti-communist groupings in Germany. Various right-wing militant groups that preached anti-communism emerged. Many were not only funded by the British and Americans but also by German factory owners who used them to break strikes.

There is no "fascist ideology" or aesthetic

The Nazi Party emerged in the mid-1920s as the main current among right-wing anti-Communist street fighters. Many different *Freikorp* factions merged into the Nazi Party, accepting its discipline and joining its very effective and brutal anti-communist street violence. Ernst Roehm, an open homosexual, was the chief of the Stormtroopers, the Nazi Party's group of armed strikebreakers who killed Communists in the streets.

The Nazi ideology drew heavily from the traditionalist German right-wing of Oswald Spengler and Ernst

Junker, glorifying the notion of a German empire. The Nazis strayed from the mainline of thinking among the German far-right by embracing populism, calling for a "people's revolution." They presented Marxism as Jewish conspiracy, and argued that Germany had only lost the First World War due to a "stab in the back" by the Marxists and Labor Unions who undermined the war effort. Nazi ideology in the early 1920s seemed to condemn capitalism, and argue that Communism was simply a foreign conspiracy invented by Jewish bankers and serving the foreign enemies in the Soviet Union, and that "true socialism" was nationalistic and loyal to the German state. However in the late 1920s, as the Nazis were being actively groomed for power, the anti-capitalism of their rhetoric toned itself down. Hitler's polemics with Gregor Strausser argued that "national socialism" simply meant that corporations would not be permitted to go against the national interest of the country. The Nazi Party dropped its calls for nationalization of industries.

R. Palm Dutt points out that the many analysts who focus on attempting to define a "fascist" ideology are completely missing the mark and that fascism is not a set of ideas or beliefs, but rather a practice. Dutt writes: "Fascism, in fact, developed as a movement in practice, in the conditions of threatening proletarian revolution, as a counter-revolutionary mass movement supported by the bourgeoisie, employing weapons of mixed social demagogy and terrorism to defeat the revolution and build up a strengthened capitalist state dictatorship; and only later endeavored to adorn and rationalize this process with a "theory." It is in this actual historical process that the reality of Fascism must be found, and not in the secondary derivative attempts post-festum at adornment with a theory.

No less unsatisfactory are the attempted anti-Fascist interpretations of Fascism in terms of ideology or abstract political conceptions. The conventional anti-Fascist ideological interpretations of Fascism see in Fascism only the principle of "dictatorship" or "violence." "Dictatorships from the Right" have existed and can exist in hundreds of forms without in any sense constituting Fascism. Tsarism was a "Dictatorship from the Right." But Tsarism was not Fascism. The White Guard dictatorships immediately after the war for crushing the revolution were "Dictatorships from the Right." But these White Guard dictatorships were not yet Fascism, and only subsequently began to develop Fascist characteristics as they began to try to organize a more permanent basis (subsequent evolution in Hungary and Finland). Fascism may be in fact a reactionary dictatorship. But not every reactionary dictatorship is Fascism. The specific character of Fascism has still to be defined. Wherein, then, lies the specific character of Fascism? The specific character of Fascism cannot be defined in terms of abstract ideology or political first principles. The specific character of Fascism can only be defined by laying bare its class-basis, the system of class-relations within which it develops and functions, and the class-role which it performs. Only so can Fascism be seen in its concrete reality, corresponding to a given historical stage of capitalist development and decay."

Put simply, there is no fascist ideology, and no fascist aesthetic. Fascism is whatever demagogy and propaganda mishmash is needed to justify the heavy-handed repression and violence used to stabilize a country amid economic crisis and the threat of socialist revolution.

The German financier Hjalmar Schacht first met with Hitler on January 5th, 1931. Weitz's biography of Schacht describes the meeting this way: "Hitler arrived dressed in a Nazi Party uniform. He seemed quite unaffected and modest... Schacht discovered what many others were to learn. A conversation with Hitler meant Hitler did most of the talking... Though Schacht reported little of the actual conversation, he soon introduced Hitler to Dr. Walther Funk, a financial journalist, who taught him some basic principles of economics. Schacht spent the following weeks lobbying Chancellor Brunning and other politicians, bringing them to consider including the Nazis in a future government."

Weitz's biography goes on to explain that after the financial downturn in September of 1931, support for Hitler became more widespread among German industrialists: "As an act of ambition and a grab for power, Alfred Hugenberg, the right-wing industrialist, instigated a rally of the so-called national opposition. It included Hugenberg's "Steel Helmet" German National Party and the Agrarian Party of the aristocratic monarchist landowners as well as the National Socialist (Nazi) Party. He arranged a mass event in the beautiful little mountain spa Bad Harzburg in the Harz mountains. It became known as the Harzburger Front... Many prominent individuals, all opponents of the democratic Weimar regime, also attended. Among them were dozens of industrialists, including: Fritz Thyssen; many titled landowners; four royal princes (two of them sons of the former Kaiser); and a gaggle of dukes: counts and barons. There were sixteen former generals."

The ascendency of Adolf Hitler to the position of German Chancellor was primarily due to the alliance he formed with the financier Hjalmar Schacht.

In the 1932 elections, the Nazi Party received 33% of the vote. The Social Democrats received 20% and the Communists received 16%. The German Centre Party, a right-wing group, received 11%. Because no party had received a clear majority, a coalition government needed to be formed among different parties.

Weitz's biography describes other sections of the German ruling class who threw their lot behind Hitler in the aftermath of the vote: "Keppler, who owned a small chemical business, was a longtime advisor to Adolf Hitler and was his contact with heavy industry.... Keppler then approached Schacht and asked him to help with men like Vogler of the steel industry and Karl Helfferich, Schacht's old opponent but now a new ally. Kepler's fund-raising activities were organized into the so-called Keppler Kries (Keppler Circle) and Schacht was not reluctant to become a member of it. He sensed the swing of the political pendulum and wanted to be involved. Many leading industrialists were still quite reluctant. Friedrich Flick, the coal-and-iron magnate, donated a token 50,000 marks to the Nazis and gave 1.8 million marks to help re-elect von Hindenburg. Von Papen met with steel king Gustav Krupp in Dusseldorf on January 7, 1933, but met resistance. The heads of the I.G. Farben, Bosch, and Siemens were equally tepid about Hitler." Franz Von Papen, the head of the German Centre Party negotiated with Nazis to form a coalition government, and on January 30th, 1933 Hitler was named chancellor of Germany. In his speech accepting the new position as head of state, Hitler asked the country "give me four years" and they would not recognize the country.

Then on February 27th, the German Parliament Building (Reichstag) was burned by an arsonist. The Communist Party was declared responsible for the arson and outlawed. The seats the Communist Party held in the parliament were handed over to the Nazi Party, which then had a majority of seats and proceeded to ratify a new constitution and establish a new authoritarian government.

Right-wing psychologist, Jordan Peterson, has told audiences that "you know we should never forget that Hitler was elected you know... when he was elected, by a large majority too, it was a landslide vote, the kind of vote that no modern democratic leader ever gets... so you know although it's difficult for people to swallow... it's hard not to assign culpability for what happened in Germany to the society at every strata."

Peterson uses this to claim human beings have a sinister nature deep down, and that populism is dangerous. However, Peterson's claim is simply historical revisionism. The Nazis never received a majority vote in the elections. The Nazis only took power through an alliance with other forces, and heavy handed political repression following what was most likely a planned false-flag operation. The Nazis were selected by the German elite and imposed on the country to prevent a revolution. They did not take power as the result of unbridled populism as Hannah Arendt, Susan Sontag, Leo Strauss, and many of the prevailing synthetic left voices proclaim in their elitist screeds.

The Nazis in Power

The Nazis made the "stormtroopers" an official government police agency, legalizing their acts of violence against Communists, Jews, and other groups. On May 17th, 1933 labor unions, strikes and lockouts were outlawed. The German Labor Front, a Nazi party organization, was the only legal labor union, and the leaders of other labor unions were arrested.

The first few months the Nazis were in power were marked by an upsurge of street chaos with newly legalized violence and terror being an aspect of daily life. After a year in office, Hitler then launched his infamous "Night of the Long Knives" and executed the leaders of the Stormtrooper organization in order to stabilize the country and end the street fighting chaos.

The new government took a number of very swift dramatic economic moves to stabilize the economy. First, thousands of leaders of the Communist Party and the Social-Democratic Party were placed in a newly constructed network of prison labor camps. Lots of money was spent building the camps, lots of people were employed as guards, and the prisoners functioned as free labor for corporations, functioning as a corporate subsidy. In essence, the Nazi government created the first prison-industrial complex, using government spending on mass incarceration and forced labor to stimulate economic growth.

Women were urged to leave the workforce, with the Nazi party launching a public relations campaign shaming unmarried women who worked outside of their homes, and paying a massive cash bonus to couples who got married. The government began hiring millions of Germans to begin the construction of the Autobahns, new highways stretching across the country. The mass imprisonment, the construction of a new system of prison camps, the push of women out of the labor force, and the construction of the autobahns all resulted in a significant decrease in unemployment.

Schacht also arranged for Germany to begin the process of rebuilding its military. According to Weitz: "In 1933, Schacht believed in the rearmament of Germany and so did Adolf Hitler. Schacht always insisted their reasons differed radically, but in 1933 their thrust was parallel... To prime the manufacture of armaments and to slice away at unemployment he founded a small shell corporation strangely named the Metallurgical Research Company, or Mefo... The purpose of Mefo was to finance large government contracts for armaments. So it was estimated there were 21 billion marks in orders. Payments were guaranteed by the Reichsbank. Some of the money came from what had been requisitioned by the so-called conversion fund. It was ironic that a portion of German rearmament was paid for with foreign money... During the next four years, the value of Mefo bonds grew from the original 1 million marks to 12 billion marks... The Mefo bonds became a very desirable investment with their rising value and guaranteed 4 percent interest."

To further stimulate the economy, the Nazis had not only created a prison industrial complex, but also a military industrial complex. Militaristic activities and training became part of the public educational system once again as they had been before the war. Hjalmar Schacht became Hitler's finance minister, and he announced that Germany would not be paying any further reparations to the allied powers and would be defaulting, and not making any further payments on loans it had received from Britain and the United States.

All of these moves resulted in an economic boom. The Nazi government eradicated unemployment, ended inflation, and oversaw a very significant rise in

The Nazis were able to reboot the German economy primarily with military spending and the creation of a slave labor underclass.

living standards. The main beneficiaries were German industrial capitalist dynasties like the Krupps and Thyssens. They had been crushed by the British and American banks at the end of the First World War, but they also hated Communism as it supported labor unions which cut into their profits and threatened to seize their property in a revolution.

Like all Bonapartism, Hitler's measures were only temporarily successful. By 1939, the German economy was crashing again. The Nazi government responded by launching the horrendous events we now know as the Second World War and the Holocaust. As Lyn Marcus explains: "Nazi military operations represented the means of securing the loot on which German capitalism depended. The Nazi military machine and its operations represented the armed forces which sustained the German capital as capital… Germany's military undertakings were launched over the strong objections of the High Command, which was systematically purged to "overcome" such objections. The Second World War was imposed upon German militarism by the hysterical demands for immediate loot of the smoke stack barons and financiers."

Bonapartism Case Study: Roosevelt's America

After the 1929 Stock Market Crash in America, it became clear that the economic downturn was long term. Mass layoffs, bank failures, home foreclosures and evictions swept the country. Homeless encampments called "Hoovervilles" sprung up across the country. Farmers went under and families fled to California to find work.

The Communist Party went from obscurity to positioning itself as the champion of the unemployed. The Communist International called March 6th 1931 "International Unemployment Day" and just as in Europe, the major cities of the United States were swept with huge protests demanding "Work or Wages NOW!" In the summer of 1932, 43,000 unemployed veterans occupied the National Mall in Washington, D.C., demanding a payment of benefits before they were cleared out by the military.

Franklin Delano Roosevelt had existed as a run of the mill Democrat from a prominent political family in New York. He had long maintained an alliance with the Rockefeller family, the descendants of John D. Rockefeller the creator of Standard Oil. Vince Copeland writes: "His early financial backers — before the convention — included the politically generous Herbert Lehman of Lehman Brothers and the Corn Exchange Bank (now Chemical Bank); Joseph P. Kennedy, father of the Kennedy brothers; the Henry Morganthaus, senior and junior; Joseph E. Davies, husband of the heir of Post cereal millions; and Jesse Strauss, then President of Macy's huge department store. In the actual campaign, the staunch Al Smith supported John J. Raskob of the Duponts and gave FDR $23,000. Another great Smith supporter, Bernard Baruch, the millionaire

Morgan messenger, gave $60,000. The Rockefellers were displeased with Hoover, but still contributed to his campaign to keep their well known inside track with the Republican Party. However, several Standard Oil families, like the Whitney's and the Harkesses, gave heavily to the Democrats."

When Roosevelt took office after winning the 1932 Presidential election it was clear he had some aspirations to be a "strongman" who could bring the country back into order. His inauguration speech spoke of "driving the money changers out of the temple" and he pushed forward the Glass Steagall Act which separated commercial and speculative banking.

Roosevelt's initial moves as President were somewhat modest. The National Industrial Recovery Act was intended to regiment industry and more closely manage it. The US department of agriculture engaged in various schemes to inflate food prices, including one that was vividly remembered by Nelson Peery, who was a boy living on a farm in Minnesota: "Conditions worsened in 1933 and 1934. One day, men from the government came to town and purchased almost half the cattle in the area. They herded the cattle into a ditch and shot them. The government agents poured lime over the carcasses and then covered them with dirt so people wouldn't eat them. When people cursed them, the government people said it was necessary to do this in order to come out of the Depression. People starved because there were too many cattle."

In 1933, US Marine Corps General Smedley Butler revealed that among the rich and powerful many felt Roosevelt's methods were too mild, and were looking to Hitler and Mussolini for inspiration. Eventually the McCormack–Dickstein Committee brought Butler in to testify what the coup plotters had discussed with him. Butler said that Connecticut businessman Gerald MacGuire had approached him saying that plans for a fascist coup against Roosevelt would have support from those connected to J.P. Morgan, Bethlehem Steel, Goodyear tires, and other major corporations. Butler says he responded to the offer for him to lead half a million soldiers to seize Washington, DC and establish a military regime by saying: "If you get 500,000 soldiers advocating anything smelling of Fascism, I am going to get 500,000 more and lick the hell out of you, and we will have a real war right at home."

The summer of 1934 marked a turning point in Roosevelt's presidency, and the history of the United States. In 1934, three major US cities were shut down by Communist-led municipal General Strikes. The Minneapolis Teamsters Strike, the San Francisco Dock Workers Strike, and the Auto-Lite Strike of Toledo, Ohio, represented a significant level of escalation in working class unrest. The National Guard was sent in to battle armed labor unionists in all three cities. Gunfire was exchanged. In Minneapolis, the Strike Committee functioned as a kind of dual government, with patrols across the city enforcing the rule "No Scab Trucks" and

In 1934, a wave of strikes led by Communists escalated the class struggle. Facing the danger of a fascist coup, Roosevelt was forced to strategically align with organized labor and the Soviet Union.

bashing in the windows of any vehicle not permitted by the union.

Textile workers and sharecroppers across the South were also on the move in Communist-led unions. A state of emergency was declared in South Carolina as impoverished workers, white and Black fought against their employers.

Talk of the need for a fascist coup to stop the Communists and labor militants increased among the rich and powerful. Roosevelt could see that he was in serious danger of being overthrown, and in 1935 the economic policies of his administration significantly shifted.

With an executive order, Roosevelt created the Works Progress Administration and hired millions of unemployed workers. He deployed them to build highways, bridges, parks, and post offices. The Civilian Conservation Corps lived in tents and wore bright green government-issued uniforms. The same year, Roosevelt also passed the Wagner Act, cementing into law that workers have the right to strike and unionize, and creating the National Labor Relations Board that negotiated industrial disagreements and certified union elections.

Hiring millions of unemployed workers, and legalizing and empowering the reformist labor leaders of the American Federation of Labor had the effect of calming the country down. However, among the rich and powerful it was decried as a Communist conspiracy. Al Smith, leader of the New York City Democratic Party formed the American Liberty League and denounced Roosevelt as a Communist. Vince Copeland explains: "Roosevelt, by intervening on behalf of millions in the way he did, kept the system from falling. It has been more or less correctly said he opposed capitalists in order to save capitalism. But in order to carry on such a hazardous operation as opposing capitalists while serving as the chief political presiding officer of the US capitalist system, Roosevelt had to gain himself a considerable social base in the enemy class —that is the working class, which includes the unemployed. And he had to be able to utilize this class against the capitalists whose system he served."

In the 1936 election, Roosevelt shifted significantly

to the left. He spoke in Madison Square Garden about how he "welcomed" the hatred of Wall Street, saying: "We had to struggle with the old enemies of peace— business and financial monopoly, speculation, reckless banking, class antagonism, sectionalism, war profiteering. They had begun to consider the Government of the United States as a mere appendage to their own affairs. We know now that Government by organized money is just as dangerous as Government by organized mob. Never before in all our history have these forces been so united against one candidate as they stand today. They are unanimous in their hate for me—and I welcome their hatred. I should like to have said of my first Administration that in it the forces of selfishness and of lust for power met their match. I should like to have it said of my second Administration that in it these forces met their master."

To be clear, Roosevelt represented one wing of the ruling class that was facing all out opposition from the rest of the rich and powerful. Roosevelt's allies included the Rockefellers, as well as a few others among the ultra-rich. In 1937 FDR Jr. married Ethel Dupont, indicating that at least one of America's top families was still on good terms with him. A few among the oil banking elite favored stability and the need to prevent all out chaos in the streets, and were willing to see the National Association of Manufacturers, Henry Ford and the Morgans accept losses in the form of union contracts and an increased welfare state.

In 1936, Earl Browder, the leader of the Communist Party, explained why his party was essentially backing Roosevelt while running their own symbolic campaign: "All the most reactionary groups in the country are gathering in one camp in order to bring fascism to the United States. Primarily through the Hearst press they have carried on a campaign against everything that is liberal or progressive in the country. They are determined to defeat Roosevelt in 1936 and place an administration in power that will carry out a program of reaction to the full satisfaction of the Morgans, the Du Ponts, and the few ruling families of the United States. Roosevelt, of course, seeks to achieve the same class objectives as his opponents from the right. In fact, he meets most of their attacks by taking a step further to the right himself... but although their goals are the same, Roosevelt pursues a different path and necessarily bases himself on different groups within the bourgeoisie. He tries to retain the support of the workers, the farmers, and the middle class groups, by posing as a liberal... He is the spokesman for those industrial and financial groups that are in conflict with the House of Morgan. To placate the masses, Roosevelt has made tangible concessions to the well-to-do farmers and miserly ones to the workers... To rely upon Roosevelt to keep fascism from coming to power, plays into the hands of the Liberty League."

When providing analysis of Roosevelt's sweeping victory in 1936, Copeland writes: "Never had an election been so badly lost with so much Wall Street money riding on the loser." Copeland goes on to explain how the bulk of the ruling class was opposed to Roosevelt: "The editorials and even front pages of most newspapers thundered against FDR, with at least 80 percent of the daily press being fiercely opposed to him and the other 20 percent only tepidly for him." Copeland explains that in the 1936 election: "The Democrats received considerable money from the very rich, too, but nothing like the golden outpouring that filled the Republican coffers to overflowing. The Wall Street money the Democrats got was not decisive. On the whole it was the same consolation money that Wall Street usually gives the party scheduled for defeat, in order that big business can still use that party on another day."

Roosevelt's victory in November of 1936 was astounding. Millions of people who had been indifferent and not voted in 1932 or 1928, poured into the polls to vote for the man who had hired them to work in the Civilian Conservation Corps, or enabled them to see an increase in their wages with a union contract as a result of the Wagner Act. Roosevelt was enacting real economic reforms and improving people's lives in a moment when malnutrition related deaths were taking place, and dead bodies of hungry and unemployed workers were regularly found on the street. A millhand in North Carolina told a reporter, in a widely quoted comment, that he voted for Roosevelt because:

"Roosevelt is the only man we ever had in the White House who would understand that my boss is a son of a bitch."

Roosevelt had referenced the fact that industrial capitalists were threatening mass layoffs if he won the election. In his Madison Square Garden speech Roosevelt explained: "The very employers and politicians and publishers who talk most loudly of class antagonism and the destruction of the American system now undermine that system by this attempt to coerce the votes of the wage earners of this country. It is the 1936 version of the old threat to close down the factory or the office if a particular candidate does not win. It is an old strategy of tyrants to delude their victims into fighting their battles for them."

In response to Roosevelt's sweeping victory at the polls, the capitalists made good on their threats and mass layoffs ensued in industry. Starting in December of 1936, workers facing layoffs began occupying their factories and refusing to leave. The Flint Sit Down Strike of 1937 in which autoworkers seized their factory turned into a national mobilization as thousands of labor unionists poured into the Michigan city to support the workers against the police and the local fascist organizations such as the Black Legion.

Roosevelt sent the military to Flint, and the crowd was shocked when the machine guns were pointed away from the factory. Roosevelt had sent the military to protect striking workers. Roosevelt's administration then proclaimed that sit-down strikes were legal. The Congress of Industrial Organizations split from the AFL as a new, much more radical labor federation that openly employed Communists as organizers. Sit down strikes swept the country.

In 1937, Roosevelt created social security and unemployment insurance. Eleanor Roosevelt, the first lady, spoke at the convention of the American Youth Congress, a Communist-led student activist group. Later organizers from the Young Communist League were invited to sleep over at the White House when facing subpoenas before a congressional committee.

In the 1940 election Roosevelt selected Henry Wallace as his Vice President. Wallace had created the food stamps program when he led the US Department of Agriculture, seeing it as a subsidy for American farmers. Wallace openly praised the Soviet Union as an anti-fascist ally, and spoke of creating a "Century for the Common Man" rather than "the American century" after defeating the Nazis. The Democratic Party forced Roosevelt to drop Wallace from the ticket in 1944 and replace him with Harry Truman.

In his final State of the Union address during the Second World War, Roosevelt proposed an Economic Bill of Rights to be added to the US constitution guaranteeing jobs, healthcare, and education to all Americans. Roosevelt died shortly before the Second World War came to its conclusion, and he remains one of the most popular Presidents in US history. Roosevelt is absolutely an example of Bonapartism, and the more threatened by his own class he became, the more he moved into a strategic alliance with Communists, labor unions, the Soviet Union and other progressive forces.

Roosevelt's Worldview

British economist John Maynard Keynes is largely considered to be the economic inspiration for the Roosevelt administration. Keynes was the prominent voice in academic economics who emerged during the 1930s to criticize neoclassical and free market economics. Keynes denounced Marxism, but argued that in order to preserve capitalism it was necessary for the government to spend money in order to prevent "underconsumption."

The most commonly used cliche to explain Keynes' economic theories is the analogy of "ditch diggers." The concept is that the government should employ a group of men to dig a ditch. Then the government should employ another group of men to fill it in. Some would see this as a waste, but with the government wages these men were paid, they buy food, pay their rent, and get the private sector of the economy moving again.

While neoclassical and more recently neoliberal economists would argue that the market naturally resolves its problems, Keynesians argue that government spending to stimulate economic activity is a necessity. Following the Second World War, academic economists were met with what is referred to as the "Keynesian

Consensus." There was an almost universal understanding that in order to prevent events like the 1930s depression, with its dramatic consequences resulting in the Second World War, free market policies had to be abandoned and the government needed to manage the economy.

The rise of Neoliberal economics during the 1970s, escalating especially following the fall of the Soviet Union, saw a repudiation of the Keynesian consensus among the circles of power. The Mont Pelerin Society of Ludwig Von Mises, the popularization of Milton Friedman, and the rise of Alan Greenspan showed that among those who held government power, there was far less interest in Keynesianism than in those who promoted notions of a more unbridled capitalism. Keynesian theories have remained dominant among academic economists, with many seeing the Chicago School, the Austrian School, and other libertarian theories to be nothing but well-funded quackery.

Regardless, the economic policies of Nazi Germany and Rooseveltian America were both more or less Keynesian. The government spent large amounts of money to stimulate economic growth amid an overall depression. However, there was a fundamental difference.

Roosevelt's administration spent money primarily on infrastructure. Roosevelt launched the Tennessee Valley Authority to bring electricity to rural areas and increase agricultural output. Roosevelt connected remote regions of the country to urban centers and the coasts with new roads and bridges. Roosevelt also improved postal access and constructed new airports.

The infrastructure Roosevelt created enabled the post-war boom in the USA to happen much more rapidly. If the power plants, roads, bridges and airports had not been constructed during the late 1930s, it would have taken much longer for US industries to explode in the 1950s as they did.

In addition to the infrastructure, Roosevelt's spending seemed to focus on making the population smarter. The Post Offices built by the WPA often contained social realist murals. Music and arts education was promoted in the schools. Vannevar Bush was hired by the Roosevelt administration to oversee government funding for scientific research and direction of technological development.

Despite Jim Crow segregation existing and being politically impossible to oppose within Roosevelt's Democratic Party, there seemed to be a subtle interest in lifting up African Americans, Jews, and other groups that faced discrimination. Henry Morgenthau, a man of Jewish heritage, functioned as Roosevelt's Secretary of the Treasury and can be credited with crafting a lot of the administration's economic policies. Eleanor Roosevelt made a point of highlighting African American musicians, and Roosevelt openly met with Black labor leader A. Philip Randolph at the White House.

Roosevelt, it should be noted, was very hostile to Zionism, despite being overwhelmingly popular among American Jews. While Roosevelt was very enthusiastic about establishing US relations with Saudi Arabia, he was noted for being frequently rude and uninterested in meeting with those who favored creating Israel. The Holocaust Museum in Washington DC goes out of its way to demonize Roosevelt, and present him as antisemitic and complicit in the Holocaust despite his excessive record of anti-fascism and support from American Jews.

Roosevelt's economic reforms were certainly the most dramatic that any American President has ever enacted. He hired millions of unemployed people, built a massive amount of infrastructure, created scores of government programs such as unemployment insurance and social security, and created many financial regulations and forms of government economic oversight.

Roosevelt's economic reforms, as confusedly negotiated as they were, fit more or less into a tradition of political economy that has been labeled the American School. Alexander Hamilton pushed for a National Bank in the immediate aftermath of the founding of the United States, and spent money on constructing lighthouses as a form of infrastructure that would facilitate the inflow of international trade. Henry Charles Carey, who Karl Marx labeled the only American economist of any merit composed an anti-slavery manifesto arguing that the southern plantation system was part of a British financier's vision of keeping the world poor.

Hamilton, Carey, and later German economists Friedrich List and his ally the socialist philosopher Eugene Duhring, rejected the notion of class struggle. They instead favored the state functioning to control the economy by balancing a "harmony of interests" to benefit the population of a specific nation-state. The belief that the state should be guided by some kind of religious or moral principles, and regulating the economy in line with them seems to have been a factor in this thinking.

This school of "American Economics" or "Christian Economy" is not to be confused with Economic Nationalism. While economic nationalism emphasizes tariffs and trade regulations along with supporting key industries as "National Champions," the Rooseveltian economic policies were rather a kind of progressive state-ism. The focus is on a good government ensuring economic growth, making the population smarter, and building a more enlightened world.

It is the kind of thinking that is associated largely with New England radicalism in the United States, and the best traditions of the American revolution. One can see the influence of Ralph Waldo Emerson and Henry David Thoreau. Henry George, whose theories about taxing land values inspired the founding of the British Liberal Democratic Party, can also be described as from this tradition.

It makes sense that Roosevelt's administration would move in such a direction while also being forced into an alliance with the Marxists in organized labor and the Soviet Union internationally. One can see such an influence on the Kennedy administration as well. The Roosevelt administration's policies were those of "old school American liberals" who believed in growth and optimism but were never radical enough to become Marxists. These folks were somewhat socially conservative and religious and did not share the attitudes of the eventually emerging "New Left."

When looking over Roosevelt's roots, the influence of Endicott Peabody, the Christian Socialist schoolmaster who educated him and many of his closest allies at an elite boarding school for the New England elite cannot be underestimated. Peabody was an Episcopal Priest who ran the Groton School for Boys, an expensive private school located five miles north of Boston. The school was known for its harsh discipline and emphasis on hard work, giving privileged young men a harshness they might not receive elsewhere in life. The school centered around a philosophy of "muscular Christianity" that emphasized athletics and keeping young men busy and closely monitored to preserve their moral purity. In addition to the spartan atmosphere, it was also known for instilling compassion and a sense of social responsibility.

Roosevelt described Peabody saying "As long as I live

Endicott Peabody, Franklin Delano Roosevelt's schoolmaster and lifelong friend, was a Christian socialist who instilled values of compassion and kindness in him as a young man.

his influence will mean more to me than that of any other people next to my father and mother." Elsewhere he described him as "the biggest influence in my life." Peabody officiated Roosevelt's wedding to first lady Eleanor. Peabody also held a special church service in Washington DC for the president-elect and his family members on the morning of his first inauguration.

The Difference Between Roosevelt-ism and Nazism

There are significant fundamental differences between Roosevelt's Bonapartism and the Bonapartism of Adolph Hitler, though they were both enacted during the 1930s in a western industrialized country.

While Roosevelt's reforms were rolled out gradually in response to threats against him, the Nazis moved very quickly, enacting their major economic changes in their first two years of power. The Nazis, unlike Roosevelt, had an absolute monopoly on political power during these years with all opposition being relegated to concentration camps or in some cases guillotined. The Nazis also seemed to more or less know what they wanted to do, whereas Roosevelt's policies were a series of compromises and negotiated solutions set to appease a variety of different social forces that made up his coalition.

Other than the Autobahn highways, the Nazi state did not really boost great infrastructure projects. Power plants were built, water systems were created, but this was all secondary. The Nazi state, unlike the Roosevelt administration, focused on stimulating the economy through degrowth. Describing how it was that the Nazi state revitalized the economy, American journalist Lothrap Stoddard observed: "How did the Nazis actually finance their ambitious projects without currency nor price inflation? They did it in a number of ways. Fluid capital was regimented and either invested according to orders or diverted into government loans. Profits were skimmed off by basic taxation. Above all, consumption was kept down and living standards were lowered by what was called a process of reverse inflation... The upshot has been that the German people have financed astounding expenditures by literally taking it out of their own hides."

Creating a class of labor camp slaves, reducing consumption, and spending huge amounts on militarism all stimulated the German economy enough to see a dramatic recovery. Weitz's biography of Nazi economist Hjalmar Schahct confirms this: "Schacht had a disdain for what he called 'ditch digging.' It was one of the things he found to criticize in FDR's Civilian Conservation Corps and publicly administered work projects."

Roosevelt hired millions of unemployed young men into the Civilian Conservation Corps, part of his Works Progress Administration that constructed infrastructure as an economic stimulus.

Rather than merely employing millions of people to build things, the Nazis' most dramatic method of curbing unemployment was mass imprisonment and driving women from the labor market. The German car industry benefited significantly from the labor of concentration camp inmates, as did armaments manufacturers. The Nazis eliminated the collective bargaining power of workers, and restored the 12-hour workday.

As Lyndon LaRouche (writing under the pseudonym Lyn Marcus) wrote in his 1975 book *Dialectical Economics:* "The two principal bases for the Nazi pseudo-recovery of 1933-1936 were fixing of wages at the lowest depression levels and the depletion of the previously idled Constant Capital of German industry. Not only were wages reduced, but their real content was further reduced by exacerbated inflation, while the intensification of exploitation of labor was accelerated. By 1936-1937, the 'success' of Nazi full-employment recovery was obviously moving to the point of crisis. In the means of production, the quality of German labor power was being depleted by intensification and lower standards of material culture. Simultaneously, the expansion of Nazi production had been based on massive issuance of fictitious values in promissory notes. The ability of the Reichsbank, and other agencies to refinance this cancerously growing mass —to cover the growth of debt service obligation beyond the scale of available product for its payment —was imminently undermined. The Reichsmark faced the prospect of early national bankruptcy."

Of course, like all bonapartist schemes to control capitalism with state power and regenerate the economy, the results were only temporarily successful. By 1939, the Nazi economy was facing a full blown slowdown and a war of expansion to conquer new markets became a necessity for Hitler's regime. Stoddard goes on to write: "By 1938, evidence accumulated that the furious pace of Nazi *Wehrwirtschaft* (really war-economy) was running into the economic law of diminishing returns and was likewise entailing serious physical and psychological overstrain in every class of society."

The Nazi state also had a particular fixation on eugenics. They believed the unrest of the previous century was rooted in a genetic defect in Jews, and that society's problems could be resolved by breeding them out. Nazis had a mystical admiration for what they termed "The Aryan Race" and the government began working hard to "purify" the population. Stoddard observed: "Nothing is so distinctive in Nazi Germany as its ideas about race. It's concept about racial matters underlies the whole National Socialist philosophy of life and profoundly influences its policies and practices."

The Nazis began euthanizing the disabled people, and publicly playing up the idea that "impure stock" was a burden on the country. Political dissidents and others deemed unfit were forcibly sterilized by a special network of courts. According to what Stoddard was told by the Nazis who ran the Eugenics High Court of Appeals, prior to the Nazi takeover: "Morons, criminals, and other anti-social elements were reproducing themselves at a rate nine times as great as that of the general population. And those lowest elements were favored in their breeding by the welfare measures of the Weimar regime." And thus when Nazis were in power "they coupled their encouragement to sound citizens with a drastic curb on the defective elements. The curb was the sterilization law."

In essence, Nazism differed from Rooseveltism in that Nazism was about glorifying the past, purging society of elements deemed impure or undesirable, and rebooting the economy through destruction and reducing consumption. Nazi economics was about slave labor, mass spending on armaments, sterilizations, political repression, and managing the population while glorifying war, while Roosevelt's economic reforms were carried out with the aim of increasing consumption and advancing technological and scientific progress.

The Nazi regime ultimately resorted to slave labor on a major scale and forcible depopulation of territories it occupied during the Second World War. As LaRouche explains: "During 1941-1945, particularly, the intensification of autocannibalism primitive accumulation proceeded along the following general lines. The working conditions of forced foreign "guest" labor were markedly worsened, the standard of living in the occupied territories generally lowered to prop up the Reichsmark. The depopulation of large sections of Slavic regions occupied by the Nazis occupying administration, emulating the salvaging of used tire carcasses by a recapping firm, as part of the slave labor system. Human bodies were squeezed of their accumulated wealth by slave-labor conditions of production, and the depleted hulks returned to the SS for replacement parts. As a further measure of capitalist economics, the welfare rolls within the concentration camps were successfully reduced by the mass extermination practices applied to the weak, the aged, women, children, depleted slave labor, and other unemployables."

Fascist Economics in the 21st Century

So, let us be clear: amid a time of economic crisis the capitalists battle each other for control of the state. This process whereby different factions among the elite battle to wrest control of the state apparatus and use it to stabilize the economy is called *bonapartism*. Fascism is a particular form of *bonapartism* in which one faction of the ruling class seizes control of the state, and seeks to reboot the economy, not with excessive state directed stimulus and growth, but rather with controlled demolition and destruction of society and the population.

With this understanding we can proceed to our analysis of the present day, and the question at hand:

Where is America going?

In the aftermath of the 2008 financial crisis, it appears that one faction that seeks to enact fascist economic policies on a global level has wrestled its hands onto the helm of power. It is persisting in its attempt to secure a total monopoly on power and enact fascist economic policies to stabilize capitalism, but it faces a wave of massive resistance and is constantly being forced to compromise and negotiate as its agenda unfolds.

After the 2008 finance crisis, the Obama administration came into office. Barack Obama appointed eco-malthusian fanatic John P. Holdren as the Presidential Science Advisor. His 1977 textbook *Ecoscience* was co-authored by Paul Erlich, the author of *The Population Bomb*. In the book Holdren wrote of the need for a "planetary regime" that could reduce the population with "repressive measures" that might include birthing licenses, mandatory abortions or punishments for procreation. Holdren cited the rise of

US President Barack Obama appointed John P. Holdren as his Science Advisor. Holdren has consistently urged for dramatic measures to forcibly depopulate the third world.

the population and living standards of Asia and Africa as a primary threat to the environment. He also spoke of a "science court" that would approve new technological inventions to make sure they are environmentally sound and won't use too many resources and damage the ecosystem.

Tracy Stone-Manning, the current director of the Bureau of Land Management for the Biden administration is a former World Wildlife Federation employee whose master's thesis was on "overpopulation." Her master's thesis included scripts for eight public service announcements urging American families not to have more children, saying: "Americans believe overpopulation is only a problem somewhere else in the world. But it's a problem here too. When we overpopulate, the earth notices it more."

Tracy Stone-Manning currently serves as Biden's Director of the Bureau of Land Management. Her academic masters thesis planned a public relations campaign to reduce the US birth rate.

From *The Global 2000 Report* of the Carter administration to the Great Reset of the World Economic Forum, the belief is more or less the same. In order to prevent global unrest and bring stability, as well as to save the planet from climate change, a large faction of the elite believe it is necessary to implement a tightly controlled capitalism in order to reduce consumption and drive down the population. Nazi economics is back in fashion amid a long term crisis of overproduction. The American elite views the "ditch digging" of China's Belt and Road Initiative or Russia's Eurasian Economic Union with the same contempt Schacht had for Roosevelt. In their view, the road to bring society back into order is depopulation and reducing living standards.

Barack Obama made it clear when he visited South Africa and told the audience that if everyone on the continent could gain access to air conditioning, modern housing and cars, it would be an ecological disaster and could not be allowed. On June 29th, 2013 Obama told his audience of African students: "Ultimately, if you think about all the youth that everybody has mentioned here in Africa, if everybody is raising living standards to the point where everybody has got a car and everybody has got air conditioning, and everybody has got a big house, well, the planet will boil over."

The actions of the west in Africa match Obama's sentiments. While China and Russia have been building up the economies of African countries, the United

States has facilitated instability with the flow of weapons and the backing of extremists. From the time Angola gained independence from Portugal in 1975 up to 2002 the United States backed UNITA, a terrorist organization in its civil war against the Angolan government. The leader of UNITA, Jonas Savembi, was a literal cannibal who waged his reign of terror with US weapons. The flow of US guns to drug gangs and anti-communist paramilitaries in South and Central America has played a similar role.

George Soros and many of the wealthiest people in the western capitalist world who position themselves as liberals, expressing concern about climate change and decrying racism and populism, have been among the biggest supporters of the International Criminal Court. This institution that presents itself as an enforcer of international law has never tried and convicted any individual who was not African.

Almost all of the African people living in Libya prior to the 2011 regime change operations had cars, modern housing, and air conditioning. Since 2011 when the US and its allies funded rebels against the Islamic Socialist government and then backed them up with cruise missiles, the country has been cast into complete poverty and chaos reducing the population to the poverty Obama deemed to be ecologically necessary. Now much of the country has no electricity, and modern day slave markets have been set up in Libya's ports. This is the result of the "revolution" against socialism, backed by western capitalism in the name of freedom.

The US-NATO military operations have significantly rolled back development in the third world. Iraq was once a wealthy oil exporting country that had presided over a significant level of industrialization. The Gulf War, a decade of crippling sanctions and then the US invasion in 2003 reduced Iraq to poverty and chaos, driving it off the global oil markets and creating millions of refugees. The US occupation of Afghanistan kept the country impoverished and in chaos for 20 years, but allowed the drug gangs which the Taliban had suppressed to set up shop once again. US troops were even stationed at some points to guard their poppy fields.

Russia and China are the primary targets of US foreign policy, because they are no longer poor. During the 20th Century both countries lifted themselves up and industrialized with socialist revolutions. Wall Street wants poor captive client states, not rival superpowers competing on the global markets.

Greta Thunberg, the teen idol of the Climate Change movement made clear she opposes raising people out of poverty, when she said to the United Nations: "Entire ecosystems are collapsing. We are in the beginning of a mass extinction, and all you can talk about is money and fairy tales of eternal economic growth. How dare you!" The message of her tear filled "made for social media" rants is that economic growth is inherently bad. Consumption and the population must be urgently reduced. This message is echoed by the "Extinction Rebellion" protesters with their hourglass logo.

Thunberg's words are similar to those of Margaret Sanger, the founder of Planned Parenthood. Sanger was originally a Marxist, but embraced Malthusianism, joining the British Neo-Malthusian society and creating the Birth Control League with funding from the Rockefellers. As far as she was concerned, the problem in the global economy was not capitalism, but rather the human desire for growth and reproduction: "Discontented workers may rally to Marxism because it places the blame for their misery outside of themselves and depicts their conditions as the result of a capitalistic conspiracy, thereby satisfying that innate tendency of every human being to shift the blame to some living person outside himself, and because it strengthens his belief that his sufferings and difficulties may be overcome by the immediate amelioration of his economic environment. In this manner, psychologists tell us, neuroses and inner compulsions are fostered. No true solution is possible, to continue this analogy, until the worker is awakened to the realization that the roots of his malady lie deep in his own nature, his own organism, his own habits. To blame everything upon the capitalist and the environment produced by capitalism is to focus attention upon merely one of the elements of the problem. The Marxian too often forgets that before there was a capitalist there was exercised the unlimited reproductive activity of mankind, which produced the first overcrowding, the first want. This goaded humanity into its industrial frenzy, into warfare and theft and slavery. Capitalism has not created the lamentable state of affairs in which the world now finds itself. It has grown out of them, armed with the inevitable power to take advantage of our swarming, spawning millions."

Sanger made clear that her belief in depopulation was tainted by racial bias. There were certain races and ethnic groups that needed to be "depopulated" much more than others, in her world view. She wrote in 1920: "Birth control itself, often denounced as a violation of natural law, is nothing more or less than the facilitation of the process of weeding out the unfit, of preventing

Margaret Sanger, the founder of the Birth Control League (now called Planned Parenthood) abandoned Marxism after seeing that the Soviet Union was not a free love sex paradise. She became an outspoken Malthusian.

the birth of defectives or of those who will become defectives." She wrote about efforts by the Birth Control League to cultivate African-American ministers to promote contraception writing: "We do not want word to go out that we want to exterminate the Negro population and the minister is the man who can straighten out that idea if it ever occurs to any of their more rebellious members."

Sanger popularized the concept of "The Cruelty of Charity" arguing that social welfare programs and charity were detrimental to society because they enabled low-income and non-white people to stay alive and reproduce rather than "naturally" perishing from poverty rooted in their inferiority, and thus clear their "inferior stock" from the gene pool.

Hillary Clinton has spoken of Margaret Sanger as one of her greatest idols. In 2009, Hillary Clinton said: "Now, I have to tell you that it was a great privilege when I was told that I would receive this award. I admire Margaret Sanger enormously, her courage, her tenacity, her vision ... And when I think about what she did all those years ago in Brooklyn, taking on archetypes, taking on attitudes and accusations flowing from all directions, I am really in awe of her."

The notion that the third world needs to be depopulated in order to save the global capitalist economy was an almost central belief of the British imperialists throughout the 1800s. This belief was used to justify the horrendous famines imposed throughout

Africa, India, and in Ireland in which millions starved to death due to "free trade" imposed at the point of bayonet. Prince Philip, Duke of Edinburgh is quoted in 1988 as saying "In the event that I am reincarnated, I would like to return as a deadly virus, to contribute something to solving overpopulation." Two years prior he wrote the foreword to a book called *People As Animals* written by Fleur Cowles, published to raise money for the World Wildlife Fund. In his introduction Prince Philip wrote: "I just wonder what it would be like to be reincarnated in an animal whose species had been so reduced in numbers that it was in danger of extinction. What would be its feelings toward the human species whose population explosion had denied it somewhere to exist... I must confess that I am tempted to ask for reincarnation as a particularly deadly virus, but that is perhaps going too far."

Prince Philip, Duke of Edinburgh, openly said he hoped to be reincarnated as a deadly virus in order to dramatically decrease the human population.

Holding back development, preventing economic growth in the third world, reducing Africa, Asia, and Latin America to impoverished "spheres of influence" has long been the aim of imperialist strategists. The belief that it is urgently necessary to stop the developing world from industrializing and developing its own economy long predates the modern hysteria about global warming. Naomi Klien's book *The Shock Doctrine* documents how Neoliberal economic policies were imposed on Eastern Europe and South America throughout the 1990s with catastrophic humanitarian results. Malthusianism and de-growth is the very essence of imperialist economics. Books such as Walter Rodney's classic *How Europe Underdeveloped Africa* go into great detail showing this.

"African economies are integrated into the very structure of the developed capitalist economies; and they are integrated in a manner that is unfavourable to Africa and ensures that Africa is dependent on the big capitalist countries."

[Walter Rodney – How Europe Underdeveloped Africa]

One can recall how the British empire burned down India's textile looms and forced a nation that had been weaving for thousands of years to import its cloth from Europe. A more recent example would be how Bill

Clinton's NAFTA brought free trade to countries like Haiti and Mexico. Nations where the population had grown its own food since long before the arrival of Christopher Columbus had their agricultural sectors demolished and now rely on importing food from US agribusiness.

Bringing Depopulation Home

While keeping the third world poor has been the longstanding nature of imperialist economics, in the 21st century, amid a long term economic crisis the imperialists are bringing their "de-growth" policies back home. As technological leaps have created a crisis of overproduction and falling rates of profit, the desperation to get the economy moving again is rising among the rich and powerful. They now take aim at Middle America.

Black Americans were the first targets of the degrowth operations. To punish Detroit for the leftist atmosphere and strength of Black Nationalism and labor unions, the city saw its factories close down during the 1980s. The Black Community was specifically targeted with predatory lending practices that stripped families of their homes. Kamala Harris rose up the ranks of California's criminal justice system riding a wave of mass incarceration. Bill Clinton, Joe Biden and the bulk of the Democratic Party oversaw a huge increase in the rate of imprisonment, playing up the fears of the public with talk of "super predators." Amy Klobuchar became a successful prosecutor in Minnesota using "gang experts" with no direct knowledge of cases to give testimony frightening jurors and convincing them to convict Black men.

The Bush administration's response to Hurricane Katrina in 2005 was seen as horrendous confirmation of what the Black community has been aware of for centuries: "they are trying to exterminate us." In the aftermath of the natural disaster the Superdome arena was turned into a mini-concentration camp with thousands held there under the gun of the national guard. The natural disaster was seized upon to "degrow" the urban African American community of New Orleans. Books like Michael Eric Dyson's *Come Hell or High Water* have gone into great detail showing how the rich and powerful seized the moment for their agenda of impoverishment.

During his 2008 campaign, Obama spoke of his enemies as a bulk of the US population who reject the idea that their living standard is too high: "You go into these small towns in Pennsylvania and, like a lot of small towns in the Midwest, the jobs have been gone now for 25 years and nothing's replaced them. And they fell through the Clinton administration, and the Bush administration, and each successive administration has said that somehow these communities are gonna regenerate and they have not. And it's not surprising they get bitter, they cling to guns or religion or antipathy to people who aren't like them or anti-immigrant sentiment or anti-trade sentiment as a way to explain their frustrations."

Hillary Clinton spoke of Trump's base as a "basket of deplorables," a collection of irredeemable people who are a burden on US society. On February 10th, 2021, Congresswoman Ilhan Omar called out the *Washington Post* on Twitter for suggesting that Trump's supporters were motivated by the economic hardships facing most of the country. Omar proclaimed: "It's not "economic anxiety" it's anxiety over losing "status and power" that's fueling Right wing extremism. There is a white supremacy radicalism in our society and we can't afford to dismiss or normalize it."

The primary barrier to implementing "degrowth" in the United States is a layer of workers who have long enjoyed a decent living standard and are unwilling to accept the emerging low wage police state. This "silent majority" that Nixon spoke of enjoyed a prosperous life since the end of the Second World War and are simply not willing to give it up in the name of saving capitalism.

The idea now widely promoted by liberals is that working class people not wanting to see their living standards decline is "racist." The white workers should be made poorer in order to atone for the poverty that has persisted for generations among Black workers, and of course, to save the environment from the scourge of human consumption. The conversation does not revolve around lifting the African-American or Latino community up to the level of prosperity once enjoyed by the white middle class, but rather of impoverishing the white workers because they have an unfair "privilege" and "sense of entitlement" and deserve to poorer as a matter of implementing social justice. Among the liberals, the great danger facing the country is "populism" i.e. the resistance to degrowth among the bulk of the population.

The roots of this particular brand of Malthusian elitism are easy to trace. Leo Strauss, the philosophical academic who is considered the ideological father of Neoconservatism spent his career extolling these principles. Strauss' thesis in *Persecution and the Art of Writing* is that philosophers, the enlightened and intelligent ones, have always done their work under the threat of the inferior masses, and had to write in code. Strauss taught his trusted inner circle of proteges that among the enlightened few there is need to manipulate and control the masses.

With no use for the white industrial middle class at the assembly line, and a need for more thorough exploitation amid an economic crisis, the "aristocracy of labor" that once held the imperialist homelands together is being terminated. The ruling class has decided to cancel middle America and abolish the "big soft middle" for which the United States has long been so famous.

While people of color, sexual minorities, and other groups can be viewed as victims on the basis of their identity, the multi-national working class majority is seen as just one ugly mass of inferiority. It is an annoying herd the US government is tasked with managing, and its living standards must be terminated.

Living conditions for African Americans, Latinos and other marginalized groups in the United States have been decreasing for quite some time. Mass incarceration, the inflow of narcotics along with the equally damaging war on drugs, the closing of factories in urban centers, have all taken a devastating toll on communities of color.

Amid all their grandstanding about Black Lives Matter and Anti-Racism, liberals do not seek to address these economic woes. Rather, the message is that the suffering that has long plagued the Black and Latino working class should now be more widely imposed and expanded on to the entire working class. Any complaint or outcry about it is "racist."

The richest of the rich are unleashing a fury of voices who preach hatred for "America," "Straight White Men," Christianity, and other targets deemed to represent the US power structure. The message is "burn it down" and "tear it down." Unlike the Communist revolutionaries of the past, these "leftists" who are promoted by CNN and MSNBC do not seek to replace the US capitalist system with a socialist one. Rather they seek to transform the country into a smoking heap of ruin in the name "justice." Furthermore, unlike the Communists and radicals of the past who aligned themselves with those resisting US imperialism, these forces are the most enthusiastic supporters of US regime change operations and proxy wars from Ukraine, to Iran, to Taiwan.

Among this layer of "woke" activists, any talk of working to improve the conditions of the working class as a whole is deemed "fascist" and "populist." The focus is instead pushing a narrative of resentment, collective guilt, and performative virtue signaling that can be used to justify driving down living standards. The "1619 Project" of the *New York Times* claims the entire formation of the United States was to protect slavery from being abolished by a supposedly virtuous British Empire. Calls for implementing national health insurance or free college are now a crime called "class reductionism" according to liberals. Jimmy Dore daring to call on the "socialist" members of Congress to actually fight for these things was deemed "violence" against "women of color" by a "white man."

The woke left hates the US working class and its high living standards, and sees them as part of an "America" that must be destroyed. While it highlights the oppression of various minority identity groups, it loathes any social-democratic consciousness. The billionaires of the Ford Foundation, Rockefeller think tanks, Open Society Institute, share their glee at seeing US living standards driven down and are happy to foot the bill for this "revolutionary activism." The foot soldiers of Nazi economics in the 21st Century, who seek to save capitalism by forcibly implementing degrowth economics, are rallying under the banner of the "woke" left.

The Distortion of Marxism

The primary argument used to justify the need for a highly controlled capitalism to force policies of degrowth, i.e. fascist economics, is the environment. The idea is that the planet has limited resources and cannot continue to sustain the population. Ha-Joon Chang, a Marxist economics professor at Cambridge University has debunked this long standing fallacy writing: "I came across this book, by a curiously named author, The Club of Rome. Flickering through the book… I became very depressed. It said we would run out of oil by 1992 or thereabouts. So, even before I turned thirty, I thought, am I supposed to start riding around in bullock carts and burn wood for heating?… The predictions of the club turned out to be right. We *have* run out of oil, that is, oil that was accessible with the technology of the 1970s. But we are still burning oil in huge quantities because we have become much more efficient in locating and extracting oil from places that were just not accessible forty years ago, especially the deep sea. Technology does not only give us access to formerly inaccessible resources, but it also expands the definition of what a resource is. Sea waves, formerly only a destructive source to be overcome, has become a major energy resource due to technological development. Coltan used to be a rare mineral of little value until the 1980s. Today, it is one the most valuable minerals in the world... Tantalum, one of the component elements of Coltan, is a key ingredient in making parts used for mobile phones and other electronic goods. At a less dramatic level, technology allows us to produce renewable resources with greater efficiency."

One must ask, why are none of the voices that blame fossil fuel consumption for the climate crisis not enthusiastic about fusion energy? China's great breakthroughs point to a higher level of energy flux density that would render fossil fuels obsolete. If humanity was still burning charcoal for heat, the planet would have certainly deforested long ago. The nature of human beings is to constantly reinvent the way they interact with nature. If fossil fuels are proving to be unsustainable, why not take the obvious route of moving to a higher energy source?

The degrowthers are not interested in Fusion Energy. The only solutions they can offer to ecological problems are reducing the population and reducing consumption. This points to the obvious reality that they have another agenda, beyond ecological sustainability. The belief that the economy's problems are due to "overpopulation" "overconsumption" or "endless growth" is re-packaging of the economic theories of Robert Thomas Malthus. Malthusian economics has long been debunked by Marxists, going back to Marx himself.

Marx devoted many pages of his economic notebooks to refuting Malthusianism. In the collection of his writings published under the name *Theories of Surplus Value*, Marx wrote "Malthus's theory of value gives rise to the whole doctrine of the necessity for continually rising unproductive consumption which this exponent of over-population (because of shortage of food) preaches so energetically... this theory, for its part, suits his purpose remarkably well—an apologia for the existing state of affairs in England, for landlordism, 'State and Church', pensioners, tax-gatherers, tenths, national debt, stock-jobbers, beadles, parsons and menial servants... Malthus also wishes to see the freest possible development of capitalist production, however only insofar as the condition of this development is the poverty of its main basis, the working classes, but at the same time he wants it to adapt itself to the 'consumption needs' of the aristocracy and its branches in State and Church, to serve as the material basis for the antiquated claims of the representatives of interests inherited from feudalism and the absolute monarchy. Malthus wants bourgeois production as long as it is not revolutionary, constitutes no historical factor of development but merely creates a broader and more comfortable material basis for the 'old' society."

In his economic notebooks, Marx showed how Malthus' conceptions of "unproductive consumers" were completely false, but served the interests of the wealthy people who had commissioned his work. Marx wrote: "Malthus's book *On Population* was a lampoon directed against the French Revolution and the contemporary ideas of reform in England (Godwin, etc.) It was an apology for the poverty of the working classes. The *theory* was plagiarized from Townsend and others. His *Essay on Rent* was a piece of polemic writing in support of the landlords against industrial capital. Its *theory* was taken from Anderson. His *Principles of Political Economy* was a polemic work written in the interests of the capitalists against the workers and in the interests of the aristocracy, Church, tax-eaters, toadies, etc., against the capitalists. Its *theory* was taken from Adam Smith. Where he inserts his own inventions, it is pitiable."

Marx's close collaborator Friedrich Engels, blasted Malthus in even more fiery language, writing that his infamous *Population* essay was "the crudest, most barbarous theory that ever existed, a system of despair which struck down all those beautiful phrases about love thy neighbor and world citizenship."

If one reads *The Communist Manifesto*, Marx makes clear what the purpose of the Communist revolution is: "We have seen above, that the first step in the revolution by the working class is to raise the proletariat to the position of ruling class to win the battle of democracy. The proletariat will use its political supremacy to wrest, by degree, all capital from the bourgeoisie, to centralize all instruments of production in the hands of the State, *i.e.*, of the proletariat organized as the ruling class; and to increase the total productive forces as rapidly as possible."

Marxism, contrary to other schools of anti-capitalism focuses on the struggle for political power. Social-Democracy focuses on gradual reforms. Anarchism focuses on economic struggles and the forming of voluntary associations. Marxism seeks for the working class to seize control of the state and use the state to create a centrally planned economy ("centralize all instruments of production in the hands of state") and with this centrally planned economy, raise the level of abundance in society ("increase the total productive forces as rapidly as possible.")

Marxist economic analysis focuses on the way capitalism holds back human productivity creating poverty amid plenty, overproduction, the tendency of the falling rate of profits, etc. Marxism argues that by liberating the means of production from the irrationality of the profit motive, a new economy can be created that is so productive that abundance will escalate. As Engels explains in the *Socialism: Utopian and Scientific:* "The expansive force of the means of production bursts the bonds that the capitalist mode of production had imposed upon them. Their deliverance from these bonds is the one precondition for an unbroken, constantly-accelerated development of the productive forces, and therefore for a practically unlimited increase of production itself. Nor is this all. The socialized appropriation of the means of production does away, not only with the present artificial restrictions upon production, but also with the positive waste and devastation of productive forces and products that are at the present time the inevitable concomitants of production, and that reach their height in the crises."

The ultimate goal of a stateless, classless world is based on this high level of abundance. As Marx explains in *Critique of the Gotha Program*: "In a higher phase of communist society, after the enslaving subordination of the individual to the division of labor, and therewith also the antithesis between mental and physical labor, has vanished; after labor has become not only a means of life but life's prime want; after the productive forces have also increased with the all-around development of the individual, and all the springs of co-operative wealth flow more abundantly — only then can the narrow horizon of bourgeois right be crossed in its entirety and society inscribe on its banners: From each according to his ability, to each according to his needs!"

Marxism has absolutely no interest in reducing consumption, imposing restraints on productive forces, or any form of "degrowth." Those who led Marxist revolutions in the Soviet Union, China, Cuba and elsewhere understood this, and used centrally planned economies to raise living standards and industrialize their countries. It is only due to conscious manipulation of Marxism by some of the richest and most powerful forces that any notion of "small is beautiful" or "less is more" has been introduced to Marxian thought.

Lyndon LaRouche, who emerged from within

Marxist intellectual circles in the late 1960s as a harsh critic of the New Left, observed this fundamental change and distortion in his text *There is No Limit To Growth*: "Marx's views were those of the Babbage variety of anti-Malthusians, and remained emphatically so throughout the remainder of his life and writings. It was for approximately a century and longer one of the leading arguments against capitalism by Marx and Marxists, that capitalism braked technological progress and that this braking caused great harm to the world's population generally. The same viewpoint was strongly professed by V.I. Lenin…"

The CIA program known as the Congress for Cultural Freedom that was launched in 1951 involved covert funding of Trotskyites, leftist academics, art galleries, and publications. The magazines *Partisan Review, Encounter, Paris Review* and *Der Monat* became king-makers in a new synthetically created intellectual circle called "The New Left." Figures like Irving Kristol, Irving Howe, Hannah Arendt, Susan Sontag and Marty McCarthy became the well-funded voices of anti-capitalism and critique of US foreign policy. They were funded primarily to counter any pro-Soviet or orthodox Marxist-Leninist voices, but their work also emphasized anti-populism. In their tirades against McCarthyism, they equated fascism and communism with all forms of "totalitarian groupthink" in which the vulgar *untermenschen* assemble to persecute their intellectual superiors.

In addition to the anti-Sovietism and anti-populism that Rockefeller think tanks, the Ford Foundation and the CIA introduced into left-wing discourse, Malthusianism drifted in as well. The critique of capitalism suddenly became a critique of "consumerism." The talking point is part of Richard Nixon's famous Kitchen Debate with Nikita Khrushchev where he belittled the Soviet Union for not being as wealthy as the United States and not being efficient in churning out consumer goods was accepted at face value. With essays like *Notes on Camp*, Sontag and others began arguing that indeed capitalism was capable of producing endless wealth and unrestricted growth, but somehow this was dehumanizing.

As right-wingers equated capitalism and the free market with "having money" and "owning stuff," the Synthetic Left echoed them, agreeing with this definition, but saying "growth is bad." The Club of Rome published their *Limits to Growth* text in 1972, two years after Democrats and Republicans united to make Lenin's birthday, April 22, a US federal holiday focused on environmentalism ("Earth Day").

Amid an economic downturn, Jimmy Carter gave his famous "malaise" speech and told Americans that they should not be so concerned about their declining wages amid inflation because: "owning things and consuming things does not satisfy our longing for meaning. We've learned that piling up material goods cannot fill the emptiness of lives which have no confidence or purpose." Amid fuel shortages, Carter lectured the American people about why they should put on sweaters instead of turning up the heat.

Ronald Reagan trounced Carter in the 1980 election. The hard-right anti-communist asked TV audiences "Are you any better off than you were four years ago?" The memo was sent out that socialists and Marxists oppose wealth, and it is now routinely repeated by libertarians and right-wingers that socialism means "making everyone equally poor." Meanwhile, all the well-funded voices of socialism echo this vulgar distortion. Michael Moore with his film *Planet of the Humans*, Jason Hickel's many screeds containing vulgar distortions of Marx's writings, the various BreadTube voices pumped across social media as the appointed representatives of socialism and anti-fascism, all repeat this mantra.

What we have seen is a complete distortion of Marxism, and assimilation of leftism into the fascist Malthusian schemes of the ultra-rich. In the direct aftermath of the 2016 election, this writer went to Wheeling, West Virginia to interview steel-workers who voted for Donald Trump. One of them explained "The Democrats don't care about the working man anymore. They have turned into a bunch of socialists."

Socialism, as the struggle for the seizure of the means of production by society, so wealth can be created on a grander scale, poverty can be eliminated, and all can become prosperous has been eliminated from US discourse. "Socialism" is now a movement of middle class intellectuals who view the working class of America as a vulgar mob of greedy racist subhumans.

Re-inventing Anti-Racism

Rather than building industrial unions and unemployment councils, the "socialists" serve as foot soldiers for the ultra-rich in their fascist degrowth scheme. Not surprisingly, these "socialists" have nothing but hatred for China, Cuba, North Korea, the former Soviet Union, Venezuela, Vietnam, and other socialist governments around the world that hold on to the populist, pro-growth, historical materialism of Marx and Lenin.

This new "socialism" should be called "woke-ism" or some other label, because it has very little interest in economics, other than promoting a general contempt for average Americans and seeking to "reduce consumption." The focus is on the fact that US society is plagued by "systemic racism" and millions of Americans have "white privilege" which they must recognize and publicly atone for.

The Communist Party USA was in the fore-front of anti-racist struggles in America, promoting an end to Jim Crow segregation and promoting civil rights for Black Americans long before Martin Luther King Jr. Paul Robeson, William L. Patterson, Henry Winston, W.E.B. Dubois and Claudia Jones were among the many Black intellectuals who praised the Soviet Union and cooperated with the Communist Party. The message was that the oppression of African-Americans as a colonized people within US borders hurt the entire working class. Black people were viewed, not as a group of people subjected to "special oppression" but as a nation within US borders subjected to national oppression.

The Communists related to the struggle for Black self-determination, taking cues from how Marx related to the Irish question in 1870 while organizing among British workers. Marx wrote: "England, as the metropolis of capital, as the power that has hitherto ruled the world market, is for the present the most important country for the workers' revolution and, in addition, the *only* country where the material conditions for this revolution have developed to a certain state of maturity. Thus, to hasten the social revolution in England is the most important objective of the International Working Men's Association. The sole means of doing so is to make Ireland independent. It is, therefore, the task of the "International" to bring the conflict between England and Ireland to the forefront everywhere, and to side with Ireland publicly everywhere. The special task of the Central Council in London is to awaken the consciousness of the English working class that, *for them, the national emancipation of Ireland* is not a question of abstract justice or humanitarian sentiment, but *the first condition of their own social emancipation*."

The Communist Party was key in organizing the Civil Rights Congress and opposing Jim Crow Segregation.

The US Department of Justice legally designated the Civil Rights Congress as a "Communist Front" in 1956.

The Communist Party felt that the struggle to free Black workers from racist oppression would uplift all workers in the process, and would set the stage for the defeat of the ultra-monopolists that sit at the center of US society. Just as Communists supported the Vietnamese and Cubans in resisting US imperialism, they supported the oppressed Black nation as well. Freeing Black people would hasten the liberation of all workers in the United States by uprooting the oppressive structures and relations that held US society together.

However, the "oppression theory" that dominates American academia has a very different interpretation. Rather than seeing Black people as victims of colonization and super-exploitation as a colonized people, it says rather that white workers enjoy "white privilege." The focus is not on liberating Black people from violations of their rights, but rather on shaming white workers for the supposed benefits they enjoy as a result of being white.

Many leftist academics have made careers writing about how white people are "settlers" and enjoy lives of extravagance and privilege at the expense of Black and Chicano people. The millions of low income white people in Appalachia, the US South, the white people who live in trailer parks, serve in the US military and inhabit the US prison apparatus, the white people living in homeless encampments near what were once prosperous suburban neighborhoods, are all written out of the "woke" narrative. "White people" are portrayed as wealthy, middle class urban professionals. "White culture" is presented as the liberal values such people espouse, and the comfortable lives such people live in relation to the nearby impoverished people of color.

After the 9/11 attacks, Ward Churchill, the top Native American scholar in the United States compared the victims of the attack to Adolf Eichmann. Churchill wrote: "As to those in the World Trade Center. . .Well, really. Let's get a grip here, shall we? True enough, they were civilians of a sort. But innocent? Gimme a break. They formed a technocratic corps at the very heart of America's global financial empire – the "mighty engine of profit" to which the military dimension of U.S. policy has always been enslaved – and they did so both willingly and knowingly. Recourse to "ignorance" – a derivative, after all, of the word "ignore" – counts as less than an excuse among this relatively well-educated elite. To the extent that any of them were unaware of the costs and consequences to others of what they were involved in – and in many cases excelling at – it was because of their absolute refusal to see. More likely, it was because they were too busy braying, incessantly and self-importantly, into their cell phones, arranging power lunches and stock transactions, each of which translated, conveniently out of sight, mind and smelling distance, into the starved and rotting flesh of infants. If there was a better, more effective, or in fact any other way of visiting some penalty befitting their participation upon the little Eichmanns inhabiting the sterile sanctuary of the twin towers, I'd really be interested in hearing about it."

In his essay he argued that average Americans are complicit in the war crimes of the United States, lamenting that there was no widespread protest movement against the US criminal sanctions on Iraq: "As a whole, the American public greeted these revelations with yawns… There were, after all, far more pressing things than the unrelenting misery/death of a few hundred thousand Iraqi tikes to be concerned with. Getting "Jeremy" and "Ellington" to their weekly soccer game, for instance, or seeing to it that little "Tiffany" and "Ashley" had just the right roll-neck sweaters to go with their new cords. And, to be sure, there was the yuppie holy war against ashtrays – for "our kids," no less – as an all-absorbing point of political focus."

While Churchill comes across as a fiery critic of US society, it is no secret that he has long been aligned with US intelligence agencies. When Russel Means, the leader of the American Indian Movement, began fundraising for the Contras of Nicaragua, Churchill functioned as his speech writer, traveling with him to Nicaragua. Churchill even composed academic essays justifying collaboration with US imperialism by indigenous people against Communism.

This hatred which Churchill spews at the American people echoes not only the other various CIA linked "leftist" voices who have spewed anti-populism since the 1960s. It also echoes the agenda of the ultra-rich.

Just as Iraq, Libya, and Syria have been "degrown" by US foreign policy, the target is now the US working class. The midwestern rust belt was once made prosperous by labor unions built by Communists. The Teamsters, the United Auto Workers and the Steelworkers union forced industrialists to sign union contracts in the late 1930s. In the 1950s, these unions had the leverage to demand high wages amid the post-war economic boom.

In the name of saving capitalism, the ultra-rich now seek to impose a heavy handed authoritarian state to force down living conditions and grind the American heartland into poverty. The aim, like the aim of the Nazis, is to save capitalism by reducing living conditions, creating an underclass of slave laborers, and setting the stage for war.

The "woke" left that has fully departed from Marxism, and embraces US foreign policy, are the primary foot soldiers of one bonapartist faction that seek to carry out a kind of 21st century fascism. The current fascist threat comes from the Synthetic Left, and its aim is to secure the power of one section of the US ruling class so that fascist economic policies can be enacted.

The Proposed High Tech Dark Ages

The Biden-Harris administration stands with the four super major oil companies, the Silicon Valley tech giants, the World Bank, the Walton Family of Wal-Mart, Jeff Bezos and the top monopolists of western capitalism in a drive to stabilize capitalism by imposing their own bonapartist model onto humanity. They face opposition from the fracking companies, the hotel and restaurant chains, the military industrial complex, and almost all the lower levels of capital who see themselves being choked. The pandemic and the proposed "Great Reset," apocalyptic warnings about climate change, all serve as justification for their plans. They accuse their opponents in the New Right of being fascists and equate populism and anti-elitism with Nazism.

Not all among the bonapartist coalition to which the Biden-Harris administration are loyal have the same vision, but the high tech dark ages they envision looks more or less like this:

1. Ultra-Monopolies Protected by the State, "Cooperative" Capitalism: They envision a society where small businesses are crushed, and the ultra-monopolies like Amazon and Wal-Mart have complete hegemony, facilitated by the government. The employees of the ultra-monopolies will all be "co-owners" and receive stock option dividends based on market activity instead of set wages. This form of crude incentive pay will be presented as "socialism" and a "worker cooperative" with the employees being powerless "co-owners." The billionaire capitalist owners will still rake in super profits, and the workers will be pushed into greater and greater poverty. Much like Mussolini's "corporate state," Franco's "National Syndicalism" or Hitler's "National Socialism," this highly controlled capitalism will be imposed by the state and utilized to stabilize capitalism with degrowth.

2. Cancel Culture: A rigid code of social conformity and obedience will be enforced. Social media will be used to immediately track and highlight all dissidents and non-conformists. Those who speak against the ruling elite or violate the imposed restrictions on activity and thought will be immediately "boycotted" by society, losing their job, expelled from their schools, losing their access to the market and perhaps even their housing. All their friends and associates will be pressured immediately to denounce them and cut them off, or face a similar shunning. Rather than executing, imprisoning, or formally punishing dissidents, they will simply be "canceled" in what appears to be a public rebuke based on consensus, but is in fact engineered and directed from above.

3. Social Engineering and Weakening of the Population: In this society every effort will be made to addict people and make them dependent on the big monopolies and distracted from pursuing bigger questions or engaging politically. Drugs, both recreational and medicinal, will be everywhere. Pornography will be as well. The population will be dazzled by constant entertainment, over-sexualization and intoxication, rendered unable to focus or think about bigger issues. An effort to make people weaker, physically and psychologically, will be carried out in order to make them easier to control.

Anti-intellectualism will accompany a campaign demonizing physical fitness and exercise. Intelligence, physical fitness, or any form of strength will be labeled "fascist" with those who display it being canceled.

4. Reducing the Population, Reducing Consumption, Atomizing Humanity: Suicide will be encouraged and romanticized in popular media. Every effort will be made to cultivate the hopelessness, depression and loneliness that leads people to take their own lives. Procreation will be discouraged. Families will be demonized as patriarchal, abusive and oppressive. Religious organizations, fraternal groups, and all associations of people will be declared "cults" and widely demonized if not forcibly broken apart. No ideology, church, or set of beliefs of any kind will be allowed to emerge and stand in the way of the mass programming of society carried out from above. Obedience to the social engineers will be described as "freedom of mind" and "thinking for yourself" and all entities that would challenge their hegemony will be accused of "brainwashing." Long term relationships and even marriage will be discouraged. Every effort will be made to break each human being down into an atomized individual with no group identity or ideology, and no way of understanding the world other than those deemed appropriate by the ruling elite.

5. Global War to Preserve Imperialism: A state of all out, constant war against Russia, China, Venezuela, Iran, and other countries that have broken out of the western financial system will be the new normal. People will constantly be mobilized and required to display their virtue by raising money, performatively making statements and otherwise supporting regime change operations. While most of the population will be kept drugged up, addicted and barely conscious, a layer of mercenary professional super soldiers will be cultivated to carry out this relentless bombardment of all headquarters of resistance around the planet.

This bonapartist scheme by the richest of the rich and the tech overlords is intended to resolve the crisis of capitalism. The endgame is reducing the population, reducing living standards, ending social unrest and opposition to austerity, crushing the global forces of resistance, and bringing the world "back into balance."

Like all the other bonapartist schemes to stabilize a naturally unstable system, it will ultimately fail. The problems of production organized for profit will not be resolved. Humanity's inherent nature as a tool-making creature that strives to reach a higher plane will ultimately win out.

The question is how greatly and how long this Neo-fascistic social engineering nightmare will be allowed to unfold, and how effective the resistance to it both globally and domestically can be.

Bonapartist struggles between rival factions in the ruling class have historically opened the door to socialist revolutions and overturning of capitalism. As is said, "It is darkest before dawn," and while this nightmare labeled "globalism" by the New Right hangs over us, the possibility of moving toward a society where human growth is no longer restrained by the irrationality of the market is also approaching. The coming period will be decisive, as the contradiction of the prolonged capitalist crisis comes to a head.

3. Counter Gangs and Revolutionaries

The Society of December 10th – The Crisis of Marxism – The Sorelian Critique of Marxist Organizing – The Fascist Weltanschauung – Counter Gangs in Kenya and Ireland – Fourth Generation Warfare – Brzezinski and the Late Cold War – Alexander Parvus and the Bolsheviks – Defeating the Kornilov Reaction – The New People's Study Society – The Long March to Power – Top and Bottom Organizing – Counter-gangs in America – 2008-2011: The Left Failed – Black Lives Matter & Antifa – The Proud Boys – BreadTube and Twitch-Streamer Leftism – Peterson-ism – The Netflix Cult Obsession – A Country Without Ideology?

Marx's understanding of how socialism would emerge to replace capitalism was based on economics. He wrote in the Communist Manifesto: "But with the development of industry, the proletariat not only increases in number; it becomes concentrated in greater masses, its strength grows, and it feels that strength more. The various interests and conditions of life within the ranks of the proletariat are more and more equalized, in proportion as machinery obliterates all distinctions of labor, and nearly everywhere reduces wages to the same low level. The growing competition among the bourgeois, and the resulting commercial crises, make the wages of the workers ever more fluctuating. The increasing improvement of machinery, ever more rapidly developing, makes their livelihood more and more precarious; the collisions between individual workmen and individual bourgeois take more and more the character of collisions between two classes. **Thereupon, the workers begin to form combinations against the bourgeois; they club together in order to keep up the rate of wages; they found permanent associations in order to make provision beforehand for these occasional revolts.** Here and there, the contest breaks out into riots. Now and then the workers are victorious, but only for a time. The real fruit of their battles lies, not in the immediate result, but in the ever expanding union of the workers. This union is helped on by the improved means of communication that are created by modern industry, and that place the workers of different localities in contact with one another. It was just this contact that was needed to centralize the numerous local struggles, all of the same character, into one national struggle between classes. But every class struggle is a political struggle… This organization of the proletarians into a class, and, consequently into a political party, is continually being upset again by the competition between the workers themselves. But it ever rises up again, stronger, firmer, mightier. It compels legislative recognition of particular interests of the workers, by taking advantage of the divisions among the bourgeoisie itself. Thus, the ten-hours' bill in England was carried."

The Society of December 10th

Marx's understanding of overproduction and the tendency of the falling rate of profits led him to conclude that unemployment would constantly be increasing, wages would continue to drop, and out of necessity the "combinations" of workers would grow. Eventually, the broad masses of workers would be organized to seize political power. With control of the state the working class would implement a rationally planned economy in which the means of production functioned for the benefit of society overall, not the profits of private owners.

Marx's vision was for a mass uprising and upsurge of democratic participation and militancy among the value-creating working class, the industrial proletariat. In his 1852 pamphlet analyzing the rise of Louis Bonaparte, Marx contrasts the mobilizations the Parisian demagogue politician built up in the streets with a revolutionary movement of the working class. Marx described the "Society of December 10th" that

Bonaparte deployed in these terms: "On the pretext of founding a benevolent society, the lumpen proletariat of Paris had been organized into secret sections, each section led by Bonapartist agents, with a Bonapartist general at the head of the whole. Alongside decayed roués with dubious means of subsistence and of dubious origin, alongside ruined and adventurous offshoots of the bourgeoisie, were vagabonds, discharged soldiers, discharged jailbirds, escaped galley slaves, swindlers, mountebanks, lazzaroni, pickpockets, tricksters, gamblers, *maquereaux*, brothel keepers, porters, literati, organ grinders, ragpickers, knife grinders, tinkers, beggars — in short, the whole indefinite, disintegrated mass, thrown hither and thither, which the French call *la bohème*; from this kindred element Bonaparte formed the core of the Society of December 10th."

Marx speaks with contempt of this mob, as not a group of wealth creators but a group of leeches on French society: "A "benevolent society" — insofar as, like Bonaparte, **all its members felt the need of benefiting themselves at the expense of the laboring nation.** This Bonaparte, who constitutes himself *chief of the lumpenproletariat*, who here alone rediscovers in mass form the interests which he personally pursues, who recognizes in this scum, offal, refuse of all classes the only class upon which he can base himself unconditionally, is the real Bonaparte, the Bonaparte *sans phrase*... What the national *ateliers* were for the socialist workers, what the *Gardes mobile* were for the bourgeois republicans, the Society of December 10th was for Bonaparte, the party fighting force peculiar to him… The Society of December 10th was to remain the private army of Bonaparte until he succeeded in transforming the public army into a Society of December 10th."

Unlike the labor unions and socialist groups with deep roots in the communities, the Society of December 10th was a collection of thugs, criminals, and elements from the margins of society. Rather than empowering millions of French people to awaken and enter politics to improve their conditions, Louis Bonaparte had simply created a gang of marginal elements to function as a hit squad and pave the way for his regime to seize power.

The contempt with which Marx described Louis Bonaparte's Society of December 10th is hardly concealed in his words. Marx wanted a broad mass movement of ordinary people to become politically aware and work in their economic interest. Louis Bonaparte, like many demagogues who emerge during capitalist crises as the rich fight among themselves, wanted an isolated group of violent fanatics and unstable semi-criminals with which to create chaos and pave the way for his seizure of power. Since 1852 when Marx laid out this understanding, the Marxist movement's perspective on this issue has greatly evolved and adjusted.

The tendency of Bonapartist figures to build up political groups of fanatics to do their bidding, as Louis Bonaparte did with the Society of December 10th, is pretty consistent. Woodrow Wilson revived and built up the Ku Klux Klan to serve this purpose. The Italian fascist Blackshirts, the Nazi stormtroopers, all more or less served this function. However, when one digs deeper one can see that there is a huge amount of overlap between revolutionary organizations and bonapartist gangs, and the role such organizations play at any given time can change.

What constitutes a genuine revolutionary working class mass movement? What constitutes a lumpen mob serving one section of the bourgeoisie? As one looks over the history of Marxist movement and political turmoil throughout the world, from Marx's day right up into the 21st century, it becomes clear that this differentiation has become completely muddled, and successful revolutionary movements and organizations often play multiple roles over the course of their development.

The more important question, obviously, is what kind of revolutionary movement is needed in our time? Finding the answer requires us to dig through lots of complex and often obscured history.

The Crisis of Marxism

On the basis of Marx's intellectual guidance, the early Marxist movement sought to create organizations much like what is described in the Communist Manifesto. They sought to cultivate "worker-politicians" or members of the wealth producing class who enter politics on their own accord, acting in their own economic interests and striving to move society toward socialism. Meanwhile, the idea of forming a group of vagrants and criminals was frowned on. While Marxists engaged in charitable work, there was a feeling that the *lumpenproletariat,* which Marx described in other writings, was particularly untrustworthy and dangerous.

The First International that Marx built ultimately fell apart due to ongoing rivalries between Marxists and the various anarchist and ultra-leftist sects that emerged. While Marx sought to build a mass working class movement, figures like Ferdinand LaSalle, Louis August Blanqui, and Mikhail Bakunin focused on adventurism, terrorism, and performative politics that kept them isolated. As William Z. Foster explains in his *History of the Three Internationals:* "The Marxist leadership of the First International fought tirelessly and effectively against the many current sectarian tendencies that aimed to misdirect the workers' efforts into channels alien to their class interests. Marx especially shattered the illusions of many around utopian socialism of various types, the radical bourgeois republicanism of Mazzini, the petty bourgeois socialism of Proudhon, the leftist phrase mongering and conspiratorial tactics of Bakunin, and the pure and simple trade unionism of the Odgers and Applegarths...

The basic reason why the First International disappeared from the world political arena was that capitalism at the time was entering a new phase of development, raising up new tasks for the working class, tasks which the First International, under the given circumstances, was in no position to fulfill."

Karl Marx died in 1883, but his ideas significantly proliferated after his death. The Second International was founded in 1889, and across Europe in the 1890s, massive Marxist parties came into existence. As Marxism became wildly popular throughout Europe during these years, the movement used the term "social democracy" to describe itself, shunning the word "communist" because it was associated with ultra-leftists and anarchists whom Marx had disagreed with.

The largest organization of the Second International was the German Social-Democratic Party led by Karl Kautsky. Labor unions, community associations, study centers, marching bands, choirs, kindergartens, and all kinds of other community associations that centered themselves around Marxist ideology emerged. The labor movement and the fight of industrial workers for their own interests on the job against the employers had its day, and Marxism was the ideology that came to give expression to this movement. Members of parliament were elected from various social-democratic and labor parties.

But around the time of 1900, the Marxist movement entered a definitive period called the "crisis of Marxism."

Marx's ideas had proliferated into a huge mass movement. Yet, the revolution Marx envisioned had not come about. Furthermore, Marx's economic predictions were not exactly correct either.

According to Marx's theories, living standards for workers in western Europe and the United States should have been continuously dropping. The problem of overproduction and the tendency of the falling rate of profits should have led to workers getting poorer and poorer, society becoming less and less stable, and the eventual revolutionary seizure of power by the industrial workers and their political movement.

However, while technology was certainly advancing, the labor movement was increasingly able to win on the picket-line. Wages for the "skilled" workers were increasing, while wages for "unskilled" workers of basic industry remained low. Society was stabilizing, and overall living standards were rising as the gigantic capitalist firms based in western countries spread their tentacles across the planet, raking in super-profits as they carved out new markets in the colonized world.

Capitalism was moving into its monopoly stage of imperialism, and it was Vladimir Lenin who had the knowledge of economics to point this out. As Lenin explained: "Imperialism *is* monopoly capitalism. Every cartel, trust, syndicate, every giant bank *is* a monopoly. Superprofits have not disappeared; they still remain. The exploitation of *all* other countries by one privileged, financially wealthy country remains and has become more intense. A handful of wealthy countries—there are only four of them, if we mean independent, really gigantic, 'modern' wealth: England, France, the United States and Germany—have developed monopoly to vast proportions, they obtain *super*profits running into hundreds, if not thousands, of millions, they 'ride on the backs' of hundreds and hundreds of millions of people in other countries and fight among themselves for the division of the particularly rich, particularly fat and particularly easy spoils... The bourgeoisie of an imperialist 'Great' Power *can economically* bribe the upper strata of 'its' workers by spending on this a hundred million or so francs a year, for its *super*profits most likely amount to about a thousand million."

As Lenin understood, the economies of the western imperialist powers were stabilizing as they raked in profits from all over the world. Meanwhile, a layer of labor leaders and "socialists" who were not revolutionary were being cultivated to maintain the imperialist system. In this context, Lenin argued that the energy in the socialist movement would come from the colonized world where workers were fighting for their nations to be free, not from the industrial workers in the western capitalist countries, who were becoming more and more comfortable and reformist. Lenin wrote: "On the one hand, there is the tendency of the bourgeoisie and the opportunists to convert a handful of very rich and privileged nations into "eternal" parasites on the body of the rest of mankind, to "rest on the laurels" of the exploitation of Negroes, Indians, etc., keeping them in subjection with the aid of the excellent weapons of extermination provided by modern militarism. On the other hand, there is the tendency of the *masses*, who are more oppressed than before and who bear the whole brunt of imperialist wars, to cast off this yoke and to overthrow the bourgeoisie. It is in the struggle between these two tendencies that the history of the labor movement will now inevitably develop. For the first tendency is not accidental; it is "substantiated" economically. In *all* countries the bourgeoisie has already begotten, fostered and secured for itself "bourgeois labor parties" of social-chauvinists…. **On the economic basis referred to above, the political institutions of modern capitalism—press, parliament associations, congresses etc.—have created *political* privileges and sops for the respectful, meek, reformist and patriotic office employees and workers, corresponding to the economic privileges and sops. Lucrative and soft jobs in the government or on the war industries committees, in parliament and on diverse committees, on the editorial staffs of "respectable", legally published newspapers or on the management councils of no less respectable and "bourgeois law-abiding" trade unions—this is the bait by which the imperialist bourgeoisie attracts and rewards the representatives and supporters of the "bourgeois labour parties"…** Wherever Marxism is popular among the workers, this political trend, this "bourgeois labor party", will swear by the name of Marx. It cannot be prohibited from doing this, just as a trading firm cannot be prohibited from using any particular label, sign or advertisement. It has always been the case in history that after the death of revolutionary leaders who were popular among the oppressed classes, their enemies have attempted to appropriate their names so as to deceive the oppressed classes."

The visible articulation of the "bourgeois labor party" tendency among the socialists of western imperialist countries came from Eduard Bernstein. Bernstein called himself a "revisionist Marxist" and broke with the Second International, proclaiming "the movement is everything, the goal is nothing," and that through universal male suffrage, labor laws and other reforms western capitalism was inching closer to socialism. Socialism, Bernstein argued, was merely the sum of reforms, a no political event horizon described as a "revolution" would take place. Bernstein's concept of "evolutionary socialism" became increasingly popular among higher paid strata of the labor movement.

The culmination of the "crisis of Marxism" was the outbreak of the First World War. The various Marxist parties of the Second International who had promised to oppose the war, changed their positions at the last minute and voted to send their working class brothers and sisters off to die in a battle to carve up the world among the European imperialist powers. In the end 20 million workers died in the "war to end all wars."

Foster explains: "The Social-Democratic Party of Germany bore the heaviest responsibility. It was the leading party of the Second International, and the labor movement looked to it for guidance. If it had made real resistance to the war, undoubtedly the bulk of the International would have followed its example." Eugene Debs in America, Rosa Luxemburg in Germany, and the Bolsheviks in Russia stood alone as anti-imperialist voices as the Marxist movement proved itself to be utterly bankrupt. Lenin denounced the Second International as a stinking corpse.

The Sorelian Critique of Marxist Organizing

In studies of the crisis of Marxism and its political interpretation, Marxists generally study the vulgar reformism of Bernstein, the less obvious reformism and opportunism of Kautsky, and the ideological breakthroughs of Lenin with his understanding of imperialism and pioneering of Bolshevism. In doing so, however, most Marxist textbooks and historians skip over a highly important political theorist from this period whose ideas are deeply important in understanding the various political organizations that have emerged since the beginning of the 20th century. This thinker is Georges Sorel.

Sorel was a French intellectual who originated among the "revisionist" school of Marxism, those who were rejecting the Second International and criticizing Marxist orthodoxy. Sorel ascended to prominence

In 1908, French Syndicalist Georges Sorel put forward a spiritual critique of the mass organizing methods of the Marxists in his book "Reflections on Violence."

when he embraced the Syndicalist wing of organized labor, rejecting social-democracy.

Syndicalism was a variation of socialist thought that favored direct action on the job, workers moving against their employers, and rejected politics. Voting was a waste of time, the Syndicalists argued. They were equally disinterested in seizing control of the government apparatus. For Syndicalists, the focus was building militant unions and training workers to be more willing to fight their employers. Syndicalism taught that the revolutionary activism and strikes of today were all preparing for the Great General Strike, when the workers of the world would lay down their tools together and rise up to seize their factories in a gigantic apocalyptic battle.

Sorel published a very widely circulated document in defense of the use of violence by striking workers and syndicalist organizations. *Reflections on Violence* was not unique in its defense of labor militancy, as many radicals argued that workers had the right to take up arms against their employers. Sorel's work stood out because it made a spiritual and psychological critique of the existing Marxist and labor movements rather than a tactical or ideological one.

Sorel spoke of violence as having a spiritual quality, reflecting on the history of Christianity and Ancient Greece. He wrote of a desire to be heroic. He argued that a strata within society of violent individuals who attain this "heroic" status should be strived for. He describes violent hazing rituals that workingmen in jobs requiring great physical strength subject each other too: "In factories and workshops customs of great brutality formerly existed, especially where it was necessary to employ men of great strength... in the end men managed to be given the task of engaging with other men, because any individual taken on by others was subjected to an infinite number of humiliations and insults; the man who wished to enter their workshop had to buy them a drink, and the following day to treat his fellow workers... There is a tendency for the old ferocity to be replaced by cunning, and many philosophers view this as real progress. Some philosophers who are not in the habit of following the opinions of the herd, do not see how exactly this constitutes progress from the point of view of morals."

Sorel also spoke of the power of myth, and how the Great General Strike the syndicalist movement strives for may never indeed happen, but the spiritual power of mythology should not be underestimated. Sorel eventually moved on from Syndicalism to traditionalist conservatism and associating with monarchists. He wrote: "It seems to me the optimism of Greek philosophers depended a great extent on economic reasons; it probably arose from the rich and commercial urban populations who were able to regard the universe as an immense shop full of excellent things to satisfy their greed. I imagine Greek pessimism sprang from the poor warlike tribes living in the mountains who were filled with enormous aristocratic pride, but whose conditions were correspondingly poor; their poets probably charmed them and made them look forward to triumphal expeditions conducted by superhuman heroes; they explained their present wretchedness to them by relating catastrophes in which semi-divine former chiefs had succumbed to fate or the jealousy of the gods. The courage of the warriors might for the moment be unable to accomplish anything, but it would not always be so; the tribe must remain faithful to old customs in order to be ready for great and victorious expeditions that might very well take place in the near future... Religions constitute a very troublesome problem for the intellectualist, for they can neither regard them as being without historical importance nor can they explain them... The ideas of socialism cannot be kept intact by diluting the phrases of Marx in verbose commentaries, but by continually adopting the spout of Marx which is capable of assuming a revolutionary aspect."

Sorel began seeing tradition, religion, nationalism and social hierarchies as necessary in unleashing the kind of violent heroism his work idealized. At the time of his death Sorel praised both Lenin and Mussolini. Edward Shils introduces Sorel's writings saying: "Heroism and a sense of the sublime are the highest virtues — they are military virtues and whether practiced inside of society as in the case of civil war or outside of society in the case of national wars, they raise the dignity of the individual and endow him with all the price that dignity requires... Sorel's ethic is the ethic of the political sect living in the midst of continuous crisis, with all the streets of purity and all the fear of contamination by the affairs of this world which mark the sect. It is the ethic of crisis, and it is of a piece with expectation of an ever deepening which is resolved ultimately only by an apocalyptic transformation in which everything is totally changed... In the life of a society, there were for Sorel only two possibilities: one, decadence, in which the ruling class of politicians and property owners, lacking in self-esteem, corrupted by the niggling procedures of pursuit and exercise of office, and too cowardly to be violent, resorts to fraud and cunning to control a mass lost in hedonistic self-gratification and individualism; and the other, renascence, in which the aspirants to rule or those already ruling, inflamed with their enthusiasm, their minds on remote goals, caring nothing for the immediate consequence of any action, but performing it because it is morally imperative."

The Italian fascists praised Sorel excessively, and their Blackshirt thugs that preached a conservative anti-capitalism along with Italian nationalism eventually set the stage for an authoritarian bonapartist regime. The Italian fascist dictator Benito Mussolini remarked: "I owe most to Georges Sorel. This master of syndicalism by his rough theories of revolutionary tactics has contributed most to form the discipline, energy and power of the fascist cohorts."

Sorel's vision of an isolated group of rigid, violent fanatics rather than a tactically flexible mass organization embedded in communities fit fascism well. Some also see elements of Sorelianism in Lenin's Bolshevik concept of the Party of New Type, but the justifications Lenin gave for his organization are quite different. Lenin viewed the ideal revolutionary organization as one staffed by professional revolutionaries who give of their whole lives and engaged in agitation and propaganda, stirring up confrontation while building up their cadre in order to seize power in a crisis.

Lenin's book *What Is To Be Done?* which was written in 1903 and built the case for this type of "vanguard party" organization remains one of the most important Marxist works in history. The book is quite difficult to read in modern times as it is filled with esoteric prose and outdated references, along with side-commentary on forces that were contemporary at the time of its publication. Even the title of *What Is To Be Done?* is a reference to a popular novel, a literary pun. But in the book, Lenin argued that the "debating society" or loose organization that was common among European Social Democracy would not be able to overthrow capitalism, and that a new model of an organization that practiced "democratic centralism" was necessary.

Sorel spoke highly of Lenin, but was not convinced he had influenced him: "I have no reason for believing Lenin made use of some ideas in my books; but if that were the case, I would be uncommonly proud for having contributed to the intellectual formation of a man who seems to be at once, the greatest theoretician socialism has had as since Marx and a head of state whose genius recalls Peter the Great… At the end of the year of 1917 the former spokesman of the Black Hundreds said that the Bolsheviks had proven that they were more Russian than the rebels Kaledin, Roussky, who betrayed the Tsar and country."

When the First World War and the various revolutionary upheavals that followed it had concluded in 1919, the situation forced many Marxists across the world to rethink their understanding of world events and the tactics they advocated. Only in Russia, a deeply impoverished   semi-feudal   country   had   the revolutionaries been able to take power. Furthermore, it had been the Bolsheviks, a leftist outlier group among Marxists, that was widely decried for its rigid and authoritarian organizing methods that had taken power. Revolution did not happen in the most advanced capitalist countries as Marx and Engels had predicted. Furthermore, the broad socialist groups that had millions of members, seats in parliaments, huge trade unions associated with them, and mass base among the wealth producing industrial working class had proved unable to stop the war and unable to take power in the political crisis that followed.

The Fascist *Weltanschauung*

In the 1920s and 30s across Europe, anti-labor militias were mobilized by the factory owners. As the threat of Communist revolution increased, in Germany the Nazi Party with its stormtroopers eventually set the stage for a bonapartist regime. In *Mein Kampf*, Hitler's autobiographical political screed, he made this interesting observation about the failure of previous German governments to crush Marxism with state repression. In 1925, as he sat in prison after a failed coup attempt, Hitler composed the following words:

"But there is something else to be said: Every *weltanschauung* (philosophy or view of life -CM), whether religious or political—and it is sometimes difficult to say where the one ends and the other begins—fights not so much for the negative destruction of the opposing world of ideas as for the positive realization of its own ideas. Thus its struggle lies in attack rather than in defense. It has the advantage of knowing where its objective lies, as this objective represents the realization of its own ideas. Inversely, it is difficult to say when the negative aim for the destruction of a hostile doctrine is reached and secured. For this reason alone a *weltanschauung* which is of an aggressive character is more definite in plan and more powerful and decisive in action than a *weltanschauung* which takes up a merely defensive attitude. If force be used to combat a spiritual power, that force remains a defensive measure only so long as the wielders of it are not the standard-bearers and apostles of a new spiritual doctrine. To sum up, the following must be borne in mind: That every attempt to combat a *weltanschauung* by means of force will turn out futile in the end if the struggle fails to take the form of an offensive for the establishment of an entirely new spiritual order of things. It is only in the struggle between two *weltanschauung* that physical force, consistently and ruthlessly applied, will eventually turn the scales in its own favor. It was here that the fight against Marxism had hitherto failed. This was also the reason why Bismarck's anti-socialist legislation failed and was bound to fail in the long run, despite everything. It lacked the basis of a new *weltanschauung* for whose development and extension the struggle might have been taken up. ... **But this was only the necessary result of the failure to find a fundamentally new *weltanschauung* which would attract devoted champions to its cause and could be established on the ground from which Marxism had been driven out.** And thus the result of the Bismarckian campaign was deplorable. During the World War, or at the beginning of it, were the conditions any different? Unfortunately, they were not. The more I then pondered over the necessity for a change in the attitude of the executive government towards Social-Democracy, as the incorporation of contemporary Marxism, **the more I realized the want of a practical substitute for this doctrine. Supposing Social-Democracy were overthrown, what had one to offer the masses in its stead?** Not a single movement existed which promised any success in attracting vast numbers of workers who would be now more or less without leaders, and holding these workers in its train. It is nonsensical to imagine that the international fanatic who has just severed his connection with a class party would forthwith join a bourgeois party, or, in other words, another class organization. For however unsatisfactory these various organizations may appear to be, it cannot be denied that bourgeois politicians look on the distinction between classes as a very important factor in social life, provided it does not turn out politically disadvantageous to them. If they deny this fact they show themselves not only impudent but also mendacious."

In these words, we find more or less a confession from Adolf Hitler that National Socialism served as an ideological substitute for Marxism. Marxism couldn't be defeated because no new *weltanschauung* had emerged to replace it. Nazism, it can be inferred, is this new *weltanschauung*.

This points to the reality that throughout Europe, and the world, during this time period, new "revolutionary movements" were being fomented by factory owners to combat the Marxist movement and its labor unions. In the United States, Father Charles Coughlin gave fiery sermons on the radio, condemning capitalism but also loudly opposing labor unions and Marxism. His broadcasts were paid for by General Motors. Anti-Communist Catholics were organized into an armed street fighting group called the Black Legion. William Dudley Pelley, the screenwriter who built his own religious sect eventually formed the Silver Legion of America (Silver Shirts) as his fascist street fighting group.

All of these groupings were more or less Sorelian, as they did not have deep roots in neighborhoods or communities, they preached a conservative anti-capitalism, and made a big point to engage in acts of violence. They all saw Communism as the main threat, but preached their own brand of right-wing anti-capitalism as the solution. Pelley's followers carried whips in honor of the "scourge of cords" with which the Bible describes Christ driving money-changers from the Temple of Jerusalem. The Black Legion murdered the father of Malcolm X in Michigan believing his proselytizing of the Marcus Garvey Back to Africa movement would create racial unrest. The Black Legion was also sent out to attack auto workers who occupied their plants during the 1937 Flint Sit Down Strike.

Fascism in various countries throughout Europe began as a "revolutionary movement" of street fighters, strike breakers, and fanatics to fight against Marxism. In Italy and Germany it eventually laid the basis for establishing an authoritarian regime as liberalism collapsed into illiberalism amid an economic crisis.

But this points to a bigger truth which is that various stormtroopers and "Society of December 10th" style organizations are created by the ruling class to serve a function, not just in defeating Marxism, but as foot soldiers in bonapartist struggles among themselves. In

Nazism presented itself as a radical mass movement that was an alternative to Communism.

fact, revolutionary Marxist organizations have frequently been used in this way by elements within the power structure as well.

Counter Gangs in Kenya and Ireland

The role of intelligence agencies makes this process even more complicated. General Sir Frank Edward Kitson oversaw low intensity military operations for the British from 1946 until he retired in 1985. One of his most successful operations was crushing the Land and Freedom Army (Mau Mau), an anti-imperialist group in Kenya, that fought the British from 1952 to 1960. During the late 1970s, Kitson oversaw British military operations in Northern Ireland focused on defeating the Provisional Irish Republican Army.

Kitson's methods for defeating insurgents were highly respected and his writings on military strategy were widely studied. In 1960 he published a book called *Gangs and Counter Gangs* describing how he had fought against the Kenyan liberation movement. The methods he used involved the creation of a network of "Counter Gangs" of Africans that engaged in covert activities. The counter gangs gathered intelligence, posing as Mau Mau fighters. The counter gangs also committed atrocities that were blamed on the Land and Freedom Army and alienated the local population from supporting the guerillas. The counter gangs spread disinformation and confused the population, sometimes claiming the Mau Mau were on the brink of surrendering and selling out the anti-colonial struggle.

In an anti-colonial war, psychological operations are extremely important, Kitson noted. The resentment of Black Africans against white colonizers had been the primary contradiction in the struggle, and served to make the Mau Mau fighters popular with the Kenyan people. The job of British military intelligence and their "Counter Gangs" was to muddy the waters and confuse the population so the Land and Freedom Army could be isolated and defeated.

Eventually Frank Kitson was sued by Mary Heenan, the widow of a man in Northern Ireland who was murdered by protestant extremists in 1973. Proof was put forward showing that the Ulster Defense Association, an extra-legal group of terrorists, who opposed the IRA were in fact being directed and armed by the British government.

It should be noted that as "The Troubles" progressed in Northern Ireland during the 1970s and 80s, culminating in the Good Friday Agreement of 1998 that ended hostilities, fighting between British troops and Irish resistance forces significantly decreased. The British government instead covertly funded protestant extremists and the IRA increasingly focused its efforts on self-defense against them. This gave the conflict more of an ethnic and religious character, making it appear much less like a national liberation struggle to observers.

The main way the British government defeated the Provisional Irish Republican Army was through following "Fourth Generation Warfare" strategies of low intensity conflict and covert operations developed by Frank Kitson.

At the same time that protestant fanatics were being funded, the United Nations, the Vatican and a variety of nonprofits and NGOs funded "peace" marches and efforts to bring Protestant and Catholic communities together. This all culminated in victory for the British government and the surrender of the Provisional IRA in 1998. Kitson's method of manipulating the terms of the conflict in Northern Ireland, reframing it as a fight between Protestants and Catholics, rather than a fight between the Irish and the British Empire proved very successful.

Fourth Generation Warfare

In the aftermath of the US invasion of Iraq, US troops occupied the country and battled against a number of different armed groups, some with ties to Iran, some with roots in the toppled Ba'ath government and others with ties to Saudi Arabia. William S. Lind, a Pentagon strategist, began writing about his concept of Fourth Generation Warfare.

In this new era, military conflicts between great powers tend to involve non-state actors. Direct flights between major countries are too dangerous, and could result in a nuclear exchange. Rather, various smaller countries that are contested and the influence of different great powers can be found are turned into battlefields, as covert support is passed on to different factions, who are loyal to different great powers. During the Cold War, the term "proxy wars" was widely used, and currently US officials often refer to "frozen conflicts." In these conflicts, the role of "non-state actors," armed or in some cases un-armed groups, are key.

Non-state actors are very different from states, and have a different set of strengths, weaknesses and rules to play by. While they may receive financing, arms and training from one country, they ultimately serve their own ends. In his writing William S. Lind describes techniques of sewing confusion and manipulating different non-state actors and armed groups against each other in order to defeat an insurgency. Lind observes: "At the heart of this phenomenon, 4th

Generation war, lies not a military evolution but a political, social and moral revolution: a crisis of legitimacy of the state. All over the world, citizens of states are transferring their primary allegiance away from the state to other entities: to tribes, ethnic groups, religions, gangs, ideologies and 'causes.' Many who are no longer willing to fight for their state will fight for their new primary loyalty."

Lind goes on to describe the mindset of shifting military tactics when battling against ideological insurgents and other non-state actors. He writes: "The military historian Martin van Creveld compares a state military that, with its vast superiority in lethality, continually turns its firepower on poorly equipped Fourth Generation opponents to an adult who administers a prolonged, violent beating to a child in a public place. Regardless of how bad the child has been or justified the beating may be, every observer sympathizes with the child. Soon, outsiders interfere, and the adult is arrested. The power mismatch is so great that the adult's action is judged a crime.... In the 3,000 years the story of David and Goliath has been told, how many listeners have identified with Goliath?"

Lind describes how winning over the local population is important. He goes on to point out that non-state actors are highly susceptible to bribery. He writes: "What artillery and air power are in Third Generation war, cash is in the Fourth Generation: the infantry's most useful supporting arm. Local commanders must have a bottomless slush fund of cash. Obviously this cash cannot be subject to normal accounting procedures as most will, necessarily and properly, be used for bribes. It is imperative that any regulations or bureaucratic obstacles to this bribery are promptly changed."

He then goes on to say efforts should be made to conceal the brutality of suppressing the non-state actors that does prove to be necessary: "One key to the Mafia's success is to conceal the use of force. If an individual needs to be whacked then it is usually done with little fanfare and in the shadows. The rule is no fingerprints. Unless there is a specific message aimed for a larger audience, people who are killed by the mafia are seldom found. This method usually requires patience. It often takes a long time for the right moment to present itself."

Strategic circles in the Pentagon and American intelligence agencies have clearly spent a long time analyzing the roots of their failures in Korea and Vietnam. It's pretty clear that as the US was losing in Vietnam, the Cold War strategy was reshuffled. When one looks at the situation currently playing out in Ukraine, Venezuela, Nicaragua, Belarus, and many other countries, it is pretty clear the United States is utilizing methods of "Fourth Generation Warfare." Non-state actors, who are often much like the isolated groups of fanatics Sorel idealized, and whose members are often much like the lumpen marginal elements who made up Louis Bonaparte's Society of December 10th, are being armed by the United States to wage a covert war against Russia, China, and various socialist and anti-imperialist states. There are, likewise, many "non-state actors" across the world who are sympathetic to Russia, China, Iran or Cuba, and oppose the United States.

Brzezinski and the Late Cold War

Zbigniew Brzezinski was a polish born academic who moved up the ranks of American strategy circles rather quickly during the 1950s and 60s. From 1960 to 1972 he headed up the Institute on Communist Affairs at Columbia University, a well-funded intelligence center, that obsessively studied the global communist movement for the purpose of defeating it. After the United States was defeated in Vietnam, Brzezinski and Henry Kissinger received funding from David Rockefeller to establish the Trilateral Commission, a think-tank to reorient US strategy in the Cold War. Brzezinski served as Jimmy Carter's National Security Advisor, and later received the Presidential Medal of Freedom from Ronald Reagan for his importance in reorienting US foreign policy operations.

In 1970, Brzezinski published a book entitled *Between Two Ages: America's Role in the Technetronic Era.* The book was published amid the massive turmoil of the Vietnam-era. Urban rebellions and a rise in Black Nationalism among African Americans, massive opposition and protests against the Vietnam War on college campuses, had culminated in a serious political crisis. Brzezinski's book contained many innovative shifts in anti-Communist strategy and thinking, and foreshadowed many things to come in the following decades.

He speaks of the "information revolution" that is sweeping the world due to technological breakthroughs, and how it would ultimately lead to the "Americanization" of the world. He wrote: "The United States is the principal global disseminator of the technetronic revolution. It is American society that is currently having the greatest impact on all other societies, prompting far-reaching cumulative transformation in their outlook and mores... Roughly 65 percent of all world communications originate in this country. Moreover, the United States has been the most active in the promotion of global communication systems by means of satellites, and its pioneering in the development of the world-wide information grid."

He wrote about how the USA has been very successful in winning over the loyalty of scientists and engineers recruited from other countries, and how American universities play the role of winning students from across the planet to have views that are more in line with the US foreign policy establishment. He described the "global ghettos" and compared the conditions in third world countries and their political results, to the situation facing impoverished urban African Americans. He described how the increasing

opportunity among African-Americans led to an
increased frustration and the rise of the civil rights
movement, much as the access to education in the third
world following the Second World War fed the wave of
anti-colonial movements and communist revolts.

Brzezinski spoke of the breakdown of orthodoxy and
commonly held beliefs that was sweeping the planet,
writing: "Today the dominant pattern seems
increasingly to be that of highly individualistic,
unstructured, changing perspectives. Institutionalized
beliefs, the result of a merger of ideas and institutions,
no longer appear to many as vital and relevant, while
the skepticism that has contributed so heavily to
undermining institutionalized beliefs now clashes with
a new emphasis on passion and involvement."

He wrote of how "institutional Marxism" in the form
of large Communist Parties and Marxist-Leninist
governments, was appearing a bit stale and unexciting
in the face of the new global wave of awareness and
involvement: "The parties bureaucratic organization,
their concern for their institutional vest interests —
even at the expense of the Marxist doctrine they are
said to embody —their fear of intellectual exploration
all have cumulatively stimulated both opposition on
the outside and sterility on the inside. Characteristic of
this sterility is the fact that the Soviet Communist Party
has not produced a single creative and influential
Marxist thinker in the fifty years since it seized power
in 1917."

Brzezinski was of course pointing to a real flaw in the Soviet Union. The fact that 15 countries had invaded after the 1917 revolution, and that 26 million people had been killed during the Second World War, had necessitated a very rigid, militarized and authoritarian atmosphere. Events like the *yezhovshchina* (Great Terror) of the late 1930s had sent the message to the population that getting involved in politics or engaging with the official Marxist-Leninist ideology too deeply might have serious consequences. The result was that Marxism, a revolutionary movement full of energy and passion, had become somewhat dry and simple when presented by the Soviet state. Brzezinski wrote: "The result has been increasing indifference to doctrine among the general membership and increasing disaffection among more creative Marxist thinkers."

What is now a matter of public record and admitted fact is that while the Soviet aligned parties had this increasing problem of bureaucratism, the US intelligence agencies were doing their best to recruit disaffected intellectuals and seize control of Marxist thought for themselves. The Frankfurt School in West Germany, with thinkers like Herbert Marcuse, Theodor Adorno and others was funded by US and British intelligence. Marxist magazines like *Partisan Review, Der Monat,* and *Encounter* were pushing an anti-soviet brand of leftist politics that focused on cultural criticism. The central entity directing these operations was the Congress for Cultural Freedom, set up by the

CIA in 1950, directed by Irving Kristol, the former Trotskyite who would eventually become the intellectual father of Neoconservatism.

Within the Soviet Union itself, US intelligence was cultivating a layer of dissident elements that would eventually overthrow socialism. In 1970, 19 years before the Berlin Wall fell, Brzezinski writes: "it may be expected that the 1970s will witness the spread to the Soviet Union of convulsions similar to those that Spain, Yugoslavia, Mexico and Poland began to undergo in the 1960s. The Soviet student population doubled during the 1960s... The 1970s will probably see the sexual revolution to the more urban Soviet centers and the party ideologues will not find it easy to accommodate within the prevailing official mores."

As a US intelligence strategist, Brzezinski announced his full support for the dissident "New Left" elements in the Soviet Union. He wrote: "It is not exaggeration to say —though some anti-communist may be loath to admit this —that the peace of mankind in large measure depends on the Soviet Union's return to the occidental Marxist tradition from which the more oriental Leninism-Stalinism had diverted it, but not necessarily the outright abandonment of Marxism."

What Brzezinski described was exactly what American intelligence did during the late Cold War years. It cultivated a layer of dissident students to sew unrest in the Eastern bloc, most of which did not want to restore capitalism, but simply to establish "socialism with a human face" or "democratic socialism." However, amid the unrest these students generated, western capitalism took control and instituted harsh neoliberal austerity. The economic devastation that followed the breakup of socialism across the former Soviet Union and Eastern Europe was devastating. Millions died, fled their countries as refugees, became victims of human trafficking, or otherwise suffered from extreme poverty.

In Brzezinski's 1970 text, he went on to describe the New Left in the United States, pointing out that it wasn't really a threat to the power structure. He wrote: "During the 1930s radical movements had a real basis for hope to radicalize the American laboring masses who were suffering due to the deprivations of the Great Depression and only then beginning to develop organizational consciousness. There was, in effect, at least potential for historical symbiosis and the frustrated and impoverished masses. Today the situation is entirely different…" Brzezinski quotes the work of those who investigated student unrest only to discover that psychological unease and depression was the primary motivation for involvement in campus activism during the 1960s: "Statistics showed that visits to psychologists and mental health professional on campuses decreased significantly during upsurges of activism, with mentally ill students finding an outlet for their feelings." He quotes observers who noted that "deep dissatisfaction with themselves and inner confusion is projected against institutions of the university first, and against all institutions of society secondarily, which are blamed for their own inner weakness."

Brzezinski's analysis of the 1960s campus activists was quite different from that of the Nixon administration and the hardline anti-communist right wing: "It is an escapist phenomenon rather than a determined revolutionary movement. It proclaims a desire to change society, but by and large only offers a refuge from society... It provides a psychological safety valve for its youthful militants and a sense of vicarious fulfillment for its more passive, affluent, older admirers."

Brzezinski warned that a heavy handed response to the student left from the government could harden young activists into real revolutionaries. He warns that a "violent left" could replace the New Left: "not from the idealistic young people who infuse it with zeal and confusion but from those among them who have been hardened, disillusioned, and embittered by their experiences in prisons and penitentiaries. These men will be psychologically prepared for real violence, and they will dismiss as child's play the sit-downs and raids on dean's offices. American society would then have to confront a real internal threat."

In essence, Brzezinski's 1970 piece laid out a re-orientation of Cold War strategy. In the 1950s, the US government cracked down on the Communist Party, as well as homosexuals, dissident intellectuals, and others. This produced a negative reaction among the public and youth in particular, whose values and relationship to authority was changing as a result of the technological revolution and new access to information.

Brzezinski argued the "New Left" that emerged in response to the failure of McCarthyism did not represent a threat of Communist revolution, but just a new wave of social liberalism and ideological deconstruction. Rather than fighting the new left, US intelligence could simply hijack it, and use it to dismantle socialism in the Eastern Bloc and win the Cold War. This, of course, involved funding, arming, and covertly supporting a lot of "Marxists" "Socialists" and "Revolutionaries" who would serve US geopolitical ends.

Brzezinski's foreign policy strategy school at Columbia University directly educated Barack Obama. Biden's administration is also dominated by this school of thought that solidified itself during the Carter years. This strand of Brzezinski-esque thinking represents the overall worldview of the many academics cultivated by the Rockefeller ultra-monopolists in oil, the government spawned Silicon Valley tech oligarchy, and a very solid axis within the US power structure.

Brzezinski spends pages reflecting on the "Americanization" of the world that will result from the information revolution. This has largely been achieved with American culture, free market policies and social liberalism going global. But in the 21st Century big sections of the world are rejecting it. Meanwhile, big sections of America also object to being "Americanized" as it means the economic and social destruction of their communities and values.

Alexander Parvus and the Bolsheviks

The strategy of covertly utilizing or manipulating leftist organizations for geopolitical aims did not begin with the United States during the late Cold War. To think that the various Marxist, Social-Democratic and Syndicalist groups of Europe prior to 1917 were not manipulated or used by various states against each other is completely naive. One of the most solid bits of proof we have that this strategy of intelligence agencies utilizing Marxists and socialist organizations in this era comes from the documented activities of Alexander Parvus.

Alexander Parvus was a Marxist born in Odessa to a family of Lithuanian Jews. He was a very prominent figure in the revolutionary movements of Europe from 1900 up to the Russian Revolution. He is also known to have been employed by the German intelligence agencies.

Leon Trotsky credits Parvus with having originated the ideas he eventually fleshed out into his Theory of Permanent Revolution. In his autobiography Trotsky wrote: "Parvus was unquestionably one of the most important of the Marxists at the turn of the century. He used the Marxian methods skillfully, was possessed of wide vision, and kept a keen eye on everything of importance in world events. This, coupled with his

Leon Trotsky's mentor, who originated the concept of Permanent Revolution, was a German Intelligence Officer and arms dealer named Alexander Parvus. He arranged for the German government to aid Lenin in returning to Russia in 1917.

fearless thinking and his virile, muscular style, made him a remarkable writer. His early studies brought me closer to the problems of the social revolution, and, for me, definitely transformed the conquest of power by the proletariat from an astronomical 'final' goal to a practical task for our own day."

The fact that Trotsky's personal mentor was an intelligence officer who eventually became financially tied in with the Ottoman Empire raises some questions about Leon Trotsky's political career in exile prior to returning to Russia and joining the Bolsheviks in July of 1917. Trotsky spent his years in exile in London, Paris, and eventually New York City. He broke with Lenin in 1903 and refused to join the Bolshevik "Party of New Type" and instead attempted to form his "August Bloc" that would be a more radical wing of the Menshevik Social-Democrats.

With Parvus as his advisor and handler, Trotsky's primary disagreement with Lenin focused on a call for a "United States of Europe." Trotsky argued that nationalism and borders were an impediment to working class solidarity, and that the socialist movement should focus on calls for some kind of European Union, a single government for all western European states. Lenin denounced the idea of unifying the imperialist powers, accusing Trotsky and the many social-democratic leaders who called for this of "working hand in glove with the imperialist bourgeoisie *precisely* towards creating an imperialist Europe on the backs of Asia and Africa."

Indeed, it seems that the notion of unifying the European mainland into a single government is something that the German imperialist bourgeoisie was strongly in favor of as a means of reducing the influence of Britain and the United States, their imperialist rivals. The fact that Trotsky would argue for such a position, with a German intelligence officer nudging him along makes perfect sense. Trotsky's

Theory of Permanent Revolution, arguing that third world countries could be seized by proletarian parties and transformed into base areas to spread communism to the West must also be examined in this light.

Parvus and the Germans were not alone in conducting such covert operations. It also seems quite well-documented that the British intelligence agencies had their fingers in various socialist, anarchist, and nationalist groups throughout the European mainland as well.

Parvus functioned as an arms dealer, owning a weapons trading company based in Istanbul. He eventually became a political advisor to the Young Turks, and a personal millionaire. As the First World War broke out, Parvus was closely involved in military operations and arms shipments between the Ottoman government and the Germans.

Amid all of this he took a trip to Switzerland where Lenin was living in exile, and established a relationship with the Bolshevik Party's leadership. Parvus began funneling money to the Bolshevik organization in Russia through Russian emigres living in Paris. In 1915 he presented the German government with a 20-page document called "A preparation of massive political strikes in Russia." The proposal indicated that the Bolsheviks could be used to cripple war production and enable the Germans to win the war.

When Tsar Nicholas II abdicated the throne in February of 1917, Parvus had further plans for his

Bolshevik friends. It is widely understood, though debated, that Parvus met with Lenin in Switzerland on April 13th. Lenin returned to Russia on April 16th with his famous "April Theses" preparing the Bolsheviks to take power, which they did in October of the same year.

How much money, weaponry, or other covert support Parvus and German intelligence provided to the Bolsheviks is unknown. Obviously, the Bolsheviks did not take power simply as the result of a German intelligence conspiracy. The Bolsheviks had no loyalty to the German Kaiser, and just a year after they took power, the new Soviet government was providing military support to armed uprisings in Germany.

Defeating the Kornilov Reaction

The primary factor in the Bolsheviks taking power was their opposition to the First World War. After the Czar abdicated, Alexander Kerensky established the provisional government, with the intention of holding an election of a Constituent Assembly that would compose a new democratic constitution for Russia. Kerensky continued fighting the war, despite the mass defections and strikes crippling the military. The Menshevik Party supported the war, as did many of the various Social-Democrats and Marxists in Russia.

The Bolshevik Party was distinguished by its opposition to the war. When Lenin returned to Russia in April of 1917, he ordered the Bolshevik Party to change its official name from the Russian

Social-Democratic Labor Party - Majority Group (Bolsheviks), to the Russian Communist Party - Majority Group (Bolsheviks). The designation of "Communist" was chosen to replace "Social Democratic" because the various Social-Democratic Parties throughout Europe had supported the war.

The Bolsheviks spent July of 1917 leading strikes with the slogan "Down with War!" It's clear that in their efforts the Bolsheviks had support from a big section of the Russian capitalist class that did business with the Germans. While the Russian state was primarily loyal to the British and Americans, their primary business partners, Germany had a lot of influence in the Russian economy. A big section, though not a majority of the Russian capitalist class, wanted to end the war and resume making profits in trade with Axis countries.

The decisive moment in the Russian Revolution came in September of 1917, when General Lavr Kornilov began marching his troops toward St. Petersburg. Kornilov felt the provisional government was too weak in crushing the anti-war strikes, and he intended to establish a military regime to aggressively continue the war and crush the unrest. The official *History of the Communist Party of the Soviet Union (Short Course)* lays out events this way: "The counter-revolutionary General Kornilov bluntly demanded that "the Committees and Soviets be abolished." Bankers, merchants and manufacturers flocked to Kornilov at General Headquarters, promising him money and support. Representatives of the "Allies," Britain and France, also came to General Kornilov, demanding that action against the revolution be not delayed. General Kornilov's plot against the revolution was coming to a head. Kornilov made his preparations openly. In order to distract attention, the conspirators started a rumor that the Bolsheviks were preparing an uprising in Petrograd to take place on August 27 — the end of the first six months of the revolution. The Provisional Government, headed by Kerensky, furiously attacked the Bolsheviks, and intensified the terror against the proletarian party. At the same time, General Kornilov massed troops in order to move them against Petrograd, abolish the Soviets and set up a military dictatorship."

The Bolsheviks mobilized a military defense of St. Petersburg from an attempted coup by General Lavr Kornilov.

Amid the crisis of a war, economic downturn, and continued revolts Kornilov was an aspiring bonapartist. He sought to liquidate the crisis as the military strongman. The Kerensky government feared for its life, and just like the anti-war capitalists, now the pro-war capitalists who favored Kerensky were forced to align with the Bolsheviks. The Bolsheviks prepared a military defense of St. Petersburg, barricading the city and arming the population. As the Bolsheviks fortified the city for the pending onslaught, it became clear that the Bolshevik militias and organizations outnumbered the official government, and had more organizational discipline and capacity. The official Bolshevik history text explains: "In face of the Kornilov revolt, the Central Committee of the Bolshevik Party called upon the workers and soldiers to put up active armed resistance to the counter-revolution. The workers hurriedly began to arm and prepared to resist. The Red Guard detachments grew enormously during these days. The trade unions mobilized their members. The revolutionary military units in Petrograd were also held in readiness for battle. Trenches were dug around Petrograd, barbed wire entanglements erected, and the railway tracks leading to the city were torn up. Several thousand armed sailors arrived from Kronstadt to defend the city. Delegates were sent to the "Savage Division" which was advancing on Petrograd; when these delegates explained the purpose of Kornilov's action to the Caucasian mountaineers of whom the

"Savage Division" was made up, they refused to advance. Agitators were also dispatched to other Kornilov units. Wherever there was danger, Revolutionary Committees and headquarters were set up to fight Kornilov. In those days the mortally terrified Socialist-Revolutionary and Menshevik leaders, Kerensky among them, turned for protection to the Bolsheviks, for they were convinced that the Bolsheviks were the only effective force in the capital that was capable of routing Kornilov. But while mobilizing the masses to crush the Kornilov revolt, the Bolsheviks did not discontinue their struggle against the Kerensky government. They exposed the government of Kerensky, the Mensheviks and the Socialist-Revolutionaries, to the masses, pointing out that their whole policy was in effect assisting Kornilov's counter-revolutionary plot."

When Kornilov's army began marching away from the city amid desertions and word of the military defense led by the Bolsheviks, this constituted a pivotal moment in the revolution: "The defeat of the Kornilov revolt further showed that the Bolshevik Party had grown to be the decisive force of the revolution and was capable of foiling any attempt at counter-revolution. Our Party was not yet the ruling party, but during the Kornilov days it acted as the real ruling power, for its instructions were unhesitatingly carried out by the workers and soldiers. Lastly, the rout of the Kornilov revolt showed that the seemingly dead Soviets actually possessed tremendous latent power of revolutionary resistance. There could be no doubt that it was the Soviets and their Revolutionary Committees that barred the way of the Kornilov troops and broke their strength. The struggle against Kornilov put new vitality into the languishing Soviets of Workers' and Soldiers' Deputies. It freed them from the sway of the policy of compromise. It led them into the open road of revolutionary struggle, and turned them towards the Bolshevik Party. The influence of the Bolsheviks in the Soviets grew stronger than ever. Their influence spread rapidly in the rural districts as well."

The Bolsheviks had protected the Provisional Government and in the process, built up their own forces to a huge significance. Shortly after defending the Kerensky government in September, the Bolsheviks toppled it in October, declaring the Soviets (revolutionary councils) to be the new government.

Were the Bolsheviks a "counter gang?" Not exactly. The Bolsheviks were not a mass party as the European Social Democrats that made up the Second International had been. They drew heavily from Russia's traditions of secret societies, from the Old Believers to the Decemberists. They required a level of fanatical devotion from their membership that forced their critics to accuse them of being organized along the lines of a monastic order or a religious cult. Their "democratic centralist" structure was labeled authoritarian by critics.

The Bolsheviks received financial support from the German government, as well as from domestic Russian capitalists who wanted to end the war. Throughout 1917, they entered multiple alliances. First, they aligned with the majority of the Russian capitalist class that wanted to remove the Czar because he was viewed as incompetent and losing the war. Then, they aligned with the German government that wanted to end the war, with German intelligence enabling Lenin to return to Russia. Then they aligned with domestic capitalists who wanted to end the war and favored doing business with Germany. Then they aligned with the provisional government against the Kornilov reaction, repelling a bonapartist seizure of power.

Because the Bolsheviks had a cadre of thousands of dedicated organizers who would carry out policies crafted from the top, they were useful friends to have. The entire time that they made themselves useful to various forces within the power structures of the day, they continued building up their own forces, and plotting to achieve their own declared mission.

The Bolsheviks seized power because they had the organizational strength and tactical wisdom to maneuver quickly within a crisis, continue building up their forces, solidifying their organizational discipline, all while the society around them was falling into chaos and confusion. When the conditions were ripe enough they then could establish themselves as the new state power.

The New People's Study Society

The Chinese Revolution, taking place in a different country at a different time, bears some important similarities to the Russian Revolution. The way the Chinese Communist Party emerged and eventually took power is completely different from the Bolsheviks, but there is some significant overlap in their historical experience.

Mao Zedong, who became the iconic leader of the Chinese revolution, was a significant activist and organizer before the founding of the Chinese Communist Party. Benjamin Schwartz's book *Chinese Communism and the Rise of Mao* describes Mao Zedong as someone who "lived on the fringes of academic life as a library employee" and "according to his own testimony, was for a time under the influence of anarchism."

The Three-Volume text *An Ideological History of the Communist Party of China* published in 2020, written by Huang Yibing, points to the role of pre-party Mao in organizing academic conferences. Huang writes: "As early as autumn of 1919, he organized a seminar in Changsha. This seminar was conducted for the purpose of studying politics, economics, social issues, education, labor, international affairs and other issues, as well as ways to unite the people, the feasibility of socialism, and issues concerning Confucianism. There were more than 140 topics in all. Mao was often deeply involved with railway workers, masonry workers, porters and other manual laborers. He made friends with them and he set up night schools and established trade unions. In order to draw nearer to the workers, he often removed his gown and wore a short tunic when he went among them. He learned the language of the workers, came to understand their demands, and became familiar with their lives."

It is in *The Morning Deluge,* Han Suyin's biography of Mao, that we find a more complex and detailed narrative of the organizational roots of Chinese Communism and its leader. According to Han, Mao spent the summer of 1917 traveling across the Chinese countryside with a friend. She writes: "Mao inquired on the conditions of crops and rain, of rent and landlords, a peasant talking to other peasants, but also a budding social scientist and researcher. Mao kept notes of what he had been told and remembered the peasant's names. He walked over three hundred miles on his trip."

Then, Han explains that after his investigative quest through the countryside, Mao launched his own political project: "Then in autumn of that year 1917, Mao Zedong founded with a friend Ho Shu-Heng, the Hsin Hsueh Hui or the New People's Study Society. The significance for the Chinese Revolution of this society cannot be overestimated, nor what is represented as training in leadership for Mao. For about a year he entertained the idea of organizing a society in which people would debate new ideas and create for themselves a new personality by debate, discussion, self-analysis and action." Han reports that Mao took out an advertisement in a newspaper calling on people to join the "organization of a society of young men, active, resolute and patriotic." She quotes Mao's recollection saying: "I specified youth who were hardened and determined and ready to make sacrifices for their country."

Mao's society apparently attracted many youths from troubled backgrounds. One early member was Tsai Chang, who "had fled to Changsha when her father had tried to betroth her against her will. With her brother's help she entered the Chounan school and was a brilliant student. She was slim and tall, with wonderful hair; she studied physical education, a revolutionary action for a girl then." Han writes that the "nucleus" of Mao's organization was made up of 13 people most of whom

When China erupted in anti-US and anti-Japanese protests in 1919, an organization called the New People's Study Society took the lead.

had "similar stories of revolt against family tradition." Mao required members of the New People's Study Society to be sexually abstinent and held them to a strict moral code: "its members engaged in neither flirtation nor romance… The manifesto of the society opposed opium smoking, gambling, drinking, concubinage, prostitution, and corruption; it advocated the reform of China and the world… In later years all thirteen of the original members of the society were to join the Chinese Communist Party, founded in 1921. By 1919 there were eighty members, of whom forty were to join the party."

The New People's Study Society intervened amid the wave of Chinese nationalism that followed the First World War. When the Treaty of Versailles handed Chinese territories, colonized by the Germans, to Japan, this led to a huge amount of outrage and rioting in China's cities. Amid this upsurge, Mao gave a lecture on Marxism. Han writes: "The students, teachers, shopkeepers, the workers of Changsha, who in 1918 already had demonstrated against Japan and carried on a very effective boycott of Japanese goods, now crowded to listen to Mao Tsetung. Mao's lecture was a great success. It ended with the assertion that only by studying Marxism could the Chinese people save themselves. In April 1919 the Marxist study group in Hunan province was founded in Changsha."

Eventually Mao's student group organized a boycott of Japanese products: "The boycott spread through the schools and their faculties to countryside small towns; even school children took part. In Changsha, teams of girls inspected and searched stores for Japanese products. When these were found they were publicly burned."

The wave of Chinese nationalism and anti-Japanese sentiment culminated a few months later in the May 4th Movement which began in Beijing. Thousands of Chinese students were arrested, and many buildings associated with the United States and Japan were burned.

In the aftermath of these uprisings, western social-democratic intellectuals Bertrand Russell and John Dewey visited China bringing a message of progressivism and reform. Mao Zedong's followers launched an ideological campaign against them, circulating a pamphlet written by Mao called *On Radicalism,* in which he argued: "The soft nonviolent kind of communism Russell preaches is good for capitalism, it can never achieve socialism." Han reports that Mao's following grew significantly in this period, and that Mao became much more picky about who was welcome to work with him: "instead of selection by intellectual ability, he recruited on the basis of ideas, enthusiasm, and radicalism. He urged the formation of investigation teams among the students, to go among the people and report on actual conditions. And he began a revolt against Chang Ching-yao, the provincial governor, who seems to have been an extremely corrupt and evil man." Eventually the New People's Study Society launched "The Anti-Militarist League for the Reconstruction of Hunan" and called for Hunan to cut ties with China's central government which they accused of being too soft on Japan and collaborating with the country's humiliation by Western colonizers.

In 1921, the New People's Study Society merged into the Chinese Communist Party. As Mao Zedong emerged to be the key leader of Chinese Communism over the course of following decades, the members of his original inner-circle rose with him, and very much set the tone for the future of the revolution.

The New People's Study Society was clearly much closer to Georges Sorel's organizational concepts than those of Second International and Marx. It was an isolated group of fanatics who lived a puritanical life, devoting themselves to achieving their goals and engaging in personal transformation. It was also not made up of the broad masses of Chinese workers and peasants, but rather of students, teenage runaways, and youth who had "similar stories of revolt against family tradition." Han writes that Mao had a particularly strong desire to recruit women to his activist organization, even though the prevailing view at the time was that women should stay out of political organizing and study.

In this sense, Mao's original organization has a lot in common with the Bolsheviks in that it was a "vanguard" formation, of people who gave "the whole of their lives."

However, much like the Bolsheviks, the New People's Study Society made itself relevant by entering strategic alliances and attaching itself to major trends in society, starting first with the wave of anti-Japanese sentiments.

The Long March to Power

Han quotes Mao as saying that "he recalled that serious disagreements arose between various tendencies; in fact, the Chinese Communist Party from its inception was far from monolithic." Mao's position within the Chinese Communist Party changed as wide-ranging debate on tactics took place. The Chinese Trotskyites wanted to focus on building labor unions among railway workers and exposing the KMT-Nationalist government of being "class collaborationist" and not as revolutionary as the Communists. Mao sided with Stalin and the majority position with the Communist International, and pushed for the Chinese Communist Party to merge into the KMT-Nationalist Party as a pro-Soviet faction. This tactic of entryism into China's ruling party that based itself on Dr. Sun Yat Sen's three principles, democracy, independence and the people's livelihood proved very successful and the Communist Party expanded their ranks to millions in a few short years.

The Soviet Union expanded its influence in China, establishing a military training school. The Communist Party functioned as the pro-Soviet wing of the KMT that favored more socialist policies, and gained significantly among the military due to Soviet training.

In 1927, Mao Zedong wrote his important essay "Report on an Investigation into the Peasant Uprisings in Hunan Province." The essay served as a fiery polemic, urging the Chinese Communists to turn their attention away from the cities and embrace the wave of rural revolts. Mao wrote: "In a very short time, in China's central, southern and northern provinces, several hundred million peasants will rise like a mighty storm, like a hurricane, a force so swift and violent that no power, however great, will be able to hold it back. They will smash all the trammels that bind them and rush forward along the road to liberation. They will sweep all the imperialists, warlords, corrupt officials, local tyrants and evil gentry into their graves. Every revolutionary party and every revolutionary comrade will be put to the test, to be accepted or rejected as they decide. There are three alternatives. To march at their head and lead them? To trail behind them, gesticulating and criticizing? Or to stand in their way and oppose them? Every Chinese person is free to choose, but events will force you to make the choice quickly."

In the essay, Mao defended the brutal vengeance the peasants were enacting against the rural aristocracy saying: "a revolution is not a dinner party, or writing an essay, or painting a picture, or doing embroidery; it cannot be so refined, so leisurely and gentle, so temperate, kind, courteous, restrained and magnanimous. Revolution is an insurrection, an act of violence by which one class overthrows another. A rural revolution is a revolution by which the peasantry overthrows the power of the feudal landlord class. Without using the greatest force, the peasants cannot possibly overthrow the deep-rooted authority of the landlords which has lasted for thousands of years. The rural areas need a mighty revolutionary upsurge, for it alone can rouse the people in their millions to become a powerful force. All the actions mentioned here which have been labeled as "going too far" flow from the power of the peasants, which has been called forth by the mighty revolutionary upsurge in the countryside."

While one can draw parallels to Sorel's belief in the spiritual power of violence, it is more important to note how Mao is once again urging the Chinese Communists to attach themselves to a bigger social force within the country. Just as the New People's Study Society attached itself to the explosion of anti-Japanese sentiments, Mao desperately urges the Communist Party to attach itself to the wave of peasant revolts.

The "White Terror" launched by Chiang Kai-Chek, in which Communists were slaughtered and driven out of the urban centers, forced the surviving Communists into the countryside. In 1927, the Chinese Communist Party established the People's Liberation Army, and Mao launched policies of "rural people's war" in which the Communists led peasants to seize liberated territory and redistribute land, as had been done spontaneously by the peasantry in Hunan. The Communists made themselves the organizational expression of the widespread desire for agrarian reform.

This led to a civil war in which the Communists controlled large swaths of territory and eventually established the Chinese Soviet Republic. As the civil war continued, the Chinese Communists eventually formed an alliance with the KMT government to fight the Japanese invaders. Then after aligning with the KMT from 1937-1945 in the Second World War, the Chinese Communists were blocked from joining a coalition government. In response to the KMT's efforts to disarm the Communist army, a new civil war was launched.

One key factor in securing the victory of the Chinese Communist Party on the mainland in 1949 was the collapse of the Gold Yuan in 1948. An article called "Hyper Inflation in Civil War China" written by Matthew Tanous, published on June 9th, 2020 quotes first hand accounts of the events. Because of China's constantly changing political system, the wealthiest Chinese families kept their assets in gold because currencies were constantly changing and often unreliable.

In 1947 Chiang Kai Chek introduced the Gold Yuan, and began forcing wealthy families to trade their gold for paper currency. His son Chiang Ching-Kuo was tasked with prosecuting "hoarders" who refused to give up their gold. He is quoted as saying: "Those who damage the new gold-based currency will have their heads chopped off!" This led to the arrest of many prominent wealthy Chinese people who did not trust the new currency. Tanous quotes Helen Zia describing a crisis within the KMT's ruling family: "Chiang Ching-kuo also arrested David Kung, the nephew of his stepmother, Madame Chiang. Upon learning that her favorite nephew was in jail, Madame Chiang stormed into her stepson's office and slapped his face."

The result of the Gold Yuan and the crackdown on hoarding was disastrous for many of China's wealthiest people: "The newly issued currency collapsed, becoming instantly worth less than the paper it was printed on. Everyone who had obeyed the government's orders to use the new currency lost everything; their assets of gold, silver, and foreign currency were now locked in Chiang Kai-shek's treasury." Solomon Adler described the situation writing "The so-called currency reform in August of 1948 robbed the impoverished middle classes of what little savings they had left

The "Gold Yuan" currency the Chinese KMT (Nationalist) government issued dramatically crashed in 1949, causing many of the wealthiest people to lose huge amounts of money and shift into an alliance with the Communists.

without any abatement of fires of inflation, and further disrupted economic intercourse between town and country... The currency introduced in August 1948 lasted only eight months and succeeding official substitutes were even shorter lived. The gap between China's economic potentialities and the ugly mess left by the Kuomintang could hardly have been greater."

In the aftermath of the Gold Yuan crash, many of China's wealthiest people came over to the communists. Mao Zedong gave assurances to urban businessmen that their property would not be touched by the Communist government during the "New Democratic" phase of the revolution, and promised that Soviet aid would strengthen the domestic economy and increase their profits.

Mao was true to his word. The property of Chinese business owners was largely not confiscated during the 1950s. Solomon Adler's 1957 study *The Chinese Economy*, writes that there were 69 millionaires in China almost a decade after the Communists took power. Adler also describes in great detail how in less than a decade the Communists had built a huge amount of railroads, greatly expanded electrification, launched literacy programs, provided medical services, cracked down on organized crime, and done many things that increased the profits of the business and middle classes.

When the Chinese Communists came to power in 1949, they did not declare China to be a socialist society, but rather a People's Democracy. The government of

China represented a "block of four classes": the workers, peasants, the petty bourgeoisie and the nationalist capitalists who were loyal to the homeland. The Communist Party sat at the center of this anti-imperialist block. They proceeded to build up state-run industries with Soviet aid.

Were the Chinese Communists a "counter gang"? Not exactly. Their roots are in a puritanical student activist group that flirted with Anarchism and Nationalism, before adopting Marxism. The Communists came to represent Soviet-influence with the KMT government, before being forcibly removed from the governing coalition. From there they attached themselves to the widespread peasant uprisings and popular movement for land reform, before entering yet another alliance to fight Japan. From there they ultimately won over even some of the wealthiest people based on their rival's economic mismanagement.

Like the Bolsheviks, the Chinese Communists were a Sorelian-style group of fanatics who expanded their influence and numbers through a series of alliances. As divisions within the ruling class intensified, the Chinese Communists attached themselves to different factions, all the while building up their own forces, until they became large enough to become the new ruling party.

Like the Bolsheviks, their strength having an ever growing army of dedicated followers who could be dispatched to carry out tasks that were useful to those with whom they were currently aligned.

Top and Bottom Organizing

Both the Russian and Chinese revolutions point to a two-pronged strategy, almost a dual nature of successful revolutionary organizations. Looking over other revolutions like those of Cuba, Nicaragua, Libya or Iran points to the same thing. Revolutionaries organize at the top and bottom of society, and take on a dual character.

On the one hand they function as Sorelian counter-gangs, isolated groups of fanatics who are useful to one section of the power structure against another. As a result they are allowed to flourish, acquire resources, and gain influence in society. Unlike the parties of the Second International, they are not mass formations, but groups of professional revolutionaries who give "the whole of their lives" to their stated purposes.

However, at some point the nature of these organizations changes and they take on a mass character, while maintaining a solid dedicated core of fanatics at the center. The groups are able to morph quickly from sects and counter gangs to mass organizations, and to some degree or other, maintain a dual character, playing both roles.

Lenin's "Party of New Type" was a hardline group of people dedicated to very specific reinterpretation of Marxism, and they allowed only "professional revolutionaries" who gave "the whole of their lives." As a fanatical sect they were useful to those at the top of society who sought to bring down the czar, to end Russian involvement in the First World War, and to repel Kornilov's coup. However, as the Bolsheviks drew closer to taking power their mass character flourished as well. Slogans like "peace, land and bread" and even the name "Bolsheviks" made a group of fanatics with a very complex specific ideology digestible and popular with millions of people.

The term Bolshevik translated to "majority group." To the average Russian, the Bolsheviks came across as a well organized group of "Majoritarians" who wanted to end the war. Their slogan "Peace, Land and Bread" was very appealing, and as they proved themselves capable of mobilizing the population, repelling Kornilov's coup, and efficiently carrying out tasks of governance, the population became convinced they should take power.

Mao's "New People's Study Society" was a group of dedicated cadres who took on a semi-monastic lifestyle. They embedded themselves within the KMT and believed in the overall goals of Chinese Nationalism, while maintaining more esoteric beliefs based on the ideology of Russian Revolution and the teachings of Marx. Eventually, they were able to become the group that incarnated the mass movement of peasants against landlords, and eventually the entire national struggle against Japanese invasion.

"Top and Bottom organizing" is the name that can be given to successful revolutionary strategy. It is a method through which an organization is capable of being both a sorelian counter gang for Bonapartist factions, and at the same time to shift and become a group that gives expression to mass sentiments and appeals to the broad masses.

In Chinese Communist literature, the concept of "The Mass Line" versus "The Party Line" is discussed. It is similar to Lenin's understanding of "agitating" to the masses but only "propagating" to the advanced.

Neither the Bolsheviks nor the Chinese Communists would have been effective if they had merely been a mass movement. They required the Sorelian energy of being a cadre organization of extremists. However, if they had merely remained as the shock troops of one faction in bonapartist struggles, they never would have come to power. They managed to transcend their fanaticism to attach to widespread sentiments among the population and overturn the established order.

This understanding of "top and bottom organizing" is extremely important for revolutionaries to grasp in a period of capitalist crisis. The understanding that revolutionaries must attach themselves to real trends in society, the battles among the elites, the mass sentiments that exist among the population, all while playing a dual role as fanatical cadres who eventually give expression to mass sentiments channeling them to overturn property relations, is key.

Examples of "top and bottom organizing" can be seen throughout the world as different societies are engulfed in a capitalist crisis. As the USA moves toward yet another military intervention in Haiti, a lot of the press is highlighting the role of G9 and Jimmy "Barbecue"

Chérizier. If one looks at the development of this powerful organization in Haiti, one can notice a very similar trajectory.

Chérizier was a figure in the Haitian National Police who ran a particularly harsh division of officers called the Unit for the Maintenance of Order. This special division of heavily armed cops was used to go after high ranking drug lords and criminals, but also served to bolster the image of certain figures in Haiti's ruling elite. However, after building up a reputation and a following for himself, Chérizier went rogue. He sat down with the very criminal organizations he had been tasked with crushing and established an alliance. He is now the leader of a self-described "Gang Federation" that has control over many key neighborhoods and can

The main anti-imperialist current in Haiti is led by Jimmy "Barbecue" Chérizier, a former high ranking police officer who formed a coalition with various criminal organizations. He engages in populist rhetoric and community organizing.

effectively block imports and shut down Haiti's economy at whim.

Now, Chérizier is not a Communist and does not seek to establish socialism in Haiti. However, he has positioned himself to be the main figure of opposition to the US-backed power structure of the country.

Time will tell whether or not Chérizier is capable of taking power, but his rise follows similar patterns of successful revolutionary movements around the world. Revolutions emerge from the failure of the old power structure, divisions in the ruling class, mass discontent, but most importantly, from effective maneuvering within such a crisis by revolutionary forces.

Lenin described a "revolutionary situation" this way: "To the Marxist it is indisputable that a revolution is impossible without a revolutionary situation; furthermore, it is not every revolutionary situation that leads to revolution. What, generally speaking, are the symptoms of a revolutionary situation? We shall certainly not be mistaken if we indicate the following three major symptoms: (1) when it is impossible for the ruling classes to maintain their rule without any change; when there is a crisis, in one form or another, among the "upper classes", a crisis in the policy of the ruling class, leading to a fissure through which the discontent and indignation of the oppressed classes burst forth. For a revolution to take place, it is usually insufficient for "the lower classes not to want" to live in the old way; it is also necessary that "the upper classes should be unable" to live in the old way; (2) when the suffering and want of the oppressed classes have grown more acute than usual; (3) when, as a consequence of the above causes, there is a considerable increase in the activity of the masses, who uncomplainingly allow themselves to be robbed in "peace time", but, in turbulent times, are drawn both by all the circumstances of the crisis *and by the "upper classes" themselves* into independent historical action. Without these objective changes, which are independent of the will, not only of individual groups and parties but even of individual classes, a revolution, as a general rule, is impossible. The totality of all these objective changes is called a revolutionary situation."

Counter-gangs in America

So, with this understanding of how illiberal organizations emerge within a capitalist crisis, and how this can lead to a socialist revolution in some circumstances, we must make a quick overview of the US political scene since the 2008 financial meltdown.

As the United States deteriorates and divisions in the ruling class intensify, US society has certainly given birth to a few entities that can accurately be described as Sorelian or counter gangs. Much like Louis Bonaparte's Society of December 10th, the various factions within the American elite that are contending for power have assembled lumpen elements to be their foot soldiers.

However, one thing that is very clear when observing the confusion of American politics since 2008 is that the ideological formations on the traditional left and traditional right, which have long existed on the margins of US politics, are not trusted to fulfill these roles. Since the 1930s most western countries have maintained a collection of Communist and Fascist sects. The Communists tend to be foot soldiers of the liberals and the Fascists tend to be the foot soldiers of the conservatives. In Europe from the 1970s to the end of the 20th century, May 1st was known as an annual day of street scuffles and brawling between various isolated sectarians.

In the United States, such groups have been much more marginal than in Europe, but they certainly have existed. The various "Hollywood Nazis" who wear outrageous costumes, espouse racial hatred, and consider themselves inheritors of National Socialism, or the various Communist groupings that proclaim themselves the true inheritors and practitioners of Mao, Trotsky, or Enver Hoxha's glorious political line have long occupied the margins of US political discourse. The groups usually have no more than a few hundred members at most, almost like obscure religious groups.

However, one would expect that amid an intense political and economic crisis, such organizations would flourish. But they have not. While the number of Americans who consider themselves Communists, Socialists, Fascists, Nazis, or whatnot has certainly increased, and interest in these ideologies is more widespread than ever as a confused public looks for answers, and the ruling class needs foot soldiers as its divisions grow more intense, these long standing fringe groups have become less relevant, not more.

In the case of the Communists, this is more or less because of their organizational inability. Following the 2008 financial crash, there was a certain amount of room for Marxists created by the political establishment. Headlines like "We're all Socialists Now" and "Marx was right" accompanied calls from figures like Warren Buffet and Jesse Jackson for some kind of "street heat" movement that would call for expansion of the welfare state and enable stabilizing reforms from the Obama administration. Michael Moore's film *Capitalism: A Love Story* was widely circulated, showing that denunciation of capitalism was now to be a permitted aspect of political discourse.

The Brecht Forum, a Marxist study center in Manhattan with former Weather Underground terrorists on its board of directors, was promoted by the *New York Times*. The workers at Republic Windows and Doors, who were organized into the radical-led UE labor union, held a successful and widely publicized sit-down strike just before Obama took office. David Harvey, Richard Wolff, Alain Badiou, and Slavoj Zizek were pushed hard in intellectual circles. The labor unions called a national rally for the first time since the "Solidarity Day" of the 1980s.

2008-2011: The Left Failed

Permission was being granted from the highest levels of the power structure for Communists to go out and do their thing, in order to help the Obama-Brzezinski faction push their reforms and bring stability in the aftermath of the crisis. It was already understood within the FBI and CIA that the hard left was no real danger to the power structure, and completely compromised. Giving them permission to amp up their activities, throwing them more grant money and media publicity than usual, was a completely safe thing for the power structure to do.

At this moment, when the Communists were more or less encouraged to become more prominent and active, they proved themselves to be even more incompetent and irrelevant than those in the ruling class who sought to use them had estimated.

Two "US Social Forums" were convened, one in Georgia and the other in Michigan. The Workers World Party staged a "Bail Out The People" March against Congress' rescue of the banks. The Left Forum went from being an obscure meeting of academics to being an event that drew big name speakers and received media publicity.

But the crowd of baby boomers who had become accustomed to operating on the fringe of US society proved incapable of "seizing the moment." Communist Party chairman Sam Webb's appearances on National Television, the endless amount of sectarian squabbling, the refusal to allow younger and more charismatic leaders to emerge all demonstrated that the Communists would not be the useful foot soldiers Warren Buffet needed. The saying "you cannot teach an old dog new tricks" seems to be applicable. These groups had functioned as fringe organizations and ego trips for various aging activist gurus, would-be philosophers and revolutionary prophets, and could not step up to be more than this.

While the "left" failed to help the Democrats, the Tea Party was mobilized by Republicans. The Tea Party had its roots among some of the rhetoric of Paleo-conservatives and Libertarians and captured some of the energy Ron Paul had stirred up with his campaigns, but it was very much a corporate mobilization. FOX news urged its regular viewers to get out into the streets to stop Obama, who they deemed to be a Communist Fascist Muslim, from expanding the welfare state.

In response to the failure of the expected foot soldiers, the Obama administration seems to have tapped into the intelligence apparatus to get the job done. Occupy Wall Street was largely directed by forces tied in with the Soros Color Revolution apparatus in Europe, including figures from Serbia's Otpor. David Graeber, a bizarre anarchist intellectual was brought in as the theoretician, and lumpen elements were mobilized along with college students to form crowds chanting "We are 99%" around the country, to back Obama against the Tea Party. The Communists, who had stage managed the very ineffective anti-Iraq war protest movement a few years prior, were marginal within Occupy Wall Street. The crowds were assembled by social media and on the ground activities were directed by a crew of foundation-linked organizers who were handsomely paid.

Occupy Wall Street was a manufactured, stage-managed mobilization by the US government's color revolution apparatus to do what they had hoped the Communists would do for them. OWS faded away almost as quickly as it sprung up. It soon gave way to Black Lives Matter and various "Stop Trump" mobilizations.

The way the Synthetic Left conducts its mobilizations includes none of the once necessary infrastructure utilized by previous social movements. Young people learn to take on a "leftist" identity as a commodity. In the same way teenagers in the 90s decided to be "punks," "goths," or "preps," young Americans decide they are "Communists" or "Anarchists" and start dressing in a certain way and taking selfies for Facebook, Instagram, and Twitter. When the mainstream media and tech giants start announcing that the trendy thing to do is assemble for protests, they run to the nearest location to join a crowd of strangers in chanting slogans and engaging in property destruction. They then run home to pat themselves on the back for all the social credit they have earned for their performative virtue, and try to outdo or "own" their peers who do not appear as revolutionary as they do on social media profiles.

Parties, organizations, communities of solidarity are not formed. The experience is an individualist one based on achieving self-validation. The Democratic Socialists of America has recruited a slew of members online, but they are merely called on around election time to campaign for democrats.

This method of "hashtag revolution" has been extremely successful for the ruling class because it prevents any real organization from emerging and keeps leftism more or less safe for the establishment, while being useful in bonapartist maneuvers. If CNN needs a crowd of people in the streets to show that sentiments that "Trump is a fascist" are widespread, it can be easily achieved. Unlike Roosevelt, the Biden administration doesn't need to compromise with Earl Browder or John L. Lewis to assemble them. The "leftist" crowds are available on command.

Social media has been quite useful in deconstructing and tearing apart any of the leftist groups that do exist. Sex allegations, rumors, exaggerations, ex-member Facebook groups have all become very useful in ripping apart whatever leftist political infrastructure has survived the confusion of this new period.

When discussing the far-left, it is worth noting that in the aftermath of the 2016 elections there was a big effort to foment a "religious left." The failure of the traditional Marxist groups and an understanding of how important religious groups are to the right-wing perhaps inspired such efforts from the Obama-Biden wing of the ruling elite. Hillary Clinton announced that she was moving toward becoming a member of the Methodist clergy. Mainstream media outlets and newspapers did stories on "the rise of the religious left" and highlighted mainline protestant churches and Reformed Jewish synagogues whose youth groups attended anti-Trump rallies. A lot of funding existed for the attempted creation of pro-LGBT hipster churches in urban centers, but these projects mostly flopped. The kind of fanaticism that the religious right of today or hardline Communist revolutionaries of the past were able to foment was pretty much impossible for grad-school post-modern liberal pastors to exude from their all-inclusive congregations pushing a watered-down reinterpretation of the Bible. The project of creating DSA adjacent churches was short lived, and has mostly been abandoned, a failed experiment by one faction of the ruling elite looking to forge its own counter-gangs.

Black Lives Matter & Antifa

The two primary street activist currents the Democratic Party wing of the ruling class has fomented are Black Lives Matter and Antifa. What is interesting about both of these entities is that they cannot exactly be called "groups." They give the impression they are hashtags, slogans, tactics, or loose associations.

The White Nationalist David Duke once said something along the lines of "Part of the reason I quit the Ku Klux Klan is because any fool anywhere in the country could put on a sheet and do something and then I would be blamed for it." Both Antifa and Black Lives Matter significantly benefit from this level of organizational vagueness. Anyone anywhere can be Black Lives Matter or Antifa. However, in addition to the wider milieu associated with them on social media, the crowds that assemble on command from social media, there is a crew of "professional activists" with funding and connections to the deep state who are tasked with stage managing bigger events, and carrying out more strong-armed and semi-illegal tactics.

While many young liberal activists will wear masks and call themselves "Antifa," a much more covert network linked to intelligence agencies carries out the work of tracking and intimidating right-wing dissidents.

When discussing Black Lives Matter, it must be pointed out that there has long been a Black Liberation movement in America. Slaves were in a constant state of rebellion. The Union League of radical republicans resisted the Ku Klux Klan in the immediate aftermath of the Civil War. Marcus Garvey gave birth to Black Nationalism as a widespread political current, and the Nation of Islam, the Temple of Moorish Science, and other entities continued with such work. The Communist Party aligned itself with the cause of Civil Rights and opposing Jim Crow segregation, and in the 1950s the civil rights movement of Dr. Martin Luther King Jr., championed it with support from the northern liberal establishment, including the Kennedy family. Black Nationalist groups of an explicitly Marxist-Leninist character emerged during the 1960s and 70s. The Honorable Minister Louis Farrakhan was a hugely important figure during the 1980s and 90s, organizing the Million Man March and leading a dedicated crew of followers.

There has long been a significant gap among Black activists. Among more working class and lower income Black liberation activists Black Nationalism has been prevalent. Social conservatism and knee-jerk support for the forces of resistance to western capitalism is more prevalent. The feeling that homosexuality and feminism are a plot to emasculate Black men and destroy the Black family, while any entity the US government is battling around the globe is "on our side" is something

The well-funded organization called "Black Lives Matter Inc." works to supplant the influence of anti-imperialist African American leaders such as Minister Louis Farrakhan.

that many working class African Americans have felt for generations. The most visible figure representing these sentiments would be Minister Farrakhan.

However, among the layer of African Americans who have moved into the middle class, becoming doctors, lawyers, and college professors, there is a similar feeling of loyalty to their demographic, but very different sentiments. The Black middle class activist currently tends to be sympathetic to the LGBT community, more pacifist in its rhetoric, and more supportive of US foreign policy. Dr. Cornel West is probably the most prominent figure representing this strata of Black activism.

It appears that in aftermath of the Ferguson uprising of 2014, and the widespread protests surrounding the death of Trayvon Martin, and the acquittal of George Zimmerman, there was an attempt to pump up and mobilize the Cornel West wing of Black politics, fearing that the politics of Farrakhan might take control of the uprising. Anger at the police state was rising among all African Americans at this time. The feeling that Obama's presidency had failed to improve things was giving rise to a serious anger, which the US power structure desperately tried to harness and control.

Yet, even the Cornel West wing was really not allowed to dominate Black politics. The organizational apparatus that controls what is now called Black Lives Matter has absolutely nothing to do with this long tradition of struggle and the many currents of Black Liberation that have existed throughout US history. If one listens to Simone Sanders or the various employed spokespeople of BLM non-profits, they have nothing to do with Marcus Garvey, Elijah Muhammad, Huey Newton, Fred Hampton, or Claudia Jones. They do not have historical context or perspective. Many of them are individuals formerly employed by Barack Obama's "Teach for America" program who were carefully vetted to weed out any deeper thinking or ideological individuals.

Their vernacular comes from academics who have written about white privilege. Their training consists of "woke-shop" sessions in which their emotional scars and wounds are manipulated to make them loyal foot-soldiers. An article by Christian Parenti exposed the influence of Scientology co-founder, Harvey Jackins, and "re-evaluation counseling."

The small core of dedicated people that make up BLM's inner core are a counter-gang created to serve a purpose by one wing of the ruling class and the intelligence apparatus. They denounce Black Nationalists as racist, sexist, homophobic, and promoting "conspiracy theories." Black Nationalists are mocked as "hoteps" for their mystical beliefs and reverence for ancient Egypt. The BLM cadre are loyal to the US government and its foreign policy. Their knowledge of "Marxism" is limited to an understanding that average white Americans are a privileged group of European settlers who are only angry they are "losing their privilege."

Antifa, much like Black Lives Matter, has a crew of vetted and ideologically weak foot soldiers who sit at the center of wider current. These well-trained, intelligence directed foot soldiers track individuals and harass them, and work to intimidate and threaten sections of the right and left that do not operate with the approval of the political establishment.

During the 1980s and 90s there was a layer of Anarchists who devoted their time to stalking and harassing Nazis. They had connections to the Southern Poverty Law Center and other well-funded outlets, and engaged in a kind of covert effort to shut down advocates of white supremacy, holocaust denial and openly racialist or fascist speech. Often this original "Antifa" cooperated with hardline Communist groups like the Progressive Labor Party to disrupt and attack Nazi gatherings.

This original Antifa had no interest in harassing run-of-the-mill Republicans, only ideological white supremacists. They also had no problem cooperating with genuine Communists in order to do so. But something began changing during the Trump-era. Antifa's target switched from the openly racist far right fringe to mainstream Republicans.

Ann Coulter, Milo Yiannopoulos, Steve Bannon, and other figures who have no links to White Nationalism or Fascist cadre groups became the target of violent protests intended to shut them down. Furthermore, the notion that Russia was a "fascist" country and all who challenged US foreign policy were somehow part of a network of "fascist" disinformation emerged.

The inner core of Antifa functions almost as a mini-intelligence agency, tracking down certain people, threatening them with violence, forcing them to lose their jobs, and cooperating with law enforcement against them.

White supremacist prison gangs such as the Aryan Brotherhood have long existed, and the far-less visible 'hit squad' that does Antifa's dirty work seems to be drawn from a similar source, perhaps rival organizations or even splinter groups from America's criminal underworld. Most of Antifas members are white, not people of color or from the marginalized groups white supremacists are known to target. Much like the cadre of BLM, the inner core of Antifa are almost completely clueless about deeper political issues.

The college kids with signs and theatrical costumes are there to give political framing and glorify "anti-fascism" on social media. But it is this ugly, semi-criminal inner core that exists in the shadows that conduct acts of violence with as much anonymity as possible. They are assigned to target specific individuals, often because of their links to foreign governments or to the semi-criminal organizations and prison gangs that espouse white supremacism. If most liberal activists and social media leftists knew the reality of what the actual, less visible crew of Antifa was like, they would probably be disgusted. The inner core are not glorious Robin Hoods fighting for marginalized communities against bigots. They are an intelligence-linked hit squad engaging in classic mafia style intimidation, acting on command from higher forces and learning not to ask questions about why.

The Proud Boys

Gavin McInnes, a comedian and co-founder of VICE magazine launched a project for creating some kind of right-wing street activist organization in 2016 to support Donald Trump. Much like similar developments on the far-left, the Proud Boys were distinctly separate from the ideological far-right that has long existed. Like the emerging currents on the left that simply demonize the right-wing and seek to purge US society of "fascism," the Proud Boys don't have a deep assessment of US society other than the need to remove a problematic element called "the left."

The group encourages young men not to masturbate and to exercise regularly. It speaks of "western civilization" as being good and opposes the narratives of leftists who promote concepts such as white privilege. The group has a violent initiation ritual and seems to market itself as being involved in street confrontations.

When pro-Trump events face far-left opposition, the Proud Boys swing into action and get into scuffles with them. The Proud Boys also stage public events in the hopes of drawing out the far-left, in order to mix it up with them in the streets. The organization known as Patriot Prayer plays a similar role in the Pacific Northwest region.

Those espousing openly anti-semitic, openly white supremacist views are generally not welcome among the Proud Boys. Rather, the organization exists to openly taunt the left and provoke it with pro-gun, pro-Trump protests, as well as to cultivate a crew of street fighters who can be on hand at wider right-wing mobilizations to counter leftist protesters and disruptors.

The slogans are "West is the Best," along with jokes about "free Helicopter rides for communists" alluding to Pinochet's method of executing dissidents. The message does not go beyond one of arguing that feminists, anti-racists, and leftists in general are annoying, and that getting into fist fights with them or provoking their outrage is a worthwhile past-time in which one can prove their masculinity.

The presence of criminal elements and those who perhaps have their origins in prison gangs is certainly worth acknowledging. However, participating in the Proud Boys activities requires such people to moderate their views or at least remain silent. What makes the Proud Boys significantly different from other right-wing currents among the population is that violence is very much part of the group's identity and marketing, and that unlike more fringe elements, the group has a level of support and approval from high ranking sections of the pro-Trump wing of the power structure.

Enrique Tarrio, a prominent member of the Proud Boys garnered media attention when it was revealed that he was a convicted felon who had been living as a career informant for law enforcement prior to joining the organization. Tarrio had been involved in security work for GPS tracking companies prior to being convicted in 2013 of rebranding and reselling diabetes tests. From 2012 to 2014 he was a "prolific" cooperator, helping the FBI and local police arrest people for offenses related to gambling, anabolic steroids, and human trafficking. Tarrio received a 155-day prison sentence for his involvement in the January 6th protests.

Much like BLM and Antifa, the Proud Boys have powerful friends. They mirror their left counterparts in

Enrique Tarrio, a high ranking member of the right-wing street fighting Proud Boys organization, was proven to be a longtime FBI informant.

watering down right-wing beliefs, and focusing on "getting the job done" i.e. engaging in provocations and violent confrontations, rather than pushing a particular message. The Proud Boys may have aspired to be a kind of "honor guard" to protect pro-Trump activists from left-wing attacks, but they quickly devolved into something a bit less rational. The group is a kind of semi-political street gang that enjoys getting into fist-fights with the left, and provoking the left to mobilize against them. In the aftermath of the January 6th events, the organization seemed to somewhat disintegrate, though many involved with it moved on to other endeavors in right-wing activism.

The core of BLM, Antifa and the Proud Boys shows the Sorelian critique of the mass socialist movement of the 1900s taken to extreme conclusions. These groups are more or less mere "cults of action." Their beliefs are shallow and almost non-existent. Their goals are to express anger and seize the opportunity to move against a hated enemy, not much more.

All of these organizations bear some resemblance to Blackshirts or Stormtroopers of pre-fascist periods in Europe. They could certainly become more prevalent as the crisis escalates, and it is clear that they all are heavily infiltrated and "handled" by the US intelligence apparatus.

BreadTube and Twitch-Streamer Leftism

Beyond the street fighting counter-gangs, there is an ideological offensive pushed at the population on social media. Socialism is now dominated by a collection of video-gaming playing, pessimistic, sarcastic "experts" loosely described as "BreadTube."

Most of their work consists of warning audiences that Trump supporters and others who disagree with the mainstream leftist narrative are somehow similar to the Nazis or Fascists. They equate existing socialist governments like China or Cuba with the Nazis. They insist socialism 'has nothing to do with the government' but is just voluntarily formed worker-cooperative enterprises. They obsess with the Trans issue, and other liberal cultural topics.

Amid their confused politics there is an underlying cynicism and pessimism. They encourage their audiences to use drugs. They mock real life activists as being "nerds." The BreadTube current is closely linked to the power structure. Hillary Clinton has highlighted the work of Natalie Wynn, known as "Contrapoints" and celebrated her efforts to debunk right-wing ideas.

Funding from the British government and its intelligence agencies has been revealed to be flowing to Abigail Thorn, whose channel "philosophytube" is dedicated to smearing those who stray from mainstream narratives and are therefore "fascist." Dr. Steve Hassan, the cult guru with a notorious past, is also lurking in the background advising BreadTubers about how to "deprogram" those won over to conservative views.

Peter Coffin, a comedian and social media personality who mentored and worked with some of the individuals who became prominent BreadTubers has written extensively about this trend of internet leftism. His texts such as *Custom Reality and You* and *Woke Ouroboros* show how the social media nature of the BreadTube leftism incentives the creation of fandoms and commodified feelings of moral superiority rather than building real organizations or movements.

Peterson-ism

BreadTube emerged, more or less, as a response to a social media trend among conservatives that can be rightly identified as "Petersonism." This is a trend of male-oriented, self-help and psychologically focused content that pushes an economic libertarian message.

The person largely responsible for pioneering the social media trend that can be called "Petersonism" is Stefan Molyneux. Molyneux is an actor who resides in Canada, and has promoted libertarian ideas with "Free Domain Radio" for over a decade. Molyneux's wife is a Freudian psychoanalyst, and under the guise of politics, Molyneux solidifies himself in the mind of listeners as their trusted counselor and advisor.

Molyneux's message seems political on the surface, but when you dig deeper it is more about interpersonal psychology. Molyneux tells an audience of mainly

Former actor and right-wing internet personality Stefan Molyneux is largely responsible for pioneering the brand of libertarian self-help directed at young men that is now largely associated with Canadian Psychologist Jordan Peterson.

young white men that the world has been unfair to them and that their pain and trauma deserves to be acknowledged. He advises them on dating and relationships. He speaks about personality theory. He advises them on getting better motivated for day to day life, cleaning their rooms, and standing up straight. The politics is standard right-wing anti-communism, resentment against feminism, along with vague utopian fantasies about a stateless world of free associating individuals i.e. "anarcho-capitalism."

Molyneux's rise began during the 2008 peak of Ron Paul's popularity and was a slow and steady uphill march. Jordan Peterson, a Canadian academic psychologist, seemed to take Molyneux's methods and message, and apply it in a less blatantly self-serving way that was deemed more safe for mass consumption. Molyneux urges his followers to "de-foo" and cut themselves off from their "Family of Origin," and embed themselves more deeply in his online community. Molyneux tells his followers they are part of an elite, special group of enlightened people.

Peterson's message is more or less the same, but it harbors no fantasy of creating an "Ancapistan" paradise, and does not seem to push the idea that he is any sort of Messiah. Peterson pushes Solzhenitsyn style anti-communism, self-help advice for young men, resentment against feminism and skepticism and annoyance with leftism and woke-ness.

Unlike Molyneux who takes calls from young men to hear them complain about their problems, Peterson gives voice to the widely experienced frustrations of young white men in lengthy sermons delivered before live audiences. Rather than stoking blatant unfiltered rage as Molyneux does, yelling in anger, Peterson puts forward the caring voice of a compassionate father-figure mixed in with a sarcastic wit, tempered by his Canadian mannerism and accent.

Jordan Peterson is the safe and watered down version of Stefan Molyneux, and "Petersonism" has exploded far beyond the two of them. There is a whole internet sphere for angry young men to get psychological self-help, have their frustrations and pain acknowledged, all while being told that Communism is responsible for the woke-ness they dislike and that free markets are the solution.

Peterson-ism is not deeply political. It is a product manufactured for a certain audience. It serves Republicans and conservatives, pushes anti-communism and echoes standard US foreign policy rhetoric about totalitarianism. Peterson-ism seems to have exploded most likely as a perceived safer alternative to the alt-right.

It carries with it certain themes that dominate right-wing spaces in our time, "incel" resentment against women and feminism, sarcasm and frustration with political correctness, nostalgia for the past, and economic libertarianism.

The Netflix Cult Obsession

Netflix, the service that allows Americans to watch TV programs and movies at their convenience, does not gain very much revenue from advertising. The corporation functions as a virtual monopoly without serious competition, and its primary means of revenue is monthly subscription fees.

Trump supporters and others have long complained that it appears Netflix is pushing a political agenda. Elon Musk has tweeted how "the woke mind virus is making Netflix unwatchable." Susan Rice, a prominent member of the Obama administration served on Netflix board until 2020 when she began working in the Biden administration. Barack Obama himself has been directly involved with overseeing a number of Netflix documentaries.

Amid its overall "woke" bias, Netflix is obsessed with "cults." Documentaries, historical fiction mini-series pieces, comedies, and so much of the content featured on Netflix seems to be inoculating viewers against involvement in illiberal organizations, be they religious, spiritual, political, self-help, exercise oriented or otherwise. The targets of Netflix anti-cult pieces go well beyond the usual targets of cult allegations such as Scientology, the Unification Church, Hare Krishnas, Mormonism, etc. The anti-cult narrative seems to be almost an attack on all religions or all mass movements. Documentaries warn the audiences of the dangers of supposed brainwashing, and need to "think for themselves." Thinking for themselves means trusting "science" of course, and believing what is told to them by the images dazzling before their eyes on the screen. Whenever the topic of cults comes up, the face of Dr. Steve Hassan is likely to pop up. Hassan has made a name for himself as the "cult expert" who is featured on CNN, MSNBC, and has authored a number of widely circulating books on "mind control."

Dr. Steve Hassan tells of his brief involvement with the Unification Church and Reverend Sun Myung Moon in the 1970s, and how his family "deprogrammed" him from their alleged "brainwashing." Hassan's latest book is *The Cult of Trump*, which alleges that Donald Trump engaged in hypnotic thought control in order to gain political power. After the January 6th events, Steve Hassan called for "deprogramming" the country on CNN, and his calls were echoed by Congresswoman Alexandria Ocasio-Cortez on Twitter.

While academics have largely debunked Hassan's "BITE Model" of thought control, Hassan's role as a talking-head and his influence on the discourse, seem rather dominant in all "cult" related conversations. However, Hassan's history is rarely discussed, but in this conversation about counter gangs, it is rather important.

Hassan came into prominence when the Unification Church became the target of congressional investigations during the late 1970s. The Carter Administration alleged that the Unification Church was involved with widespread illegal lobbying and political influencing operations conducted by the South Korean government, then led by military strongman Park Chung-hee. Park had overseen massive economic development of the cities in South Korea, while also crushing leftist protest movements and student dissidents. Park was a Bonapartist who the United States had propped up during the 1960s, after Sygman Rhee, the previous US-backed military dictator had been toppled in the April Revolution.

In the late 1970s, Park was moving South Korea in a more independent direction. He announced his intent for South Korea to develop its own nuclear weapons to deter any attack from North Korea, and eventually remove the presence of US troops from the country. The nuclear program of South Korea moved ahead, with Park claiming South Korea would test its own atomic bomb by 1983. Outrage from the international community and France's refusal to cooperate with South Korea's atomic energy program finally forced Park to relent. South Korea ratified the Nuclear Non-Proliferation Treaty on April 23rd, 1975. However, investigations from the International Atomic Energy Agency have shown that Park continued top secret research with unreported plutonium and uranium after signing the treaty. Park went ahead with setting the stage for possibly restarting the nuclear weapons program, successfully testing the Nike Hercules Missile Korea-1 in 1978.

US leaders increasingly denounced South Korea as moving in a renegade direction, and a US media campaign and congressional investigation of Korean lobbying in America accompanied widespread demonization of the Rev. Sun Myung Moon, the anti-Communist pastor who was operating in the United States, and recruiting young Americans to his religious movement.

On October 26th, 1979, Park Chung-hee was murdered in his home by Kim Jae-gyu, the head of the Korean Central Intelligence Agency. The circumstances of the killing are widely debated and questioned, even up to today. Kim Jae-gyu was executed quickly afterwards, without ever clearly stating his motive.

Steve Hassan was an expert witness before Congress and in the media, demonizing Moon as a foreign agent supposedly brainwashing young people. *The Washington Post* described his testimony before a Congressional Committee in a report published March 14th, 1980: "Steven Hassan, a soft-spoken, 26-year-old wearing tinted glasses and a pin-striped suit, recalled following orders like a "true soldier" when he was the church's chief Maryland fundraiser from 1974 to 1976… After being "deprogrammed" — persuaded to renounce the church — Hassan recalled today that he slept only three hours a day for months while he was a Moonie."

After Congress was unable to produce any evidence proving Sun Myung Moon was functioning as an illegal

lobbyist or engaging in the scores of crimes his angry
detractors accused him of, Moon was ultimately
indicted in 1981 on tax violations and conspiracy
charges. After being convicted, he served 13 months in
federal prison. A diverse chorus of voices spoke up in
Moon's defense at the time of his imprisonment, among
them Minister Louis Farrakhan, Jerry Falwell, and the
American Civil Liberties Union. The Unification
Church is now headed by his lifelong spouse, Hak Ja
Han, "Mother" Moon, and continues to maintain
influence among American conservatives, owning the
Washington Times newspaper. Various breakaways,
including the very vocally pro-Second Amendment
Sanctuary Church run by Moon's son also maintain
influence in conservative circles.

Steve Hassan's career as the central talking head in
the late 1970s and early 80s "cult scare" (now continued
by Netflix) was essentially solidified by his involvement
in setting the stage for an individual associated with an
increasingly independent South Korea to be imprisoned.
Hassan became the mentee of Robert Jay Lifton, the
top-US military psychiatrist who had first introduced
the concept of "brainwashing" to the US public. Lifton's
work laid the basis for the CIA's project MK-ULTRA
with his research into Chinese prisons during the Mao
era and their methods of "Thought Reform."

Steve Hassan and his associates became involved
with something called the Cult Awareness Network, an
organization that was eventually shut down by lawsuits

for its practice of kidnapping legal adults against their will in order to forcibly detain them in isolation while they were persuaded to renounce their beliefs. Steve Hassan admits in his writings and interviews that he was involved in "forcible deprogramming" of individuals, but says he no longer supports this practice.

Signed affidavits from individuals such as Arthur Roselle describe Hassan imprisoning people, holding them against their will, and brow beating them with the intention of changing their religious beliefs. Ted Patrick, an associate of Hassan, was eventually imprisoned for kidnapping. The Cult Awareness Network (CAN) was eventually shut down by a 1995

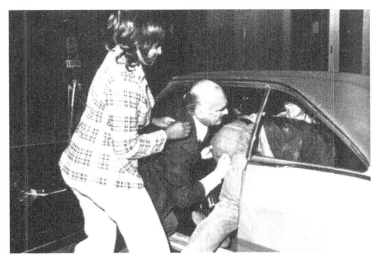

Many individuals who feature prominently in the "anti-cult" messaging of Netflix and mainstream media have links to the Cult Awareness Network and its history of forcible deprogramming, i.e. kidnapping.

lawsuit by Jason Scott who was kidnapped by CAN associate Rick Alan Ross.

Among those who Hassan has worked with in his "deprogramming" efforts is Ginnie Thomas, the wife of US Supreme Court justice Clarence Thomas. When Ginnie Thomas became a figure within the January 6th investigations, Steve Hassan began releasing videos of her describing her experience being "brainwashed" and later getting involved with Hassan's anti-cult activism. Hassan describes the QAnon internet conspiracy circles and those like Ginnie Thomas who question the 2020 election results as "brainwashed."

In a YouTube interview posted on July 13th, 2021, a former member of a British Trotskyist group described to Hassan how he was "brainwashed": "I despised Corbyn, I hated him, I thought he was a terrorist supporter. I thought he was an enemy of the West. I saw him as the embodiment of evil, but then I joined the IMT [International Marxist Tendency] which was practicing entryism in Labour, which was strongly supporting Corbyn, and here I was campaigning for him… I had been a strong supporter of Israel before that and **they brainwashed me into thinking that Israel was this uniquely evil country**… I played down the whole anti-semitism fury that was going on because there was genuine anti-semitism…"

The partisan political nature of Steve Hassan's work as an outspoken liberal Democrat and supporter of US foreign policy objectives and Israel should seem obvious. In the interview the young ex-Trotskyist describes how selling newspapers, calling people to invite them to party meetings, holding forums on Black history and other routine political activities were prime examples of "cultism" he had been "brainwashed" into doing. He then describes how he suddenly came to "think for himself" once again: "just to clear my mind of Trotskyism and read other stuff, other material that wasn't just IMT propaganda, *I rediscovered my hero Nietzsche who had been a strong influence on me before I joined the cult and was told that he was a reactionary and I should stop reading him. I rediscovered people like Hitchens.* Christopher Hitchens who had been an idol of mine, but he of course, was a famous renegade who abandoned the left, so he was spoken of badly off in the cult and I was brainwashed to disavow him."

Steve Hassan frequently says "China is the world's largest political cult" in his interviews, lectures and videos. He says Russia is also a political cult, and warns audiences not to be "brainwashed" by TV networks and websites that challenge US media narratives about foreign policy. Hassan has often pushed the debunked notion that somehow Russia is responsible for Donald Trump winning the 2016 election.

The irony of Hassan and his anti-cult political movement, is that all of their materials could easily be used to target and demonize the US government apparatus. The techniques used in US military boot camps or the training of FBI agents fit his criteria of brainwashing and are more intensely practiced in these government institutions than in anything done by legal religious organizations.

Hassan and his associates espouse an ideology of "freedom of mind" and "think for yourself" echoed by Netflix. The irony is that the very American and western liberal power structures they defend from the danger of "cults" are propped up by illiberal, authoritarian institutions.

When one listens to the liberal deconstructionism espoused by the anti-cult "experts'' such as Hassan, one is forced to think of the CIA's project MK-ULTRA and its results. Hassan warns his audiences that singing, chanting, declarations of loyalty, eye-contact and other routine activities are "mind control techniques." Hassan works to push his audiences to a place of postmodern cynicism where no real truth exists, no cause is worth fighting for, and any figure capable of generating loyalty and enthusiasm is viewed as a predatory "malignant narcissist."

John Marks' book *The Search for the Manchurian Candidate* describes how US intelligence officials tracked the political and ideological value of hallucinogenic drugs. Marks' quotes a CIA officer reporting on his experience with drugs: "you tend to have a more global view of things. I found it awfully hard when stoned to maintain the notion: I am a US citizen — my country right or wrong... You tend to have these good higher feelings. You tend to have a brotherhood-of-man idea and are more susceptible to the seamy sides of your own society... I think this is exactly what happened during the 1960s, but it didn't make people more Communist. It just made them less inclined to identify with the US. They took a plague-on-both-your-houses position."

This points to the built in problems of liberal deconstructionism. It takes everything apart, not just the targeted enemies. It leaves a pessimism and cynicism in place of the loyalties and dedication that hold societies together.

As Netflix urges its audiences not to be "brainwashed" by cults, religions, causes, or ideologies, its real goal is not very hard to uncover. The social media giants, the tech monopolists, the board of Netflix, and the intelligence apparatus want to break Americans down into atomized individuals upon whom no organized group can have influence. This gives social media, mainstream media, and the entrenched powers a complete monopoly of influence over the minds of the public.

Essentially, Americans are told to "think for themselves" by allowing only the most powerful people to direct their thoughts without any interference from a community. As the social engineers of Silicon Valley and the intelligence apparatus see it, brainwashing is their job, and no one else's. Any religion, political organization, community or family that would interfere must be gotten rid of in the name of "free thought."

For those seeking to break the public down into atomized individuals who can be programmed by the tech monopolists, the pandemic lockdowns were highly convenient.

A Country Without Ideology?

The liberal order rails against all ideology and all mass movements as totalitarian. However, as it does this it is maneuvering behind the scenes in experiments to create counter gangs and illiberal movements of its own to liquidate the crisis.

Beyond the economic crisis, the liberalism of US society is spawning a psychological crisis. Young Americans are not being raised to salute the flag and pray to God, but rather to believe "there is no truth" and "think for yourself." They enter adulthood without the psychological foundations that supply the identity and passion that societies historically have provided. Human beings have always had ideologies, and the belief that US society can function without ideology, in a post-modern existence seems to be a very toxic delusion.

Many in America want to believe in something, to know who they are, and to have a cause and purpose to live for and to fight for. The bulk of the ruling class knows this, but also recognizes any such force could emerge to establish an illiberal regime, or at minimum, be useful to its political rivals in bonapartist struggles.

As the crisis intensifies, the natural course of western capitalist societies is to become more and more chaotic until liberalism collapses into illiberalism. US capitalism, left to its own devices, will naturally collapse into some kind of illiberal fascism to try and resolve the crisis. As the ruling class goes all out pushing radical postmodern liberalism, it also experiments with various "safe" forms of illiberalism it is nervously and carefully cultivating.

The backdrop for all of this, however, is the rising anti-imperialist bloc and alternative global economy. The new economy centered around Russia, China, Iran, Venezuela, Cuba, and other anti-imperialist states is openly displaying the effectiveness of a non-fascist, growth-centered form of illiberalism.

The US ruling class is terrified of 21st Century Socialism and even in the most western aligned, anti-communist forms of illiberalism, it sees reflections of it. The endless comparisons of Donald Trump to Kim Jong-Un, Stalin, and other anti-imperialists were not simply bombast. They reflected real fears of the illiberal tone of Trump's four-year presidency.

One wonders if the US ruling class would be capable of forming a solid block strong enough to enact fascism. The "degrowth" woke current is the primary source of power within the US ruling class at this time, but even it is very loose and contains many rival factions and contradictory agendas.

Karl Marx himself recognized back in 1848 that the bonapartist struggles of the ruling class are what brings the working class into politics. He wrote: "The bourgeoisie finds itself involved in a constant battle. At first with the aristocracy; later on, with those portions of the bourgeoisie itself, whose interests have become antagonistic to the progress of industry; at all time with the bourgeoisie of foreign countries. **In all these battles, it sees itself compelled to appeal to the proletariat, to ask for help, and thus, to drag it into the political arena. The bourgeoisie itself, therefore, supplies the proletariat with its own elements of political and general education, in other words, it furnishes the proletariat with weapons for fighting the bourgeoisie...** Finally, in times when the class struggle nears the decisive hour, the progress of dissolution going on within the ruling class, in fact within the whole range of old society, assumes such a violent, glaring character, that a small section of the ruling class cuts itself adrift, and joins the revolutionary class, the class that holds the future in its hands. **Just as, therefore, at an earlier period, a section of the nobility went over to the bourgeoisie, so now a portion of the bourgeoisie goes over to the proletariat**, and in particular, a portion of the bourgeois ideologists, who have raised themselves to the level of comprehending theoretically the historical movement as a whole."

As working class people are brought into politics ("compelled to appeal to the proletariat... drag it into the political arena") at first they are the foot-soldiers of one faction of capitalists against others. However, as the crisis intensifies Marx predicts that the working class becomes the dominant partner in the coalition. The politicized workers go from being foot soldiers of the ruling class, to having sections of the ruling class align with them. As Marx wrote, they do so "in the decisive hour" when "the whole range of society assumes such a violent character," i.e. liberal bourgeois society collapses into illiberalism.

The understanding that capitalism is naturally moving society toward fascism, and that therefore Communists should position themselves at the center of an anti-fascist coalition was the basis of the late-1930s Popular Front strategy. The chain of events leading to the Bolshevik revolution of 1917, the victory of the Chinese Revolution in 1949, and many other moments that created non-capitalist societies serve as confirmation of this process as well.

The age of a politically disengaged US public is long gone. Americans are digging into obscure political ideas and looking for answers.

As the American capitalists scramble to manage the crisis and battle against each other, they are opening the door for forces that could eventually overturn US capitalism to emerge.

4. The Coming Triumph of Illiberalism

Philosophical Irrationalism – Where is Julius Caesar? – The Last "Yankee and Cowboy War" – The New Battleground – The Communist Party and the Anti-Monopoly Coalition – The New Communist Movement – The Boston Trap – The Great Retreat – The Bolivarian Coalitions – Defending American Values – "Country Joe and the Fish" – "Out of the Movement, to the Masses!"

When the First World War broke out, a Marxist revolutionary activist named Rosa Luxemburg composed a pamphlet to express her outrage. She turned her primary anger at the German Social-Democratic Party which had sold out and voted for war credits.

In the first chapter of her famous *Junius Pamphlet,* Luxemburg framed things in what some considered an overdramatic and alarmist way. She wrote: "Socialism is the first popular movement in world history that has set itself the goal of bringing human consciousness, and thereby free will, into play in the social actions of mankind. For this reason, Friedrich Engels designated the final victory of the socialist proletariat a leap of humanity from the animal world into the realm of freedom. This "leap" is also an iron law of history bound to the thousands of seeds of a prior torment-filled and all-too-slow development. But this can never be realized until the development of complex material conditions strikes the incendiary spark of conscious will in the great masses. The victory of socialism will not descend from heaven. It can only be won by a long chain of violent tests of strength between the old and the new powers. The international proletariat under the leadership of the Social Democrats will thereby learn to try to take its history into its own hands; instead of remaining a will-less football, it will take the tiller of social life and become the pilot to the goal of its own history. Friedrich Engels once said: "Bourgeois society stands at the crossroads, either transition to socialism or regression into barbarism." What does "regression into barbarism" mean to our lofty European civilization? Until now, we have all probably read and repeated these words thoughtlessly, without suspecting their fearsome seriousness. A look around us at this moment shows what the regression of bourgeois society into barbarism means. **This world war is a regression into barbarism. The triumph of imperialism leads to the annihilation of civilization.** At first, this happens sporadically for the duration of a modern war, but then when the period of unlimited wars begins it progresses toward its inevitable consequences. **Today, we face the choice exactly as Friedrich Engels foresaw it a generation ago: either the triumph of imperialism and the collapse of all civilization as in ancient Rome, depopulation, desolation, degeneration – a great cemetery. Or the victory of socialism, that means the conscious active struggle of the international proletariat against imperialism and its method of war.** This is a dilemma of world history, and either/or; the scales are wavering before the decision of the class-conscious proletariat. The future of civilization and humanity depends on whether or not the proletariat resolves manfully to throw its revolutionary broadsword into the scales. In this war imperialism has won. Its bloody sword of genocide has brutally tilted the scale toward the abyss of misery. **The only compensation for all the misery and all the shame would be if we learn from the war how the proletariat can seize mastery of its own destiny and escape the role of the lackey to the ruling classes."**

This question of "Socialism or Barbarism" became a famous one, often quoted and attributed to Luxembourg in eulogies and articles memorializing her great sacrifices, but rarely understood or examined. Rosa Luxemburg was pointing out that the new form of capitalism in its monopoly stage, in which Western powers spread their tentacles across the planet holding back development, was gradually eroding the political, moral, spiritual and rational frameworks that held the imperialist homelands together. She was arguing that left unchanged, imperialism would disembowel the societies of western Europe and America and cast them into a chaos much like the period of regression that followed the fall of the Roman Empire.

Philosophical Irrationalism

What is ironic is that while Luxemburg, a revolutionary opponent of Western civilization, was warning about imperialism planting the seeds of societal collapse, a school of thought descended from Friedrich Nietzsche was celebrating the very things that pointed to the eventual downfall. Georg Lukacs' famed philosophical text *The Destruction of Reason* goes into great detail showing that the basis of Nazism and the horrendous atrocities committed during the Second World War, is the philosophical irrationalism that emerged during the rise of capitalism in its imperialist stage. Summarizing the groundbreaking Marxist text, John Bellamy Foster explained: "In this work, Lukács had charted the relation of philosophical irrationalism—which first emerged on the European Continent, particularly in Germany, with the defeat of the 1848 revolutions, and that became a dominant force near the end of the century—to the rise of the imperialist stage of capitalism. For Lukács, irrationalism, including its ultimate coalescence with Nazism, was no fortuitous development, but rather a product of capitalism itself."

While rationalist philosophy argues that truth can be acquired through the use of reason and the scientific method, philosophical irrationalism argues that feelings and instincts are superior. Rationalists, like Marx and Engels, argued that human beings had a special ability to reinvent their relationship with mother nature and that their intelligence separated them from other animals. The irrationalists, however, saw human intellect as inherently flawed and human beings as a species no better than other animals. They pointed toward the persistence of war, poverty, cruelty and man's inhumanity to man as proof that the ability of the human mind to reason did not indicate that a better world could be achieved. Philosophical irrationalism celebrated feelings over logic, was pessimistic rather than optimistic, and held a generally negative perception of the human race.

When explaining the basis of Nietzsche's philosophy, Lukacs wrote: "Whereas the popular fellow-apologists, concentrating on an idealization of capitalist man, strove to dismiss all capitalism's darker aspects and contradictions, Nietzsche's writings centered exactly on what was problematic about capitalist society, on everything that was bad in it. Of course he too went in for idealizing; but what he emphasized with his ironic criticism and poeticizing pathos were the capitalist's egotistic, barbaric and bestial features, seen as attributes of a type desirable for the good of mankind."

Nietzsche saw imperialism reducing the western man to a mindset of "might makes right '' and the law of the jungle and perceived this as a positive development. He wrote of the "blonde beast" and celebrated the fact that in becoming an imperialist plunderer, the Western man was shedding the moralistic and religious mindsets that were restraining him. Nietzsche saw Christianity and Socialism as the greatest evils and equated them with each other. Lukacs quotes Nietzsche's words on this: "And let us not underestimate the destiny that has crept all the way from Christianity into politics! Today, nobody has any longer the courage of special rights, or rights of command, or a sense of respect towards oneself and one's peers — a *pathos of distance* ... Our politics are *sick* through this absence of courage! The fib of the equality of souls undermined the aristocratic outlook in the most insidious way; and while faith in the "prerogative of the most" is making and *will make* revolutions — it is Christianity, let there be no mistake about it, and it is *Christian* judgements that turn every revolution into mere crime and bloodshed! Christianity is the revolt of all groveling creatures against that which has *stature:* the gospel of the "lowly" *makes for* lowliness..."

The religious structures and platitudes that had held medieval European feudalism together were ripped apart by the emergence of capitalism. Marx wrote about this saying there was "no remaining nexus between man and man but naked self interest, callous cash payment." The ascension of capitalism in Europe into its monopoly stage of imperialism pushed this process further along to the point that morality itself, and the basic notion of human solidarity was being repudiated among the elite. The "blonde beast" was emerging. The pretenses of morality were vanishing.

Sigmund Freud ended his 1929 book *Civilization and its Discontents* by asking if humans were not indeed better off as primitive savages, and saying he was neutral on the matter. He wrote: "For a wide variety of reasons, it is far from my intention to express an opinion upon the value of human civilization. I have endeavored to guard myself against the enthusiastic prejudice which holds that we possess or could acquire and that its path will lead to unimaginable perfection."

He preceded his statement of neutrality by pointing to flaws in Christian ethics: "The commandment 'love thy neighbor as thyself' is the strongest defense against human aggressiveness and an excellent example of the un-psychological proceedings of the cultural superego. The commandment is impossible to fulfill; such an enormous inflation of love can only lower its value and not get rid of the difficulty... But anyone who follows such a precept in modern day civilization merely puts himself at a disadvantage vis-a-vis the person who disregards it."

The novel *Atlas Shrugged* is cited by Paul Ryan, Stacey Abrams and other prominent US political figures as a primary source of inspiration. The novel tells of rich capitalists of the world going on strike against the inferior and ungrateful masses. The climax of Ayn Rand's magnum opus is the famous "John Galt Speech" that contains the following: "Your acceptance of the code of selflessness has made you fear the man who has a dollar less than you because it makes you feel that that dollar is rightfully his. You hate the man with a dollar more than you because the dollar he's keeping is rightfully yours. Your code has made it impossible to know when to give and when to grab. You know that you can't give away everything and starve yourself. You've forced yourselves to live with undeserved, irrational guilt. Is it ever proper to help another man? No, if he demands it as his right or as a duty that you owe him. Yes, if it's your own free choice based on your judgment of the value of that person and his struggle. This country wasn't built by men who sought handouts. In its brilliant youth, this country showed the rest of the world what greatness was possible to Man and what happiness is possible on Earth. Then it began apologizing for its greatness and began giving away its wealth, feeling guilty for having produced more than its neighbors. Twelve years ago, I saw what was wrong with the world and where the battle for Life had to be fought. **I saw that the enemy was an inverted morality and that my acceptance of that morality was its only power. I was the first of the men who refused to give up the pursuit of his own happiness in order to serve others.**"

What Georg Lukacs correctly identified as "philosophical irrationalism" has become the dominant mode of thinking among the western elite, and as US society enters a greater crisis and information technology is more widespread, these conceptions are seeping into the wider population.

Leo Strauss, the academic largely pointed to as the intellectual inspiration for Neoconservatism, pushed his own version of this teaching. His works such as *Persecution and the Art of Writing* present a narrative of great Platonic "philosopher kings" living in fear of the rabble, the mob, who would force them to conform. The sentiment echoes Ayn Rand and Nietzsche's sentiments of an *ubermensch* persecuted by the inferior masses.

Strauss' worldview focused on the notion that the population must be controlled and manipulated to make sure that they could never assemble and threaten the intellectual superiors. The complexities and nuances of the world should be reserved only for the trusted intellectual class. An article from *The Nation* published on June 2nd, 2005 describes Strauss perspective: "Intellectuals, he believed, would have to spread an ideology of good and evil, whether they believed it or not, so that the American people could be mobilized against the enemies of freedom. For this reason Strauss, we learn in one of many telling asides, was a huge fan of the TV series *Gunsmoke* and its Manichean depiction of good and evil."

The Straussian Neoconservative school of thinking seems to have been quite influential in how US political discourse was framed. Two Presidents, Ronald Reagan and George W. Bush explicitly cultivated a cowboy persona as they told "noble lies" in order to justify military operations against "evil doers."

The primary voices of leftist thought have equally been cultivated to espouse philosophical irrationalism. Susan Sontag and Hannah Arendt, two left-wing intellectuals promoted by the CIA's Congress for Cultural Freedom pushed the notion that fascism was synonymous with any form of group conformity or mass mobilizations. Sontag's *Fascinating Fascism* equates Nazism with exercising, group cohesion, athletics, and admiration of a leader. Arendt's *Eichmann in Jerusalem* presents Nazism and its crimes, not as the result of capitalism in decay, but in the "banality of evil" i.e. the evil inherent in all ordinary people which is unleashed by any populist mobilization.

Philosophical irrationalism's contempt for morality and humanity walks hand in hand with the Malthusian projects discussed among the ultra-rich. In their view the human race is nothing but a dangerous horde of bloodthirsty inferiors. The herd must be culled, and those who remain living must have their minds controlled. The activities of the masses must be carefully regulated and every effort must be made to prevent any kind of upsurge of democratic involvement or mass movement.

This kind of thinking, espoused by Nietzsche, Strauss, and many others was intended only for those they perceived to be *ubermensch*. But as these ideas seep into the population overall, they have resulted in a demoralization and cynicism that has made the political crisis spawned by the economic crisis quite unique.

Society is becoming less and less stable, with the ruling elite no longer bound together by any sense of loyalty or mission. The population is following the lead of the elite and viewing human life as nothing more than a contest between criminals where "survival of the fittest" is law. As the roads, bridges, highways, water treatment facilities and power plants become rustic and start to crumble, the ability of the policing agencies and government bodies to rally around a consistent agenda is also eroding. The concepts and ideas on which US society once seemed to be somewhat unified are taken less and less seriously. While the multinational corporations and houses of finance stretch their arms across the planet, the western homelands, most especially the United States, are coming apart on many different levels.

The Malthusian ultra-rich long for some kind of Hitlerian Bonapartist to emerge with the charisma to mobilize the dramatic enactment of one of their various "degrowth" schemes. This would be done, of course, to rescue capitalism from itself and reboot the economy with destruction. However, the cynicism and barbaric thinking the ultra-rich once reserved for their own circles has become so widespread, it is unlikely the masses would respond to such a fascist mobilization. It also is unlikely that enough unity could be formed among the elite themselves to push forward a fascist program and fully collapse the country into authoritarianism.

Where is Julius Caesar?

As the era of western hegemony winds toward its conclusion, the result is looking to be similar to the "depopulation, desolation, degeneration" Luxemburg predicted.

When examining the demise of the Roman Republic, we can certainly draw certain historical parallels and lessons. Rome was a military city state built on the economic foundation of slavery. Rome traveled across the world extracting crops, tools and slaves from various nations in order to enrich itself. Rome functioned as the middleman in all international trade, with "all roads" leading to and being controlled by it. The Roman Empire was certainly the prototype for the Atlanticist form of conquest described in Lenin's *Imperialism: The Highest Stage of Capitalism* or the writings of Henry Charles Carey describing "The English System."

As Rome ascended, it faced a serious problem as its mode of production stagnated. In his key text *The Foundations of Christianity,* Karl Kautsky wrote: "The slave economy... did not denote a technical advance, but a step backward. Not only did it make the masters impotent and incapable of working, and increase the number of unproductive workers in society, but it also cut down the productivity of the productive workers and checked the progress of technology, with the possible exception of some luxury trades…. Like every mode of production that is founded on contradictions, the ancient slave economy dug its own grave. In the form it finally took in the Roman world empire, it was based on war. It was only continual victorious wars, continual subjugation of new nations, continual extension of the territory of the Empire that could supply the masses of cheap slave material it required."

Slavery is a highly inefficient mode of production, because the slave has no real motivation to work other than avoiding punishment. The bigger the Roman Empire became, the less efficient and productive its plantations, mines, and craftsmen were.

The fact that Rome was a republic with a hereditary Senate and an elected National Assembly had been a strength in its period of ascendency. Rather than concentrating the power in the hands of one family, the land owning Patricians and Plebeians all felt that they had stock in the empire, and had input in how the loot was distributed.

As Rome stagnated in the first century B.C.E politics became filled with *Popularis*, i.e. populists, who drew political strength from Rome's less wealthy inhabitants who they weaponized against their rivals among the elite. The problem of *popularis* ultimately forced the Roman elite to abolish the Republic and establish a hereditary monarchy, an Emperor proclaimed to be a living God. This move set the stage for Rome's gradual deterioration.

The demise of the Roman Republic came about when a politician and military leader emerged who threatened to completely reverse the course of the Empire. Gaius Julius Caesar was populist who gained his political strength by functioning as a champion of the property-less *proletari,* the wage-worker underclass within the city who owned no property, but were not slaves. Michael Parenti's groundbreaking book *The Assassination of Julius Caesar: A People's History of Ancient Rome* described how the military figure came

Julius Caesar was stabbed to death by wealthy Roman Senators because his plans to reinvent the Roman Empire to be more multi-polar and sustainable cut into their profits.

to dominate Roman politics: "He used state power to effect some limited benefits to small farmers, debtors, and the urban proletariat, at the expense of the wealthy few. No matter how limited these reforms proved to be, the oligarchs never forgave him. And so Caesar met the same fate as other Roman reformers before him."

Caesar's program of populist reforms soon evolved into a program to save the Roman Empire from itself. He had plans to grant "citizenship not merely on individuals but on entire nations and provinces." He proposed redistributing land in laws that "provided almost the whole of Campania be divided among the poor and needy."

Parenti described the assassination of Caesar on March 15th, 44 BC as happening because "Caesar was branded a traitor to his class by members of that class. He committed the unforgivable sin of trying to redistribute, albeit in modest portions, some of the wealth that the very rich tirelessly siphon from state coffers and from the labor of the many. It was unforgivable that he should tamper with the system of upward expropriation that they embraced as their birthright. Caesar seems not to have comprehended that in the conflict between the haves and the have-nots, the haves are really have-it-alls. The Roman aristocrats lambasted the palest reforms as the worst kind of thievery, the beginning of a calamitous revolutionary leveling, necessitating extreme counter measures. And they presented their violent retaliation not as an ugly class expediency but as an honorable act on behalf of republican liberty."

If Caesar had succeeded in granting citizenship to residents of various city states across the Empire, and building up these respective cities as prosperous trading hubs, the Roman world order would have been much more sustainable in Europe. Likewise, if Caesar had expanded land ownership among the population and stopped its concentration among a small elite, Roman society would have been much less stratified. Caesar's emphasis on education, his construction of public libraries and other institutions could have brought a new level of strength and stability.

Caesar was a military man and Rome was a military state. Being the head of the army enabled Caesar to have a more collectivist vision for the long term sustainability and health of his society, looking past his own short term gains. Much like Bonapartist figures of centuries later, Caesar tried to "imagine himself elevated above class antagonism" as a figure working in the interest of society as a whole.

Caesar looked at the Roman Empire much like he looked at his own army on the battlefield. The concentration of wealth and influence had to be diffused across a wider geographic space in order for the entire empire to be sustained. Likewise new commanders needed to emerge, and a broader strategy than simply enriching a single city-state had to be employed. For Caesar it was not a question of morality, but rather one of efficiency and long term thinking. The only way the Roman Empire could survive was to change its economic relationship with Europe, the Middle East and North Africa. The method of plundering the world to enrich a single city was doomed to failure.

Caesar failed because those who opposed him among the rich and powerful were numerous. Caesar rallied the proletarians to push back against those in his own class who opposed him. The more power Caesar gained, the more of a threat he was to the wealthy Senators and landowners. Ultimately they stabbed him to death, and after his fall and subsequent demise of the Republic, Rome continued on its trajectory of deterioration.

The Last "Yankee and Cowboy War"

In order to realistically assess how the United States could avoid balkanization, deterioration and depopulation, the set course of its current trajectory, it must be understood that some sort of Caesarian figure or faction is likely to emerge within the US military.

The USA, like Rome, is a military state. Since the Second World War, the military industrial complex, a government funded network of private corporations that profit from war, has been an essential part of the US economy. The role of the military industrial complex in US politics was widely discussed by leftists in the 1960s, but in the context of the crisis, it is changing.

Carl Ogelsby's book *The Yankee and Cowboy War*, published in 1976, presents post-war US politics as a fight between two factions of the elite. He quotes Carroll Quigley, the respected academic who mentored Bill Clinton who wrote: "By the 1964 election, the major political issue in the country was the financial struggle behind the scenes between the old wealth, civilized and cultured in its foundations, and the new wealth, virile and uninformed, arising from the flowing of profits of government-dependent corporations in the Southwest and West."

The "government dependent corporations" was a euphemism for the military industrial complex. Weapons manufacturers and others tied in with the huge Pentagon budget were steeped in fanatical anti-Communism and McCarthyism. They

Carl Ogelsby's book "The Yankee and Cowboy War" interprets the political turmoil of the 1960s as a fight between the military industrial complex and the old money "Eastern Establishment."

enthusiastically supported the Vietnam War and were suspicious of the Civil Rights movement. Meanwhile, "the souls most calmly able to accept losses and pull back tended to argue from an Atlanticist, Council on Foreign Relations, NATO-haunted kind of position."

Ogelsby notes how right-wing literature from the 1950s and 60s seethed with rage against the Rockefellers, the Duponts, the Morgans, and other entrenched wealthy families who did not share their militarism and right-wing nationalism. This "Eastern Establishment" was interested in stabilizing society and gradually rolling back the influence of the Soviet Union, not in big wars abroad and an authoritarian fascist state at home. Ogelsby describes these rival wings of the American elite this way: "Yankee is the Council on Foreign Relations, the secret Round Table, Eleanor Roosevelt, Bundles for Britain, and at a certain point, the Dulles brothers and the doctrine of massive retaliation. Cowboy is Johnson the rancher and Nixon the city slicker, Howard Hunt and the bay of pigs team. Yankee is Kennedy, Cowboy is Connally."

Ogelsby writes "The Yankee mind, of global scope, is at home in the great world, used to regarding it as a whole thing integrated in the far-flung activities of western exploration, conquest, and commerce. The Yankee believes the basis of a good world order is the health of alliances across the North Atlantic, the relations with western democracies from which our tradition mainly flows… The Cowboy mind has no room for the assumption that American and European culture are continuous."

This interpretation of the US political landscape by Marxists generally saw the "globalists" of the old money in New England as the "democratic bourgeoisie" who leftists should be aligned with against the "fascists" of the military industrial complex. While Birchers and McCarthyists want to outlaw dissident groups and push US society into an anti-Communist frenzy, the more educated and long term thinking elites wanted detente and progressive social reforms.

Sam Marcy, the leader of the Workers World Party, composed a pamphlet entitled *Generals Over The White House* describing how in the 1980 election, it seemed that the military industrial complex was in revolt against Jimmy Carter. Marcy observed: "Perhaps more than any other event, the open letter by 170 admirals and generals, which appeared in the New York Times and other capitalist newspapers on January 21 [1979], indicates the scale of the military threat and the ready capitulation of the Carter administration. It indicates the danger the military poses from the point of view of retaining any semblance of bourgeois democracy against its continuing encroachments. This letter was a virtual ultimatum to no less than the President. It opposed SALT, it demanded a furious pace of rearmament, and called for military superiority over the Soviet Union. Carter embraced all three."

Marcy observed "the new militarism" in revolt against the geostrategic methods of the Carter administration: "The new militarism has been in the making for several years. It differs from the old militarism only in form. As against the crude, vulgar, and offensive outpourings of the type of Generals Patton and Curtis LeMay, the new militarism has broadened its base by virtue of its more sophisticated, more deceptive approaches. It handles itself with urbanity and goes out of its way to cultivate its long-standing ties with the universities, the press, and other public institutions of the capitalist establishment."

Marcy linked the rise of Ronald Reagan to the discontent of the military with Jimmy Carter: "The new militarism has its counterpart in the civilian population

Mass right-wing mobilizations in response to the Iran hostage crisis laid the basis for Ronald Reagan and the military industrial complex to defeat Jimmy Carter in 1980.

in the growth of the new right. The latter is a loose, conglomerate coalition of all the old reactionary and right-wing groupings under new names and masquerading more recently under single-issue-oriented labels such as Right to Life and so on."

The Communist Party USA, the Workers World Party, the Socialist Workers Party, and other major leftist groups of the era embedded themselves in anti-war activism, and soon in the movement against nuclear power, seeing themselves as pushing back against Reaganism and the military industrial complex, which was the main danger. This was the orientation leftists received from the Soviet Union, which saw the escalation of the arms race as the most immediate threat.

Throughout the 1960s there had been protests against nuclear weapons proliferation. Groups like SANE/ FREEZE and "Ban the Bomb" had called for nuclear disarmament. However, starting in the Carter Years the movement opposing nuclear energy combined itself with the larger movement against nuclear weapons. Opposition to nuclear power had one key financial backer: Big oil.

According to an article published by Forbes on July 13th, 2016: "In 1970, a leader of the petroleum industry and the head of the Atlantic Richfield Co. named Robert O. Anderson contributed $200,000 to fund Friends of the Earth, an organization that is strident in its opposition to nuclear energy, citing both safety and cost issues… The oil industry had long-been concerned that "atomic fission" could replace oil, or at a minimum, significantly undercut its price. Fission occurs when an atom is split into two parts and it results in the generation of electricity from a nuclear power plant. Skeptics have long expressed concern over the use of such technology for warfare. Adams says that the fossil fuel industry has also glommed on to this argument as a matter of convenience."

Big oil, it is worth noting, is also the property of New England old money, the Eastern Establishment that opposed the military industrial complex. Eric Walberg explained the process in his book *Postmodern Imperialism: Geopolitics and the Great Games*: "Their logic was to discourage widespread use of nuclear power to replace high cost oil energy… Its widespread use would leave big oil with falling profits and would mean the end of big oil's economic hegemony. The concern of big oil, rather than to simply prevent countries from building bombs, the intent of the Nuclear Non-Proliferation Treaty (1970) is to limit the use of nuclear power in general. Thus the manipulation of the growing ecological movement by oil-funded foundations made sure that anti-nuclear energy focus was at the ecological activists' agenda. This is confirmed by analysis of the green movement from the 1960s on. Leading green or ecology organizations such as Greenpeace, Nature Conservancy, Sierra Club and others have all received backing from the oil industry…"

Because it was corporations tied in with the military industrial complex that were building nuclear power plants, it seems the "Yankee and Cowboy War" was continuing in the 1980s, with the CIA-Big Oil-Eastern Establishment facing off with military corporations and lower level capitalists that wanted nuclear power. The various communist groups threw their weight solidly behind the CIA Eastern Establishment forces, decrying Reagan as a "fascist."

Among Marxists, one lone voice seemed to be putting forward the opposite view. This was Lyn Marcus, the leader of the National Caucus of Labor Committees, who later reverted to using his birth name, Lyndon H. LaRouche. He argued throughout the 1970s that the greatest threat came from the old money liberals whose ideology he linked with fascism, Malthusianism, and sophisticated efforts to psychologically manipulate the population while transitioning the United States to a "post-industrial" society.

LaRouche's followers got into fist fights with the Communist Party, and were labeled "fascist" by most leftists. LaRouche was praised by Ronald Reagan in 1980, and is credited with originating the Strategic Defense Initiative which the White House put forward in 1983. LaRouche's followers supported nuclear power, seeing the main force against it coming from anti-science Malthusian elements linked to big oil and the Eastern Establishment.

Describing what Ogelsby called "Yankee" LaRouche wrote "It was, as we have reported, one incestuously inter-married mass constituting an extended family. McGeorge Bundy is nominally a "Lowell," a family traced from the Bristol African slave trading port in England to Newbury... In addition to New England families, and the New York and other families associated with the Aaron Burr networks, there are two categories of additions added to the Eastern Establishment today. In some cases, such as the House of Morgan, the new families were created as joint operations of the British and New England... In a second categorical case, the networks of agents deployed by August Belmont, Judah Benjamin and the Slidells in building the Confederacy... These families are generally organized on the Venetian model, the *fondo*. The *fondo* is a financial trust, from which heirs may enjoy the use of assigned properties and may draw income, but may not individually draw down the capital... The *fondo* is managed professionally by a group of persons who may or may not include members of the biological family..."

Most leftists were repulsed by LaRouche's analysis and in line with his thinking, seeing the military industrial complex as the better faction, LaRouche spoke very harshly against the Soviet Union. Eventually LaRouche and his supporters denounced Marxism and embraced the economics of Friedrich List and Henry Carey. While LaRouche was sympathetic to Reagan, George H.W. Bush was seen as an old money Wall Street

Republican. When Bush ascended to the Presidency after Reagan, LaRouche was prosecuted and imprisoned by the US Department of Justice at Bush's direction.

The Communist Party at first resisted the all out opposition to nuclear power among leftists, but eventually gave-in and became fully opposed to atomic energy. Workers World Party leader Sam Marcy always insisted his followers not say they were against nuclear power, but rather that they advocated workers control of all public utilities. The logic of "building the movement" and following the middle class leftist currents left over from the 1960s forced the Communist groups to fit themselves into the anti-nuclear movement.

The US anti-nuclear movement, it should be noted, actively courted the Gorbachev wing of the Soviet Communist Party as allies against the "hardliners." Joint "days of action" against nuclear power and weapons were held in the Soviet Union and the United States. As the USSR moved toward dissolving, the role of the US Synthetic Left and liberal academics in helping cultivate the liquidationist wing of the Soviet bureaucracy became very obvious. Angela Davis and a number of her allies left the Communist Party USA when it supported the arrest of Gorbachev. Following the fall of the USSR, the bulk of the Communist Party's members in academia and the labor bureaucracy resigned to form Committees of Correspondence for Democracy and Socialism.

The New Battleground

When one fasts forward to the 2020s, one can certainly see the similarities in our contemporary political divide. Biden and his allies are decried as "globalists" while the Trump MAGA movement is denounced as "fascists" and "nationalists." The intelligence community, known to cooperate closely with the Ford Foundation and Rockefeller Think Tanks, leaked and worked against the Trump White House relentlessly. Trump's hardcore allies were Pentagon figures like Michael Flynn.

But some key things have changed.

Firstly, information technology has pushed into reality Brzezinski's fantasies of a "Technetronic Era." Social media has given the Eastern Establishment a key upper hand and advantage. Since the Obama administration it has been clear that Silicon Valley walks hand in hand with the liberals, and sees the right-wing as "spreading disinformation" and weakening the interests of US imperialism.

Secondly, the pandemic has more effectively secured the monopolies of certain mega-corporations like Wal-Mart and Amazon while weakening the lower level capitalists who supported Trump and Reagan a generation before. The low oil prices of the pandemic nearly wiped out the "fracking cowboys" who raged against Big Oil and its ally Barack Obama. The group had already been devastated by the Obama-Saudi price drop in 2014, but the pandemic seems to have finished them off as an effective political force. Now as oil prices surge due to the Ukraine conflict and US efforts to completely isolate Russia, big oil faces no serious competition within the United States. Its monopoly is secured.

Thirdly, while the "military industrial complex" is still right-wing, nationalistic, and fired up with opposition to the old money "globalists," this weakened section of the US economy is more anti-war and more sympathetic to Russia and China. Hard-right libertarian Congressman Ron Paul garnered huge amounts of support from military personnel in Presidential Campaigns. Lt. Col. Tulsi Gabbard, a soldier who was elected to the House of Representatives in Hawaii, became the primary anti-war voice. She has since left Congress and the Democratic Party and appears regularly on FOX news.

Lt. Col. Tulsi Gabbard, former Congresswoman from Hawaii, has positioned herself as a primary anti-war voice in US politics.

Retired General Michael Flynn was forced out of being Trump's national security advisor and faced persecution from the Department of Justice after being friendly with the Russian Ambassador. FOX news host Tucker Carlson continues to run segments questioning US foreign policy, warning of the danger of escalating toward a new world war, and asking why politicians are not putting "America First." It is QAnon-linked Congresswoman Marjorie Taylor Green who has been the most outspoken in opposition to the US arming of Ukraine against Russia.

Why is the military more anti-war than the liberal old money establishment? One factor is that many within the US military want to prevent events like 9/11 from happening. In their desire to "keep Americans safe" they are more concerned with fighting Al-Qaeda than toppling Assad and Gaddafi. What is widely pointed out by Russia and China, that the so-called "war on terror" has actually strengthened terrorist groups by toppling the socialist and anti-imperialist governments that restrained them, is also apparent to many Pentagon analysts.

But beyond this obvious contradiction, the liberal establishment has long been tasked with strategically planning out mechanisms to secure the hegemony of the United States. Brzezinski wrote about how the information revolution could be used to "Americanize" the world. With Russia and China rising, Bolivarianism on the march in South America, and the Axis of

Resistance expanding in the Middle East, this task requires increasing aggressiveness. The USA is losing the "information war" as Hillary Clinton told her audiences, but also losing the economic war as the Belt and Road and Eurasian Economic Union get stronger. The Eastern Establishment is now more hawkish, as it focuses on keeping the US and Britain at the center of the world economy. The military industrial complex would be satisfied to just keep selling weapons.

The military industrial complex and lower levels of capital are less interested in the long term global dominance of western monopoly capital. They just want to make money and making money means maintaining economic growth. The military industrial complex is concerned with the domestic US economy which is continuing to grow more dire as the "post-industrial" vision of some globally minded elites plays out. They reject the degrowth agenda intended to stabilize capitalism as it will cut into the profits, and lock them out of decision-making.

Furthermore, the military strength and potential human costs of a war with Russia and China are much more apparent to those who sit in the Pentagon calculating the risks and running scenarios each day. Behind many of Tulsi Gabbard and Tucker Carlson's warnings about escalation with Russia is a knowledge of facts that the "Dr. Strangelove '' type academics refuse to acknowledge. Unlike intelligence linked occultist guru Marilyn Ferguson, who served as Al

Gore's spiritual advisors, the Pentagon wing of the US deep state is not fantasizing about the libidinal release of a massive conflagration that would "bring the world back into balance with nature." The pagan-primitivism of new left occultism and its destructive fantasies horrify many of the evangelicals and conservative minded thinkers in the lower levels of the elite.

While the Eastern Establishment is hell-bent on propping up the decaying western order, the military industrial complex just wants to make money. Among many of the wealthy there is a growing desire for an economic reboot here at home. The knowledge that a wave of investment and partnerships with China and its allies around the world could make this happen remains an unspoken truth. For those in the United States whose only concern is expanding their profit margins, not securing the monopoly of US bankers, peace and economic cooperation with the explosion of development led by China around the world should be very appealing.

There is also an ideological component to this reshuffling of US political discourse. After the political confusion of the 1970s, the US military establishment rebuilt its strength with "the Christian right." This was a new synthesis of rock and roll music, watered down religious revivalism, patriotism, and social conservatism. After neoconservatism died with the 2008 financial crisis, the liberal order that now has the upper hand has made support for homosexuality and transgenderism, along with opposition to religion, as one of its primary focuses.

The liberal order wants to break down all forms of authority that could form as the basis of opposition. The patriarchal father figure, the priest, the pastor, the military strongman, all could get in the way of the social engineering planned by Silicon Valley. Netflix is constantly inoculating its viewers against any voice that inspires passion and claims to represent universal truth.

The liberal order wants to abolish ideology, abolish all ties that bind human beings to each other, and allow for itself to have a complete monopoly over the mind of the public. The military brass is made up of people with a much more illiberal mindset, for whom religion and ideological structure have always been key.

Tulsi Gabbard, for example, is a Hindu, an adherent of one of the groups that broke away from the Hare Krishna movement, a Hindu sect that proliferated in the US during the 1960s and 70s. Her organization is not Christian or rooted in European practices, but it opposes gay marriage and sexual promiscuity and urges its adherents to live a regimented life. While similar groups were promoted by the US intelligence apparatus in the 1970s as an alternative to Communism, they now find themselves targeted by the liberal order and back into a reluctant alliance or sympathy with Russia and China.

Just as the liberal order seeks to destroy the ideology of Marxism-Leninism, Bolivarian Socialism, Shia Islam and Russian Nationalism, it also wants to destroy the ideology of protestant evangelical Christians, the Catholic Church, and any other illiberal institution or organization. The liberal order is just as much a threat to the way of life and worldview of the Pentagon brass as it is to socialists and communists.

This all lays the basis for an anti-imperialist bloc to emerge in US politics. The lower level capitalists and the military want to see the domestic US economy revived. The labor unions and the bulk of the population, excluding the urban middle class, want to see this as well. Such an economic revival is in the interests of Russia and China as well, and trading with them to make it happen is likely a necessity, and would possibly help shield them from imperialist attacks.

The bulk of US society, the overwhelming majority, do not benefit from degrowth policies and war agenda of the ultra rich. This alignment of direct material interests leaves the big monopolies with their urban middle class foot-soldiers pretty alone and outnumbered. The only hope the imperialists have is mesmerizing wider chunks of society with social media or sewing division. If polarization along these specific lines of direct material interest matures, the emergence of a revolutionary anti-imperialist government in America is the logical conclusion.

The kind of polarization against the imperialists that once took place in formerly colonized nations seems to be fitting for the United States in this era of capitalism in decay.

Even today, the Chinese government bears the name "The People's Republic." China's form of government is described in its constitution as a "People's Democratic Dictatorship" i.e. a coalition government representing anti-fascist and anti-imperialist forces under the leadership of the Communist Party. This follows the theory of "People's Democracy" which was the basis for the foundation of governments led by Communist Parties across the planet following the Second World War.

The Chinese flag bears one big yellow star, with four smaller yellow stars next to it. The four small yellow stars symbolize the "block of four great classes" which came together to establish the People's Republic. These Four Great Classes were the peasantry, the working class, the land-owning middle peasants and the national bourgeoisie (i.e. capitalists who were loyal to China against US and British imperialism). The large yellow star represents the Communist Party that directs the four great classes with its proletarian ideology and understanding of the objective laws of history. The Communist Party, while representing most specifically the interests of the proletarian class, positioned itself as the liberator of the entire country, at the center of a broad coalition to build a new China free from the oppression of the imperialists.

The 4 small stars on the Chinese Flag represent the peasants, the workers, the middle peasants and the national capitalists, the Block of Four Great Classes. The large star represents the Communist Party which unified them against the imperialists.

The Communist Party and the Anti-Monopoly Coalition

In 1948, just a year before the Chinese Communists took power, William Z. Foster explained the vision of the US Communists for building a similar United Front: "In order for the people to put the United States firmly on the path toward peace, democracy, and general well-being the power of the monopolists who dominate our country must be curbed and finally broken, and the people themselves must take political charge, under the leadership of the working class. The struggle for socialism grows inevitably out of the everyday fight of the workers and their allies, especially against the present menaces of economic chaos, fascism, and war. In all good times the American people, on the basis of their existing conditions, will decide how and in what forms they will introduce socialism. The way our party foresees the possible development of the future is along the following general lines:

First, we propose the regular election of a democratic coalition government, based on a broad united front combination of workers, small farmers, Negroes, professionals, small business groups, and other democratic elements who are ready to fight against monopoly, economic breakdown, fascism, and war. This type of united front government could well have behind it an overwhelming majority of the people, as it has in other lands. It goes without saying that the election of such a democratic government could only be brought about in the face of powerful and very surely violent opposition from organized reaction.

The whole history of the American class struggle, which is full of examples of employer violence in strikes and in other mass struggles, teaches this lesson with unmistakable clarity.... Obviously, it would be an extremely difficult proposition to elect a truly democratic government in the face of this strong, violent, and reactionary opposition.

Second, our party contends that such an anti-fascist, anti-war, democratic coalition government, once in power, would be compelled either to move to the Left or to die. With state power in its hands, it would be forced to pass over from the more or less defensive program upon which it was elected to an offensive policy. Confronted with the sabotage and open resistance of big business, it would have no other alternative than this, if it hoped to realize any of the progressive legislation of its program and to ensure its staying in power.

A people's government would be forced to proceed directly to curb and undermine the power of the monopolies by adopting far-reaching policies of nationalization of the banks and major industries, the break-up of big land holdings, the beginnings of a planned economy, the elimination of reactionary elements from the control of the army, schools, and industry, as well as various other measures to weaken monopoly and to strengthen the working class as the leading progressive force in the nation.

Third, a democratic, anti-fascist, anti-war government, under the violent attacks of the capitalists and in its efforts to find solutions to the burning economic and political problems, if it were to survive, would necessarily move leftward, towards socialism, much as the People's Democracies of Eastern and Central Europe are now doing.

Some liberals believe that a united front coalition

government in this country would introduce a regime of "progressive capitalism," but this is a naive and dangerous illusion. Capitalism is now in its monopoly stage and is hopelessly reactionary. Any people's government in our times, in order to be progressive (or even to live), inevitably must move towards socialism.

American socialism, beyond question, will have its own specific forms and methods, but basically it will be the same as socialism in other countries, with monopoly capital completely defeated, the industries and national resources in the hands of the people, production for general use instead of for profit, and the working class the leader of the whole people.

Only in this way will this country and the world be finally freed of the dangers of poverty, economic chaos, fascist slavery, and murderous war. These steps could be taken legally by a people's government, notwithstanding the opposition of the capitalists, however violent.

To promote the election of a progressive, coalition government of this type which, by force of circumstances, would move to the Left and, eventually, to socialism, on the general pattern of the European People's Democracies, is obviously not to advocate a program of force and violence, the enemies of the Communist Party to the contrary notwithstanding.

The charge by the Department of Justice that our party advocates the forcible overthrow of the government is a brazen conscious lie…

Is it possible to elect such a democratic coalition, anti-monopoly government in the United States, the stronghold of world capitalism? It is a sinister fact that civil rights in this country, notably since the end of the war, have been seriously whittled away; but the United States is by no means at the stage of fascism. Nor do we Communists consider American fascism to be inevitable.

The big popular upsurge in the recent presidential elections was a dramatic justification of our faith in the democratic strength of the American people. It showed a profound anti-fascist, anti-war sentiment among the masses. In the event of an economic crisis or a war, this mass democratic upsurge would be vastly greater and more clear-sighted. Our party's political line is thus based upon the assumption that it is possible, under present political conditions in the United States, for the broad masses of the people, militantly led by the trade unions and a strong mass political party, to elect a coalition, anti-monopoly government. How long this possibility may last in the face of the fascist trends in this country is problematical. But if we should get fascism, if the United States were to be reduced to the level of fascist Spain, then the Communists will also know how to reshape their policies to meet that kind of situation.

It may well be asked, what resistance will American capitalism be able to make when the great masses of

**the people finally decide, as they surely will, to
establish socialism? Today American capitalism is
strong; but it is not as strong as it appears to be, nor
has it got a permanent lien on its present strength.
Now, it is true, Wall Street is the world bully and is
busy trying to organize civil wars in various countries
and to arm itself and other capitalist countries for
another world war.**

But what will its power of resistance to socialism be
when, as may be likely, the vast bulk of the rest of the
world has "gone Socialist," when its own foreign markets
have largely dried up, when it is undermined by
economic crises, when it may have just about wrecked
itself by its projected world war, and when its working
class has developed a Marxist-Leninist ideology and
sets out to bring about socialism?

**It may well turn out that it will be far easier for the
American working class, in the midst of a socialist
world, to establish socialism in this country than
now appears to be the case, with American capitalism
at the peak of its strength. Who can foretell these
things? Certainly we Marxist-Leninists do not
indulge in such prophecy."**

In the midst of the McCarthyite witch-hunts and
prosecution from the Department of Justice, the
Communist Party USA understood what its job was.
They were to try and build what William Z. Foster later
called it an "Anti-Monopoly Coalition." In the name of
peace, higher wages, the labor movement, racial

equality and anti-fascism the broad majority of the American people were to be brought together in a coalition to reject Wall Street and its agenda of war and fascism. A government that represented all the forces of opposition was to be brought to power and defended from the onslaught of opposition from the American power structure. In order to defeat the attacks of the big monopolies and the US power structure, such a government would then be forced to change the nature of the policing agencies, the military, and the economy and establish what Marx called "The Dictatorship of the Proletariat." With the state in its hands, the Communist Party and its allies could begin transforming

In 1948, US Communist Party leader William Z. Foster laid out the strategy of building an anti-monopoly coalition to fight for an anti-war government.

the United States into a prosperous socialist society no longer held back by the shortcomings of capitalism and its restraints on human productivity.

Unfortunately, the Communist Party was unable to achieve this goal. The FBI and the mobilization of the public around anti-Communist hysteria in the post-war years effectively weakened the party, reducing it to a core of less than 10,000 members, two thirds of which lived in New York City. The Communist Party was forced to operate in a semi-clandestine manner, with the national board sent to prison and publications banned from the mail.

After the death of Stalin, the media's repudiation of Joe McCarthy and the execution of the Rosenbergs, as the Cold War began to thaw, the Communist Party gradually emerged to publicly function again. When Khrushchev gave his "Secret Speech" in 1956 at the 20th Party Congress of the Soviet Communist Party, the remaining loyal cadre who had endured so much persecution felt utterly demoralized. The leader of the Soviet Union was saying that all the allegations made against Stalin in the US media were in fact true. Many resigned and abandoned Communism immediately.

Then in 1957 the US Supreme Court legalized the Communist Party in the *Yates v. The United States* ruling, saying the party could legally exist as long as it did not advocate violence, engage in espionage or function as unregistered agents of a foreign government. What the court solidified had already become the practice of US officials prior to the ruling. Starting amid 1956 the Communist Party was free to have a public office in Manhattan again and hold meetings in New York City. It appears this was seen as some kind of favor to the Soviet Union, a diplomatic gesture showing that the US was more willing to negotiate with the Khrushchevites who had just taken power.

Eugene Dennis emerged as the Communist Party's new public spokesperson having an event in Madison Square Garden proposing a merger with Norman Thomas' Socialist Party. A document called *The Communists Take A New Look* was widely circulated by the party announcing that at the upcoming convention the Communist Party was considering officially dropping Marxism-Leninism as its ideology and terminating its relationship with the Soviet Union. This coincided with Khrushchev's "de-Stalinization" campaign in the Soviet Union and Mao's "Hundred Flowers" campaign in China.

In 1957, the Communist Party leadership battled against two dissident factions. The first faction led by William Z. Foster and many African American leaders that refused to embrace Khrushchev's denunciation of Stalin. This faction also held on to the Black Belt Thesis that presented African Americans as an oppressed nationality. The hardliners were roundly defeated. Nelson Peery writes about his departure from the Communist Party: "The effect on the American Communist Party was catastrophic. Hundreds of militant comrades, declaring Khrushchev had destroyed socialism, quit the party. I never would have left the CP just because I disagreed with its projections or disliked some of its leaders, any more than I would have deserted my platoon because I hated George Patton or because Douglas MacArthur had referred to us as a 'bunch of n——rs'... spontaneously, the party began to break up into the factions that had once formed its base. I thought somebody should do something, but I no longer belonged to the party and there was nothing I could do."

Eugene Dennis and his allies such as Elizabeth Gurly Flynn defeated Foster by aligning with another dissident faction led by John Gates. Gates favored liquidating the Communist Party, cutting ties to the Soviet Union and becoming a "mass party of socialism." While Foster went into retirement as chairman emeritus, most of his allies resigned or were expelled laying the basis for the "anti-revisionist" groups of the coming years. The first attempt at a regroupment among those from the Foster faction was the Provisional Organizing Committee, though later the Progressive Labor Party (PLP) and Hammer and Steel emerged as "anti-revisionist" breakaways.

Joseph R. Starobin's *American Communism in Crisis 1943-1957* describes how the fallout of Khrushchev's secret speech really rendered the CPUSA completely impotent. He writes "In 1958 no regeneration of the CP seemed probable... the party no longer had the participation, even indirectly, of those it had once considered its most valuable supporters. No other political force on the left had any impact on the Communist Party's ultimate crisis; no other wing of the left could inherit those who could not remain Communists. None of American Communism's ideological kinfolk benefited from the debacle, though hopes rose in different sects and groups… Neither the CP's strict adherence to Marxism-Leninism over a decade, nor its acceptance of revisionism for the second time enabled it to maintain political momentum. Nor did the CP recover from the debacle once the revisionists of 1956-57 had withdrawn. Within a few years most of the old leaders were to pass away after obscure, internecine battles. What remained of the Communist Party has played a most inconsequential role in the sixties. The new left is phenomenon which owes little to communism, does not understand its lessons, and does not seem to care."

Shortly after the 1958 convention, John Gates and his allies were pushed out of the Communist Party as well, as ties to the Soviet Union were seen as non-negotiable. Gus Hall emerged from federal prison to become the Communist Party's primary public face for the coming decades. The ranks of the Communist Party from then on have always been less than 2,000 members, except for a slight uptick during the early 1970s.

It appears that when the Communist Party resurfaced in 1956, it was doing so under the direct permission and supervision of American intelligence agencies, most specifically the FBI. Most of the leaders had been imprisoned and released on supervised parole. Later it was revealed national committee member Morris Childs was an FBI informant from the early 1950s onward, and that he was tasked with smuggling millions of dollars in cash from the Soviet Union to fund the Communist Party's activities. Morris Childs received the Presidential Medal of Freedom from Ronald Reagan for his activities managing and controlling the Communist Party under the direction of the FBI.

From 1957 onward, the Communist Party's existence was a gesture to the Soviet Union. The Communist Party was used to help American intelligence court the "reformist" wing of the Soviet government that eventually oversaw the collapse in 1991. The Communist Party sewed the illusion that the Democratic Party wanted detente and that only the hard right-wing wanted to destroy Russia. Within the United States the Communist Party worked hard to channel US dissidents away from militant actions and into functioning as volunteers for the Democratic Party.

Today, the Communist Party USA exists to serve similar purposes. It works to court China, Vietnam and Cuba's leaders to be allies of the Democratic Party. It also works to channel youth who are interested in Communism toward being Democratic Party activists. Communist Party leaders monitor and track other leftist groups, reporting on their activities to Democratic Party leaders and indirectly to US government agencies.

Jacobin magazine, Democratic Socialists of America, and the Committees of Correspondence for Democracy and Socialism play a similar role. These are the "state department socialists" of our time, and they have a particular grudge against the leaders of contemporary Russia, most of whom come from the wing of the Soviet bureaucracy and the KGB who rejected their overtures and became more socially conservative and nationalistic during the final years of the Soviet Union. The Communist Party has also cut ties with the Democratic People's Republic of Korea, opposing its proliferation of nuclear weapons.

The New Communist Movement

It is fair to say that from 1956 onward the US Communist Party stopped working to build an anti-monopoly coalition and became a vehicle for Cold War intrigue and backchannel communications and intelligence operations. However, during the 1970s there were a few other organizations that emerged and took it upon themselves to carry out the tasks the Communist Party set for itself in 1948.

The civil rights and anti-Vietnam war protest movements of the 1960s, the New Left, spawned a generation of young Americans who were interested in Communism. Among young Black activists associated with the Student Non-Violent Coordinating Committee, a secret Communist organization called the Revolutionary Action Movement was formed in

The New Communist Movement was rooted in 1960s civil rights and anti-war activists who sought to build a new mass communist party aligned with China.

1962. The group set out to build a new communist party that would fight for the liberation of Black people in America. It took inspiration from the radio broadcasts of Robert F. William "Radio Free Dixie" transmitted across the US south from Havana.

Malcolm X met with RAM members and voiced support for their efforts, and some clandestine armed groups were able to recruit and operate among the wider trend of Black nationalism. Eventually, two activists associated with RAM, Huey Newton and Bobby Seale, broke away to form the Black Panther Party for Self-Defense, which emerged as the primary Black communist organization in the United States, attracting the admiration of millions and tens of thousands of active members. The Black Panthers faced heavy FBI repression and infiltration with Fred Hampton being assassinated.

In 1969, Eldridge Cleaver and his followers broke away from the Black Panther Party and launched a series of left adventurist attacks on police officers. Huey Newton then steered the rest of the party toward pursuing policies called "survival pending revolution" such as the Free Breakfast Program. The Black Panthers aimed to eventually merge into a multi-national party with white, Latino, Asian, and Chicano activists as part of Newton's theory of "Inter-communalism."

During the same period, many white anti-war activists joined Students for a Democratic Society, which had originated as liberal pacifist organization. By 1969, Students for a Democratic Society was dominated by the Progressive Labor Party and the Revolutionary Youth Movement (RYM), two Marxist-Leninist factions whose stated goal was to build a new communist party to defeat American imperialism.

After the breakup of SDS at the 1969 convention, PLP cut ties with China and Vietnam and also expressed hostility to the Black Panthers. RYM leadership began calling for militant street activism and left adventurist terrorism, eventually dissolving into the Weather Underground Organization and carrying out symbolic bombings.

Those in RYM who rejected the Left Adventurist tactics of the Weathermen and continued looking to

China, Vietnam and the Black Panthers as allies, formed "Revolutionary Youth Movement 2" (RYM 2). RYM 2 took instruction from the Black Panthers and aimed to build a communist organization among white industrial workers that would support the Black Panthers, China and global anti-imperialist forces.

RYM 2 laid the basis for what has been called the New Communist Movement, a trend of US politics during the 1970s that has been documented in books such as Max Elbaum's *Revolution in the Air*, Aaron Leonard's *Heavy Radicals: The FBI's Secret War on America's Maoists, Detroit: I Do Mind Dying* by Dan Georgakas, and many other academic works.

The NCM rejected the hippie counterculture. Its members cut their hair short, abstained from drug use and often denounced sexual promiscuity and homosexuality as "bourgeois decadence." The movement broke up into many different sects and tendencies, all of whom looked to China for inspiration and sought to bring Communist politics out of radical intellectual circles and to the broader American working class. Most NCM organizations oriented their members to work in factories and attempted to form "shop nuclei" as the Communist Party had done during the 1920s and 30s.

Detroit is the only city where the NCM that was significantly successful. In the mostly African-American city the League of Revolutionary Black Workers led by lawyer Kenneth Kockrell recruited hundreds of members and had significant influence among autoworkers. Mel Ravitz, a lawyer who openly called himself a Maoist Communist was elected for a term as a Criminal Court Judge and served many different stints on Detroit's City Council. Coleman Young, a Black activist who was a close-friend of the Communist Party USA and had briefly been a member of the anti-revisionist Provisional Organizing Committee during the late 1950s, became Mayor in 1974. The Communist Labor Party led by Nelson Peery maintained a significant layer of influence in Detroit during the 1970s and even up into the 80s with General Gordon Baker being considered an influential figure.

The successes of the New Communist Movement were limited, but in Detroit the Dodge Revolutionary Union Movement, a radical faction of the Autoworkers Union, gained significant influence.

Detroit City Council Member Joanne Watson also began her career in politics as an NCM activist.

The 1970s NCM was able to make significant alliances with the Arab American population of Dearborn, Michigan near Detroit. Dearborn is the highest concentration of Arab Americans in the United States, with significant Iraqi, Yemeni, and Syrian communities. Protests against Israel, and activism in solidarity with Libya and the Democratic People's Republic of Yemen took place.

However, beyond Detroit the NCM was largely unsuccessful. The reason was that the US economy was still strong, the US industrial working class enjoyed union wages and a high living standard, and as a result was uninterested in Communism and Anti-Imperialism. The problem of "Labor Aristocracy" that Lenin described decades earlier was a major factor, and the US had not yet been de-industrialized.

The Boston Trap

The NCM made a point veering away from standard left-wing politics, understanding that the counterculture elements were marginal and that it was necessary to build a base among the broader US working class. This led to some interesting instances of cooperation with the right-wing.

For example, in 1974, evangelical Christians who objected to Darwin's theory of evolution and other cultural conservatives in Kanawha County West

Virginia engaged in a series of riots and bomb threats in response to the new school textbooks selected by the County School Board. One bystander was shot during a protest and schools closed for extended periods in response to threats. The Revolutionary Union and other NCM organizations supported these right-wing "textbook riots" on the grounds that working class people had the right to choose what curriculum their children should study in school. The rhetoric of the Maoist communists condemned middle class liberals who looked down on the Appalachian coal miners, and hailed the militancy and use of firearms by the local population in response to outrage about liberal textbooks.

The most blatant and widely condemned example of NCM activists cooperating with the right-wing was in 1974 when racist riots took place against school desegregation. White residents of Boston who objected to their children going to racially integrated schools formed an organization called Restore Our Alienated Rights (ROAR). From 1974 to 1976, 40 different riots occurred in which white Bostonians targeted Black high school students. A number of stabbings, shootings, and bombings took place. Tear gas was deployed and thousands were arrested in the wave of unrest.

It was not only the racist white Irish-American Bostonians who opposed busing, though they were the ones engaging the rioting and targeting Black students labeled "de-segs" with street violence. The Nation of

The mistaken decision of some New Communist Movement groups to support the 1974 racist anti-busing riots in Boston pushed many leftists into the trap of assuming it is never acceptable to support anything labelled "right wing."

Islam and the Black Panther Party also opposed school desegregation, saying they wanted Black schools for Black children and that racial integration was a plot by white liberals.

It is also worth noting that school desegregation was promoted not only by civil rights activists and leftists, but also by the Ford Foundation, the Rockefeller Think Tanks, and some of the most wealthy institutions in America. The Catholic urban political machines of Boston and many other urban centers were a barrier against austerity. The labor unions and community voting blocks of many ethnic neighborhoods represented a force to contend with in the effort to bring about cuts in government jobs and enact privatizations. The neoliberal wing of the Democratic Party understood that breaking apart these nepotistic, and often very racist centers of local power was necessary to furthering their economic agenda.

In the context of the racist riots, Black nationalist opposition to busing, and support for busing and condemnation of the riots by the mainstream media, a few of the NCM groups voiced support for the anti-busing riots. The Revolutionary Union proclaimed "The People Must Unite To Smash The Boston Busing Plan" on the front page of its newspaper. The Revolutionary Union defended its position writing: "Those who think that the only way to stand with Black people and other oppressed nationalities is to attack white workers as simply a bunch of racists, who think the ruling class is a friend of the oppressed, can at best only drag at the tail of the struggle, and if they continue in this path, can only end up falling over backwards completely into the camp of the ruling class." The October League, another NCM grouping, promoted the writings of Black Nationalists who opposed busing.

Meanwhile, the Workers World Party dispatched almost its entire membership to Boston to organize a protest called "We Say No To Racism!" WWP members hide their Communist views, and the protest that attracted around 20,000 people to oppose the racist anti-busing riots featured Democratic Party speakers and local elected officials. At the march, Workers World

Party sought to lead the crowd to defy police orders but marshals from the Socialist Workers Party actively prevented a wider confrontation with the police from breaking out.

The Revolutionary Union and its successor organization the Revolutionary Communist Party were widely condemned for "pandering to racism" and supporting ROAR. The book *Heavy Radicals: The FBI's Secret War on America's Maoists* describes how "the RU's position was ridiculed widely on the left, and inside its own ranks it created serious dissension… The political fallout would have lasting consequences for the RU in terms of loss of prestige if not legitimacy in certain quarters."

The incident led to a consensus among US communist activists that one must never support "the right-wing" and make the mistake of the activists who supported the anti-busing riots. The NCM's instinct of breaking with the mainstream left and finding common ground with backward workers who were engaged in a confrontation with the US political establishment was seen as a deep flaw.

This assumption that every movement or sentiment labeled "right-wing" must be condemned, and that any effort to distance oneself from the liberals and find common ground with such people is a huge blunder is rightly called 'The Boston Trap.' It was certainly incorrect for the Maoists to align with the textbook rioters and the racist Bostonians, but this historical moment cannot be projected onto all circumstances.

Trump supporters and MAGA conservatives in the 2020s, for the most part, are not racist mobs attacking Black children. Their views are wildly incorrect, but their targets of opposition and political goals are often not far from those of anti-imperialists. Liberalism and the Synthetic Left have deteriorated into a defense of US military interventions, the FBI, economically devastating lockdowns, cancel culture, and the US political establishment itself. Many Americans labeled "right-wing" openly seek an end to the police state, an end to the wars, and the economic rejuvenation of the rust belt. The words quoted above from the RU's defense of its mistaken position are oddly prophetic. Decades later it appears most "socialists" have fallen over backwards "completely into the camp of the ruling class."

The Great Retreat

The failure of the various NCM groups to expand their base of support or recruit new cadres became a source of frustration as the 1970s proceeded. It was accompanied by the fact that the country to which they turned for political guidance was rapidly changing. The Gang of Four put forward the notion that China could reach "a higher stage in poverty" and that full communism could be achieved without industrialization and economic development, on the basis of having the correct political line. China's foreign policy shifted in the early 1970s aligning with the United States against the Soviet Union. The Gang of Four condemned "Soviet Social Imperialism" which they labeled "the main danger."

As the cultural revolution grew uglier, the Gang of Four's politics became more absurd and pessimistic. American writer William Hinton presented China's foreign policy views in an interview with *The Guardian* published May 5th, 1976, saying that a third world war was considered inevitable. Stating what he assessed as the main foreign policy view of Beijing during the last years of the Gang of Four he stated: "We asked about war — can a third world war be prevented? The thinking in China is that short of revolution in the U.S. and the USSR, a third world war is inevitable. The people of the world can take measures that may delay war but as long as these two great powers — the American and the Russian — exist in their present form and content for dominance, war is bound to come. Detente is an illusion, a smoke screen that covers up underlying stark reality — an arms buildup leading to war...

"The thinking in Peking seems to be: in three to five years, war is unlikely; in 10 years, it is a possibility, if one thinks in terms of a 30-year period (the time that has elapsed since World War 2), it is likely to be sooner rather than later. Another 30 years without a world war? Impossible. Does world war mean nuclear war? Not necessarily. The feeling is that a major world war might well be fought with conventional arms. Even a nuclear war will not destroy mankind. 'Mankind will

destroy the bomb, the bomb will not destroy mankind.'
At least half the human race will survive. War will
hasten revolution and revolution will solve problems
that have long been unsolved…

"Today, there is still a major contradiction between
the peoples of the world and the two superpowers, but
as between the two superpowers, one — the Soviet
Union — is more dangerous than the other. It is, in
fact, the main danger confronting the whole world
today. So now a more appropriate slogan would be
'Mobilize the third world, unite all the forces of the
second world willing to struggle, neutralize the United
States and strike the main blow at the Soviet Union.'
China judges world leaders by how well they
understand this new relationship of forces. Thus they
prefer Heath to Wilson, Strauss to Brandt and
Schlesinger to Kissinger."

The NCM groups were heavily competitive with
each other for China's approval, often engaging in
strange behaviors intended to follow Beijing. For
example, the October League held a protest against the
teaching of Confucius at an American University to
show support for the "Criticize Lin Biao, Criticize
Confucius" campaign launched by the Red Guards in
China. In 1976, Chinese Foreign Minister Zhou Enlai
died and his state funeral turned into an anti-
communist riot. Young intellectuals saw Zhou Enlai as
one of their few allies against the Red Guards and Gang
of Four that were actively preventing China from

economically developing.

In 1978, Deng Xiaoping declared that the Cultural Revolution in China was over and the Gang of Four were arrested for counter-revolutionary crimes. China began its "Reform and Opening Up" causing yet more confusion among its international allies.

This shift in China's politics coincided with a significant economic downturn in the United States, as well as an upsurge of anti-imperialism around the world. The 1978 Saur Revolution in Afghanistan was followed by the Islamic Revolution of Iran and the Sandinista revolution in Nicaragua. In these circumstances, many of the NCM organizations moved into a tragic desperation.

Communist Workers Party members in North Carolina challenged the Ku Klux Klan to a fight. They held a permitted protest in Greensboro called "Death to the Klan" and sent a provocative letter to the KKK, challenging them to "show their faces." The Klan responded by coming to the event and shooting five Communist activists. The events have been referred to as the Greensboro Massacre.

The KKK members were acquitted and the Carter administration refused to bring federal charges. One of the people riding in the KKK caravan was Frazier Glenn Miller, who spent years in the FBI's witness protection program, and later went on to carry out a mass shooting at a Jewish Community Center in Overland Park Kansas in 2014, killing three people.

On November 3rd, 1979 in Greensboro, North Carolina, five members of the Communist Workers Party were killed by the Ku Klux Klan.

The Revolutionary Communist Party split, with a large percentage of the members staying loyal to China and advocating that the party pursue United Front tactics. This faction was expelled or resigned forming the Revolutionary Worker Headquarters and eventually laying the basis for Freedom Road Socialist Organization. The remaining members of the RCP declared that China had restored capitalism and rallied around Bob Avakian as their chairman.

The RCP members staged a "Death to Deng Xiaoping" protest outside the White House with mass arrests and violence on January 29th, 1979, with many people arrested and facing serious criminal charges as a result. The RCP followed up with a very provocative "May Day

1980" campaign that resulted in scuffles with police and mobs of right-wing workers attacking RCP members across the country. The RCP made a point of publicly supporting the Iranian hostage takers and provoking right-wing crowds to attack them by burning flags.

Steve Hamilton, who had been a founder of the Revolutionary Union, looked at the events with disappointment. *Heavy Radicals* quotes him as saying: "Now, in 1979, the RCP seems to have regressed to the kind of Left Adventurism that is reminiscent of the Weatherman days, also reminiscent of the later years of PL when it found itself an isolated sect and a kind of "go for broke" mentality set in."

Internally, the RCP became much more harsh and rigid: "It was particularly feverish within the East Coast May Day Brigade. In a public mass meeting in New York, comrades were criticized and expelled from the party. The tone was ugly and dangerous… Leaders were removed and new leaders installed, actions the party had encouraged just weeks before were now denounced as rightist. Overall the bearings of the group were run amok." (*Heavy Radicals*, 2014)

The desperation and adventurism of the NCM groups reflected an understanding that after a decade in the factories attempting to build a new Communist party, they were seeing little progress. Meanwhile the international situation was changing in ways they could not really understand.

The economic downturn of 1978 resulted in a rightward shift among most white American workers. Ronald Reagan swept the 1980 elections. In response, the NCM began to fizzle out. Michael Harrington and his associates formed the Democratic Socialists of America and with a well-funded publication called *In These Times* they began recruiting ex-Communists into the Democratic Party and labor bureaucracy. The Democratic Workers Party and the Communist Party (Marxist-Leninist) previously known as the October League, dissolved.

The Revolutionary Communist Party declared that only the "lumpen proletariat" had revolutionary potential, and argued that most white American workers were "bourgeoisified." The RCP began putting forward scenarios for a "people's war" in America that would involve rioting among the urban Black population supported by a neutral or sympathetic middle class "movement."

Bob Avakian describes a moment at a Jimmy Buffet concert where he was surrounded by intoxicated youths as being pivotal in his shifting perspective, rejecting the need to win over the broad masses. Avakian recalls: "… as the struggle with these Mensheviks was developing and sharpening up a bit, after the revisionist coup in China, I went to a Jimmy Buffet concert. I had listened to some Jimmy Buffet songs because Jimmy Buffet sort of had one foot in youth culture and one foot in the country western culture. He came to Chicago and he had his band which was called the Coral Reefer Band; and of course reefer was a play on words—on the one hand it referred to the Caribbean influences in his music but then it was also… reefer. And at this Jimmy Buffet concert there were lots of reefer; there were a lot of jokes from the stage from Jimmy Buffet and the band about reefer and a lot of people in the audience were smoking reefer. In the audience there were a lot of youth from the middle class, but there were also a lot of young white proletarians there, who were into all of this. And this might seem odd, but even in the form of all this talk about reefer, and the people joking about it, there was a certain rebellious edge, and it made me think: we've gotten into tailing after more intermediate sections of the workers, or even the more backward among the white workers. There are workers, including among the white youth, who are more alienated and rebellious than many of the more stable and more conservative tending workers among whom we had been focusing much of our work. It is right to have a strategic orientation toward winning as many as possible among the more intermediate workers, and even more backward workers, to socialism, but this should not be our main focus. In a way, this Jimmy Buffet concert, while in and of itself a small thing, was part of provoking questions in my mind politically and ideologically."

This notion that it was better to appeal to a "rebellious edge" among the youth rather than seeking to build class consciousness among the broad masses of workers spread further than the RCP. Anti-populism and the idea that average working class Americans were the enemy seeped into almost all of the Communist movement.

The 1984 Jesse Jackson Presidential Campaign in the Democratic primary and Harold Washington's campaign for Mayor of Chicago attracted significant support from Communists and ex-communists. But overall, the early 1980s marked what can accurately be described as "The Great Retreat." Communist organizations in America largely declined in membership and those who remained focused on a specific niche on the fringes of US society for recruitment, no longer aiming to win over the bulk of the population to an anti-imperialist united front.

The Communist Party USA became almost invisible, working within the Democratic Party claiming that Republicans represented "creeping fascism." The Workers World Party focused on staging liberal rallies and "taking over the movement '' becoming the stage managers and facilitators of regroupments of the 1960s peace marchers. Various Trotskyite and Maoist sects went into the labor union bureaucracy and attempted to maneuver and push more radical politics. Many former Communists became academics and received grant money to write screeds about identity politics and postmodernism.

The concept of "White Skin Privilege" was developed in academia by Noel Ignatin, an NCM activist and labor organizer who became a professor at Harvard University. He argued that "white skin privilege" was what had prevented the NCM from being successful in winning over white workers to anti-imperialism during the 1970s.

The anti-populism of "woke" pseudo-leftism may have originally begun as an honest attempt to interpret the failure of the NCM by former Communists. However, in the early years of the 20th Century it became clear that writings about postmodernism and identity politics were being promoted by the Ford Foundation, the Rockefeller think tanks, and the Ivy League Universities. Voices like those of bell hooks, Robin DiAngelo and Judith Butler were being used to craft a new ideology that saw white workers as the enemy, and felt it was the duty of the morally superior college educated whites to keep them in line. "Intersectionality" was intended to help purify the image of the United States so it could go around the world toppling governments in the name of human rights. The academic "woke" current rejects Marxism as "class reductionist" and is heavily tied in with US intelligence and its color revolution regime change apparatus, and essentially just continued the work of Susan Sontag, Hannah Arendt, and Irving Howe, *Partisan Review* and the Congress for Cultural Freedom.

The decision of most remaining Marxist sects in America to cooperate with the efforts of the well-funded "woke" apparatus is based on the assumption, "learned" during the NCM that average Americans have no revolutionary potential. It also fits in with the logic of the Boston trap, that offering support or engaging in dialogue with any section of society declared "right-wing" or "fascist" by the establishment is a tragic, almost unforgivable blunder.

At this time Americans are more anti-war, more class conscious, more critical of the police state and more open to class struggle rhetoric than ever before. The only reason we have not seen a revolutionary upsurge in the United States amid what should be a perfect storm is the conscious infiltration and manipulation of Communist groups, and their confused belief that average Americans are unreachable and undesirable.

If there is to be any hope for moving the United States toward anti-imperialism and socialism, conscious Communist activists must repudiate the "great retreat" and the "Boston trap." They must instead find a way to go "out of the movement, to the masses" and build a base among the sections of the population that are at odds with the establishment.

The Bolivarian Coalitions

One of the biggest developments in international politics so far in the 21st Century has been the Bolivarian movement of Latin America. It is worth carefully examining how it is that a mass, anti-imperialist and socialist movement was able to take power in many different countries throughout the western hemisphere, and hold on to this power amid a huge effort to roll it back.

The first thing to understand is that throughout the Cold War, the United States largely backed military governments in South and Central America. Bonapartist authoritarian regimes served to lock societies down and prevent what had happened in Cuba from spreading to other countries in what the United States considered its "back yard."

Figures like Somoza in Nicaragua, Rios Montt in Guatemala, and various military juntas that held power throughout the region were based among the light skinned military elite that inherited its wealth and position from Spanish colonialism. These forces were viciously anti-Communist and saw indigenous peoples as inferior savages. However, they were also fiercely nationalistic and held on to power by "handing out the goods" among their own social caste.

These regimes backed by the United States made it impossible for Communists to organize among the urban proletariat. Student activists and labor agitators were routinely "disappeared" by the regimes. Communists throughout South and Central America were forced to wage guerrilla warfare in the countryside. The Cuban government served as an organizing center for the various armed factions that emerged in the 60s and 70s to fight the military juntas. The Tricontinental Congress founded by Che Guevara aimed to help various Guevaran focoist and Maoist guerrilla campaigns to be successful. The Cuban revolution came to power in this manner in 1959. In Nicaragua, the Sandinistas were able to take power with such tactics two decades later. However, the United States was able to offer military and intelligence support and enable the prevention of such victories elsewhere.

The horrors of the Contra war in Nicaragua, the various paramilitaries in Colombia, the arming of drug cartels and the counter insurgency operations that transformed into genocidal massacres of indigenous people have been revealed in decades since. The flow of US weapons and the arming of some of the most ruthless forces still haunts the region, and the inflow of migrants to the United States has been a direct consequence. The body count of US policy in Central and South America, if one ads up all those killed in massacres of indigenous people, killed by drug cartels and paramilitaries armed by the United States, as well as deaths resulting from chronic poverty and underdevelopment kept intact by US operations to prevent socialism and development is probably in the millions, perhaps tens of millions.

Regardless, as the Soviet Union was in decline and the danger of Communist revolution in Latin America faded, the United States turned on many of its long-standing allies. The Communists who protested for an end to military rule and civil liberties were joined by well-funded "human rights" activists who wanted an "open society." George Soros and the CIA's color revolution apparatus helped secure an end to military rule and the establishment of free elections in various countries.

This was done to serve the needs of Wall Street. Austerity policies are much easier to impose in the context of a weak government that is constantly going bankrupt and begging the IMF for more development loans. The American economist, Jeffrey Sachs, oversaw Bolivia selling off its state assets and shredding its domestic industries with a "democratic" government making it happen. Ecuador went through a similar process.

In 1989 the capital city of Venezuela exploded in rage in response to a dramatic increase in the costs of public transportation. The riot was known as "The Caracazo" and it laid the basis for a military leader named Hugo Chavez to attempt a coup in February of 1992. Chavez failed to seize power and was imprisoned, but he was released later because many among the Venezuelan elite sympathized with him and wanted to stop the economic demolition the country had been enduring at the hands of the neoliberal economists, and the US-led international institutions.

During the 1990s, Cuba and the various Communist parties of Latin America reoriented their strategy. In the context of "open societies" they could publicly organize and operate within urban centers again. Cuba held international conferences about neoliberalism, and oriented the Communists away from guerrilla warfare toward a strategy of building united fronts against economic cutbacks. The strategy of building up a large coalition against neoliberalism, and mobilizing big sectors of the population to become politically involved became the new tactical orientation for the new situation.

The FARC rebels in Colombia refused to abandon armed struggle in 1992 after their political wing, the Communist Party, voted to enter the government. As a result, Cuba terminated its relationship with the FARC and Fidel Castro denounced the group for fetishizing armed struggle and not shifting its tactics. Explaining

The victory of Bolivarian socialism in Venezuela and other parts of Latin America has been the result of anti-imperialist united fronts polarizing society against neoliberal economics.

why Cuba ended its relationship with FARC, Fidel Castro wrote: "The Colombian Communist Party never contemplated the idea of conquering power through the armed struggle. The guerrilla was a resistance front and not the basic instrument to conquer revolutionary power, as it had been the case in Cuba... (FARC Leader Manuel Marulanda) conceived a long and extended struggle; I disagreed with this point of view. But I never had the chance to talk with him. ... I have expressed, very clearly, our position in favor of peace in Colombia; but we are neither in favor of foreign military intervention nor of the policy of force that the United States intends to impose at all costs on that long-suffering and industrious people. ... I have honestly and strongly criticized the objectively cruel methods of kidnapping and retaining prisoners under the conditions of the jungle."

The victory of Hugo Chavez in the 1998 elections was the result of a very big coalition being created to support his Movement for the Fifth Republic. Chavez said he was a "Bolivarian" after Simon Bolivar, the hero of South American anti-colonialism. In his early years Chavez said he did not believe in capitalism or socialism but "the third way" and what was best for Venezuela. He promised to end the neoliberal policies that were weakening the Venezuelan nation. After getting elected, Chavez deployed the military and mobilized the population to help those affected by mudslides and heavy rains. Chavez used his TV broadcasts to whip up an atmosphere of brotherhood and solidarity, having his supporters build "Bolivarian circles" in their communities to mobilize disaster relief. In the wave of patriotism and enthusiastic community service that followed, he was able to push through a new constitution.

Chavez then faced an attempted coup in 2002, but was brought back into power due to an uprising of rank-and-file soldiers. The following year, Chavez announced he was moving Venezuela toward "21st Century Socialism" and solidified the country's relationship with Cuba. Cuban doctors were brought in to provide healthcare for low-income people and Cuban literacy volunteers began providing education. The indigenous peoples of the country who had long been left out of the political process suddenly became empowered as Chavez foot soldiers against the elite. Revenue from the state-run oil company paid for it, and Chinese investment also facilitated Venezuela's economic expansion.

In Bolivia, a similar process was carried out with Evo Morales, a man of indigenous heritage who voiced support for the miner's strikes and fights against the privatization of water. After being elected President Morales began the process of transitioning his country toward 21st Century Socialism, aligning with Cuba and China. At the same time, the Sandinistas returned to power in Nicaragua in 2006.

Bolivarian Socialism in Latin America, which has held on to power in Venezuela and Nicaragua despite an onslaught and series of defeats elsewhere, was an expression of a number of different trends. It represented the political awakening of the dark-skinned majority in Latin America which had previously been left out of politics. It represented a rejection of neoliberal economics and the total erosion of domestic industries overseen by the United States during the 1990s. Bolivarianism was dependent on two major factors in order to stay in power, the first being the dramatically high oil prices created by the Bush administration and its invasion of Iraq, the second is the inflow of investment and the construction of infrastructure that China oversaw.

A number of different trends in Latin America came together, and in certain areas revolutionaries were able to tactically maneuver and oversee a transition to socialism. A kind of "perfect storm" and society-wide crisis had erupted, and some were able to seize the moment. This required dramatically changing their tactics for a new situation.

The politics espoused by Bolivarian socialism is certainly not traditional Marxism-Leninism. It is a mixture of Marxism, Economic Populism, Nationalism, Liberation Theology, Indigenous traditions and spiritual practices, and much more. Bolivarian socialism is quite diverse and uses different emphasis and messaging in different countries. Bolivarianism more or less gives voice to a number of different trends within Latin American society, and ideas that are already quite widespread among the population.

This is how a serious political movement operates. One can compare this with how the "Socialism with Chinese Characteristics" that developed as a result of Mao's revolution gave voice to aspects of Chinese culture and tradition. Mao Zedong was able to harness the power of the already existing peasant movement in China to take power. In his 1927 essay he urged the Chinese Communist Party to drastically reorient its tactics in order to capture the energy of peasant rebellions. He wrote: "In a very short time, in China's central, southern and northern provinces, several hundred million peasants will rise like a mighty storm, like a hurricane, a force so swift and violent that no power, however great, will be able to hold it back. They will smash all the trammels that bind them and rush forward along the road to liberation. They will sweep all the imperialists, warlords, corrupt officials, local tyrants and evil gentry into their graves. Every revolutionary party and every revolutionary comrade will be put to the test, to be accepted or rejected as they decide. There are three alternatives. To march at their head and lead them? To trail behind them, gesticulating and criticizing? Or to stand in their way and oppose them? Every Chinese person is free to choose, but events will force you to make the choice quickly."

Successful revolutionaries do not create unrest and divisions in order to take power. Rather, they capture the energy of the unrest and divisions that have already been created by material conditions. They maneuver within the wider existing social forces, strategically positioning themselves and entering alliances to give voice to much bigger, widespread currents. This scientific understanding of how revolutions occur and how societies can be transformed needs to be grasped by those operating within the United States as the country proceeds on the path of a long-term crisis.

Defending American Values

What feelings among Americans could be given expression by a mass socialist and anti-imperialist movement? It may be too early to give definite answers and this may be clearer as the crisis develops, but some speculation is certainly permissible.

In his 1937 text *Freud and Marx: A Dialectical Study* the British Marxist R. Osbourne quoted Georgi Dimitrov's observation about fascists' ability to capture the souls of countries and communism's weakness in doing so. Dimitrov wrote "One of the weakest aspects of the anti-Fascist struggle of our parties lies in the fact that they react inadequately and too slowly to the demagogy of Fascism, and to this day continue to look with disdain upon the problems of the struggle against Fascist ideology... We must under no circumstances underrate this Fascist capacity for ideological infection. On the contrary, we must develop for our part an extensive ideological struggle on the basis of clear, popular argument and a correct, well thought-out approach to the peculiarities of the national psychology of the masses of the people. **The Fascists are rummaging through the entire history of every nation so as to be able to pose as the heirs and continuers of all that was exalted and heroic in its past, while all that was degrading or offensive to the national sentiments of the people they make use of as weapons against the enemies of Fascism.** The new-baked National-Socialist historians try to depict the history of Germany as if for the last two thousand years, by virtue of some 'historical law,' a certain line of development had run through it like a red thread, which led to the appearance on the historical scene of a national 'savior,' a 'Messiah' of the German people, a certain 'corporal' of Austrian extraction... Mussolini makes every effort to capitalize the heroic figure of Garibaldi. The French Fascists bring to the fore, as their heroine, Joan of Arc. The American Fascists appeal to the traditions of the American War of Independence, the traditions of Washington and Lincoln. The Bulgarian Fascists make use of the national liberation movement of the seventies, and its heroes beloved of the people—Vassil Levsky, Stephan Karaj, and others. **Communists who suppose that all this has nothing to do with the cause of the working class... voluntarily relinquish to the Fascists falsifiers all that is valuable in the historical past of the nation, in order that the Fascists may bamboozle the masses."**

Osbourne accompanies his quotation from Dimitrov by saying: "We have defined leadership, from the psychoanalytic standpoint, as the capacity to stand in the emotional relationship of the father of childhood days. Whether this definition is agreed with or not, there are certain emotional factors whose existence will raise no dispute. A need for protection, for someone to love, who will shoulder one's burdens and accept one's responsibilities — these are universal factors in leadership. It is irrelevant for the moment that some leaders deceive the people into believing that they can and will give this protection. The fact is that they are believed, and consequently attract the emotional allegiance of which I have spoken. That the need for leadership is universal is hardly disputable. Sometimes it may be highly rationalized in allegiance to abstract ideas of love and truth, or admiration for a person because of the intellectual quality of his works, but most often the emotional nature of the need is very apparent. What is also easily established is that the leaders of movements, groups, and religious bodies become endowed with qualities which mark them out from the common run of mankind. In some cases this belief is consciously nurtured... But it is not only necessary for Communists to associate their present struggle with the heroic figures of past struggles; they must also identify those traditional figures who are loved and respected with someone in the present. That is part of the successful technique of the Fascist leaders, who have claimed to be the modern counterpart of the heroic figures in national history... If people have this capacity to love and to idealize individuals, it is better, after all, that they expend it on individuals whose lives and deeds have really deserved for them this love and reverence. And it is a psychologically sound measure to keep such people before the masses as an incentive and guide to the overcoming of difficulties on the road of social progress."

Those who seek to push the US into the anti-imperialist camp and toward socialism must present themselves as the defenders and inheritors of all that the American people already love. In the current circumstances, this may prove to be much easier than expected.

For centuries, America has been known as the land of innovators and hard workers. Alexis De Tocqueville wrote: "It seemed as if New England was a region given up to the dreams of fancy and the unrestrained experiments of innovators." Anna Louise Strong

The deeply held religiousness of many Americans is currently at odds with the liberal order.

described how Americans are known around the world for being "motor minded" and fanatical in their pursuits. Across the planet, the USA has cultivated an image for itself as a land of "work hard and achieve your dreams."

It should not therefore be shocking that the lockdowns, the degrowth fascism, and the cynicism of the low-wage police state are extremely unpopular. A so-called "nation of immigrants" that have been pumped with Horatio Alger "rags to riches" stories since childhood does not appreciate having cold water poured on its inner enthusiasm.

It is also worth noting that the United States, far more than most western countries, is a stronghold of religious fanaticism. Two US states have opted not to outlaw the practice of snake handling. Various religious sects and divergent brands of spiritual practice proliferate among the US public. While liberalism seeks to impose itself on society at large, with Netflix psyching up its audiences about cults and promoting religious skepticism, a big chunk of the US public maintains an illiberal worldview. Many Americans have been brought up from childhood to believe that the greatest way to live one's life is in devotion to a cause.

In 1934, *Liberty* magazine commissioned exiled ex-Bolshevik Leon Trotsky to write an essay called "If America Should Go Communist." In his essay, Trotsky wrote that he did not believe religious fanaticism would be a barrier to the eventual socialist revolution in

America, and that in fact it would probably aid in the process. Trotsky wrote: "Even the intensity and devotion of religious sentiment in America will not prove an obstacle to the revolution. If one assumes the perspective of soviets in America, none of the psychological brakes will prove firm enough to retard the pressure of the social crisis. This has been demonstrated more than once in history. Besides, it should not be forgotten that the Gospels themselves contain some pretty explosive aphorisms."

It is an odd twist of fate that two of the key components of Americanism that have laid the basis of anti-communism are now at odds with the liberal order. For years, Americans were told to hate Russia and China, because in our land of free markets anyone who works hard enough can become a millionaire. Now, the US elite urges Americans to accept poverty to stop climate change. The American elite is working to convince the public that "Less is More" while China surges ahead with a new millionaire every day and hundreds of millions lifted from poverty.

Americans have likewise been told for generations to hate Communism because the atheistic adherents of dialectical materialism oppose the faith of their fathers and would cut them off from the beauty of spiritual life and the clarity of belief. But now the American elite tells them to be lukewarm and passionless and to view every cause and creed with skepticism. Meanwhile, socialism in Latin America is rising with slogans like

"Christianity, Socialism and Solidarity." Hugo Chavez told his followers that "Jesus Christ was the greatest socialist in all of history." While the west descends into a land of cynicism and hopelessness, it is the anti-imperialists of the world that boil with passion, willing to die for the cause of defeating the satanic order of greed and bringing in a new world of compassion and human brotherhood.

Even American patriotism is at this point being condemned by the American elite. Americans have been told Communism is "un-American" and contrary to the country's foundational principles of freedom. Becoming an adherent of Marx means spitting on the declaration of independence, the founding fathers, the pledge of allegiance and the beauty of the American flag. Yet, now social media is mobilizing young people to tear down monuments. The founding fathers are commonly described as racist slaveholders. The American people are told that rather than being proud of their country, they should put on a sackcloth and repent for centuries of white privilege and a lack of racial awareness, as the country collapses into the open international system and deeper poverty. Americans who want to see their wages and living standards increase are told this is "racist" because the economic deterioration is simply "losing their privilege."

This, of course, creates an opening for socialists to become the bearers of a new kind of patriotism. We can tell the American people to not be full of shame but to be proud of their heritage in defeating the British empire, defeating the London-aligned confederates, building the labor movement, standing with Russia and China against the Nazis, and much more. As bourgeois patriotism steeped in anti-Communism dies, and even the US military faces an attempted "woke-ification" the revolutionaries can bring forward pride in the heritage of John Brown, Harriet Tubman, Gus Hall, Huey Newton and Elizabeth Gurly Flynn. Patriotism is being handed to us as a gift by the ruling class, along with religion and passion, and American innovation.

Everything that America has been said to stand for is now being abandoned and chucked into the garbage by the ruling class as they move to lockdown society amid an economic crisis. They are handing it to us and to anti-imperialism as a gift. The deeply held sentiments of the masses, their desire to live and not be "degrown" to save the profits of the elite are just waiting to be hijacked by those with serious political vision. The homeless encampments across the major cities and rage-filled youth trapped in debt and hopelessness are just waiting to be transformed into an army of liberation, a mass movement of resistance. The question is whether or not those who want a real socialist movement in America will be smart enough to seize hold all of this great potential.

"Country Joe and the Fish"

Seizing the moment will require adopting a new mindset in relation to the American people. Mao Zedong and Joseph Stalin, the two key leaders of Communism in the 20th Century, were effective mass organizers because they had a deep understanding and connection with their own respective peoples.

One of the Rock & Roll bands that performed at Woodstock was called "Country Joe and the Fish." While it may come as a surprise, the performers were the children of Communist Party USA members, and their name was an homage to Stalin and Mao. Mao Zedong instructed his followers that "the masses are the water, revolutionaries are the fish." He urged Chinese Communists to become deeply connected with the population, to lose any elitist notions they held onto and go among the people. Mao wrote: "How should we judge whether a youth is a revolutionary? How can we tell? There can only be one criterion, namely, whether or not he is willing to integrate himself with the broad masses of workers and peasants and does so in practice. If he is willing to do so and actually does so, he is a revolutionary; otherwise he is a non-revolutionary or a counter-revolutionary. If today he integrates himself with the masses of workers and peasants, then today he is a revolutionary."

Like Mao was a fish, swimming among the masses, Stalin was "Country Joe," the son of a boot-maker from a small village in Georgia. Stalin's teen years were spent

The 1960s Rock Band "Country Joe and the Fish" drew its name from rural village-born Joseph Stalin ("Country Joe") and Mao Zedong ("the masses are the water, revolutionaries are the fish.")

in a Russian Orthodox Seminary being trained for the priesthood. Historian Simon Montifore described Stalin's mass organizing methods this way: "Stalin was hostile to bumptious intellectuals, but he was less with the less educated worker-revolutionaries, who did not arouse his inferiority complex, he played the teacher — the priest… The workers listened reverently to this young preacher — and it was no coincidence that many of the revolutionaries were seminarists, and the workers often pious ex-peasants… Trotsky, agitating in another city, remembered that many of the workers thought the movement resembled the early Christians and had to be taught that they should be atheists."

Che Guevara is widely quoted as having said: "At the risk of seeming ridiculous, let me say that the true revolutionary is guided by a great feeling of love. It is impossible to think of a genuine revolutionary lacking this quality." Communists in America must actively learn to have "great feelings of love" for the people, and know them better than they know even themselves.

A real revolutionary movement in America will require the bulk of the population, the broad masses in their millions, to become involved in the political process and take history into their own hands. Communists must approach them as such. It is them, not us, who will be the decisive factor. They will do things that amaze us and far surpass our own bravery and strength. All we can hope to do is offer the guidance and direction to point the explosion that is coming in the right direction. Ultimately, they will be the protagonists, the leading actors of the struggle to come. We will simply function as stage managers and producers, enabling them to shine before the world and perform the magical acts of beauty we know they have always been capable of. Mao Zedong wrote: "The masses are the real heroes, while we ourselves are often childish and ignorant, and without this understanding, it is impossible to acquire even the most rudimentary knowledge."

"Out of the Movement, to the Masses!"

As the crisis in the United States and the rest of the world deepens, much is unclear but a few things can be safely predicted.

First, the ruling class of the United States will become more thoroughly divided. The ultra-rich and their loyalty to the global financial system will put them at further odds with the military industrial complex and the lower levels of capital that seek to see their profits expand. The efforts to transition the United States to a society that fits into an Atlanticist model of international trade, with southern California and New York City as globalist trading hubs, and the rest of the country as an unused "flyover country" will garner more and more opposition.

Second, the economic consequences of the breakdown of capitalism will leave more and more people behind.

Desperation will grow greater, hunger and homelessness will expand. The efforts to eradicate the aristocracy of labor and collapse the United States into the open international system will create more and more resistance among different layers of the population.

Third, in addition to the economic crisis, the spiritual and ideological crisis will also grow deeper. The lack of ideology, the lack of collective identity and meaning, will cause more and more younger Americans to search for a purpose in life and a movement they can join to find meaning. Some will be succumbed by the pessimism and hopelessness, the cynical wrecker mentality. But others will not and will press forward and join in an optimistic current of resistance.

The tasks once taken on by the Communist Party and the New Communist Movement are now continued by the Center for Political Innovation.

CPI was conceived in 2020 as a vehicle for doing what is largely not being done: promoting a brand of anti-imperialist and socialist politics that is aimed at the bulk of the American people.

CPI has put forward its four-point economic plan. CPI has also published a number of books and convened conferences in a variety of different corners of the country, intended for the purpose of cultivating a group of people dedicated to these politics. The CPI maintains a relationship with various anti-imperialist forces around the world, and works to publicize and create sympathy for them among the US working class, while promoting opposition to the big monopolies and their low-wage police state.

Unlike the various Marxist groupings that have emerged in the last two decades, CPI maintains no illusions of being the vanguard party. We are not a Leninist party formation or an electoral entity. Rather, the CPI is simply an educational project, taking on the specific task of laying the ideological and intellectual foundations of the coming revolution.

CPI will carry out a strategy of "top and bottom organizing." While we win over, utilize and train more and more people in our own movement of anti-imperialism and our unique ideological tradition, we will also make ourselves useful to forces within the power structure that are resisting the drive toward de-growth, fascism and a new world war. As US society continues to polarize around the question of imperialism and war, we will position ourselves solidly with those opposed.

CPI already fits into a much bigger trend within US society. A mishmash of forces of diverse political origins are coming together to denounce the flow of weapons to Ukraine, to oppose censorship and police state repression, and to demand the economic rebirth of the country. The "Rage Against The War Machine" protests involving Libertarians and Socialists together are a big step forward. As these trends proliferate, different forces will take on different tasks, running for office, organizing protests, building international and domestic relationships, etc. CPI will play only one specific role, the role of teaching ideology and building community around it, laying the foundations for others to do important work in different areas.

There is no question that if current trends continue, at some point the crisis will take on a more severe character. The divisions in the ruling class will become far deeper, and the suffering of the masses will become much more acute and intolerable. In such circumstances, CPI will have laid the foundations for something much different to be formed to serve the needs of this historic moment.

It will be the Center for Political Innovation and its organizational and ideological successors that will have laid the foundations and created the network necessary for resisting fascism. We will have popularized the notion of a "Government of Action That Fights for Working Families" and put forward serious policy solutions to liquidate the economic crisis.

Our work will enable the people to know what they are fighting for and to know who their natural allies around the world will be as they resist the rise of a low wage police state.

Liberalism, the worldview that puts the individual above all else, is doomed. Human beings are collective creatures, and all that human beings have ever achieved has been collective in nature. Human beings always seek to advance toward a higher plane, a higher mode of production, a larger population, a more comfortable life, and a more sustainable relationship with nature. Humanity will continue to march forward beyond the narrow confines of the irrational profit system.

Illiberalism will triumph and the United States will join the rest of the world in abandoning an economic system that puts profits before people and creates poverty amid abundance. Technology will be freed from the artificial restraints of the capitalist system, and the human race will soar to new heights. New sources of energy will be discovered, humanity will expand its existence beyond this single planet. A life that is unimaginable to us in our time will be enjoyed by our descendants as the epic march of human progress continues at an even faster pace.

The 21st Century will undoubtedly be remembered as a difficult period of transition, filled with hardships, setbacks and victories. But those in future generations will undoubtedly celebrate and admire our courage, and our ability to keep pressing forward when it seemed the entire weight of the old order was coming down on us.

Marx wrote: "proletarian revolutions, like those of the nineteenth century, constantly criticize themselves, constantly interrupt themselves in their own course, return to the apparently accomplished, in order to begin anew; they deride with cruel thoroughness the half-measures, weaknesses, and paltriness of their first attempts, seem to throw down their opponents only so the latter may draw new strength from the earth and rise before them again more gigantic than ever, recoil constantly from the indefinite colossalness of their own goals – until a situation is created which makes all turning back impossible, and the conditions themselves call out: Hic Rhodus, hic salta! (Here's the rose, now dance!)"

We must keep with us the words of the man did so much to start China on the road of colossal transformation and national resurrection, and never forget that our own conscious actions and the boldness to carry them out despite the risks can be decisive in changing the course of history: "Dare to Struggle, Dare to Win!"

At the opening ceremony of the 2022 Chicago Conference, members of the Center for Political Innovation display anti-imperialist flags along with the US flag as the national anthem plays.

Appendix #1: Timeline 1978-1981

At one point, when looking over the various literature published by the Workers World Party, the Revolutionary Communist Party, and the Socialist Workers Party, I was forced to raise the question: Why was so much of it published during the Carter administration?

A huge amount of attention is given by leftist historians to the events that took place from the year from 1968 up into the early 70s. These were the years of Martin Luther King Jr's assassination and the ensuing urban rebellions, the chaos at the Chicago Democratic National Convention, increasing unrest on college campuses, the rising influence of the Black Panthers, the election of Richard Nixon, COINTELPRO, the assassination of Fred Hampton, the music festival Woodstock, the collapse of Students for a Democracy Society, the Kent and Jackson State Massacres, the trial of Angela Davis, and many other events that were rather pivotal in the history of US radicalism.

However, the events of a decade later are remembered

by boomers with much less nostalgia. The economic downturn, followed by the Iranian and Nicaraguan revolutions, all culminated in the ascension of Ronald Reagan. These are the years when the New Communist Movement began to disintegrate, and the seeds of the fall of the USSR were being planted by what would be the Color Revolution industry. The world Communist movement was in utter confusion, leftist influence on US political discourse was declining, and the "late Cold War" normal was setting in. Neoconservatism was setting up shop in Washington to become the primary ideological trend among the US elite.

However, having an understanding of the events of 1978-1981 is very important for those seeking to utilize divisions in the ruling class, build up some kind of revolutionary organization, construct a United Front against the imperialists, and eventually move the United States toward socialism.

In the process of digging into the history of various political movements in the United States as well as geopolitical events, I was forced to compile this timeline of 1978 to 1981.

A decade after the late 1960s political upsurge, Jimmy Carter was President, the US economy was facing a downturn, the global communist movement was at the height of its strength, but also more divided and confused than it had been since 1917. US foreign policy was being reshuffled by Brzezinski and Kissinger in light of the defeat in Vietnam.

In essence, the Malthusian ultra-rich Eastern establishment faced an explosive rebellion from lower level capitalists and the military industrial complex. The economic consequences of Carter's policies and the inability of the White House to build up public support for US military interventions shook up Washington DC. Many of the hard-right anti-Communists in the United States and around the world saw Carter's degrowth agenda as a threat to them. In the context of the Iranian and Nicaraguan revolutions, and the US proxy war with the Soviet Union in Afghanistan, the lower levels of capital, with the aid of the Pentagon and the FBI moved against Carter. Ronald Reagan moved from the far-right fringe of the Republican Party to become the primary candidate.

Within the United States, various political and religious "counter gangs" became chess pieces in an elaborate power struggle. Globally, many armed insurgent groups, intelligence linked movements, and political figures were used in a similar manner.

When the dust finally cleared, Reagan was President but his anti-establishment right-wing tendencies had been tamed. The Carter aligned wing of the US deep state went into retreat and accepted its position as a kind of semi-loyal but ever present opposition guiding academia and the intel apparatus.

The fight did not reopen until 2008 when the US economy crashed. With the ascendancy of Obama, Brzezinski and his crew were back in power in

Washington DC. A fight that seemed to almost reach an armistice in 1981 reopened with a vigor, and is now raging across America's headlines as the economy continues to crash and burn while Eurasia rises.

In such a context, serious revolutionaries must look over this elaborate chain of events while contemplating what role we can play in our time, and how to maneuver within this current crisis to stop the looming danger of a new world war and win justice for working families.

1978

January 1, 1978 – The book *Dope, Inc.* is published by followers of Lyndon LaRouche. The text documents the role of the British Empire and US intelligence agencies in promoting drug use from the 1600s up to today.

April 30th, 1978 – The Democratic Republic of Afghanistan is declared following the Saur Revolution.

May 7th, 1978 – In Houston, Texas the "Moody Park Riots" erupt as local Chicanos rebel against police brutality. Three members of the Revolutionary Communist Party are charged with inciting the riot, but their convictions are overturned on appeal.

August 8, 1978 – A police attempt to evict members of the Black Radical MOVE organization in Philadelphia results in a shoot-out. The "Move 9" are sent to prison as a result.

October 9th, 1978 – Korean Businessman Tongsun Park testifies before Congress about allegations of illegal lobbying by the South Korean government in the

United States, the "Koreagate" scandal. At the time
South Korea was headed by the military strongman
Park Chung Hee, a hardline anti-Communist and
bonapartist who is largely responsible for using state
and military power to industrialize South Korea.

November 2nd, 1978 – US Congress releases a 447
page document accusing Rev. Sun Myung Moon, the
leader of the Unification Church of violating US tax
and immigration law, money laundering and illegally
lobbying for the South Korean government. A
widespread media campaign accuses the Unification
Church of being a "cult" that "brainwashes" young
Americans.

November 13th, 1978 – Strikes across Iran spread to
the oil industry. Oil prices significantly rise as unrest
spreads across the country, intensifying the ongoing
US energy crisis.

November 18, 1978 – Followers of Rev. Jim Jones
commit mass suicide in Guyana. 909 people drink
cyanide on command. The Peoples Temple was a
religious sect that operated in San Francisco and had
ties to the leftist wing of the Democratic Party. Jones
had taken his followers to Guyana after a media
campaign revealed ugly details of the Church's internal
life.

November 27, 1978 – San Francisco Mayor George
Moscone & Alderman Harvey Milk, both of whom had
been supported by Jim Jones are assassinated by a
former police officer. Dianne Feinstein, who had run

against Moscone who she considered too far left, was sworn in as Mayor of San Francisco in the aftermath of the assassinations.

1979

January 7th, 1979 – Vietnamese forces, aligned with the Soviet Union, take Phnom Penh and the US-China backed government of Pol Pot in Cambodia is forced to retreat.

January 16th, 1979 – The Shah of Iran flees the country amid an ongoing uprising.

January 21st, 1979 – 170 Retired Generals and Admirals publish an ad in the *New York Times* condemning Jimmy Carter's SALT treaty with the Soviet Union and calling for an increase in military spending.

January 25th, 1979 – Revolutionary Communist Party vandalizes the Chinese Embassy in Washington DC shortly after it opens, as the US establishes diplomatic relations with China.

January 29th, 1979 – Revolutionary Communist Party holds a "Death to Deng Xiaoping" rally at the White House. 200 RCP members are arrested and charged. 2 RCP members run at Deng Xiaoping on White House grounds waving Mao's Little Red Book after being given press credentials by the US Air Force.

February 1st, 1979 – Ayatollah Khomeini returns to Iran from exile, greeted by thousands of supporters at the airport. Ten days later the government collapses and the Islamic Revolution is declared victorious.

May 21st, 1979 – The former police officer who shot Harvey Milk and George Moscone in San Francisco is acquitted for murder and only convicted of "voluntary manslaughter." He is given a 7 year sentence. At his trial he used the infamous "twinkie defense" saying junk food had caused him to be mentally ill. San Francisco lights up with the "White Night Riots" and 140 people are injured as LGBT activists take to the streets burning cars and attacking police. Police then raid gay bars in retaliation, beating and injuring many people.

July 15th, 1979 – Jimmy Carter delivers his "crisis of confidence" aka Malaise Speech, bemoaning the energy crisis, high costs of gas, and telling Americans that "owning things" will not make them happy.

July 19th, 1979 – The Sandinistas declare victory in Nicaragua, successfully toppling the US backed dictator Somoza after a two-year civil war. The Sandinista National Liberation Front (FSLN) is a broad coalition of leftist forces, and Liberation Theology is central to the beliefs of the new government, with Christian socialist language being added to the new constitution.

October 8th, 1979 – The *New York Times* publishes a hit piece on Lyndon LaRouche with the headline "One Man Leads US Labor Party on its erratic path." The article accuses him of anti-semitism, and running a terrorist training school.

October 26th, 1979 – South Korean military dictator Park Chung Hee is assassinated in his home by the head of the Korean Central Intelligence Agency. The assassin is summarily executed and the motive is unclear.

November 1st, 1979 – Walter Guevara, the elected President of Bolivia, is toppled by a US-backed military coup. 100 protesters supporting him are killed in the All Saints Day Massacre shortly afterward.

Nov. 3rd, 1979 – The Greensboro Massacre takes place in North Carolina. Five members of the Communist Workers Party are gunned down by the Ku Klux Klan on live TV. The Communists staged a "Death to the Klan" rally and sent the KKK a threatening letter challenging them to show up. The Communists agreed not to carry firearms when negotiating their parade permit with the local police. One of the Communists did not observe this rule and fired a pistol into the air when the KKK caravan was driving by. The KKK members then parked their car, got out their rifles and opened fire on the Communists, killing five of them.

Nov. 4, 1979 – Iranian revolutionary youth seize the US embassy in Tehran, taking over 50 Americans hostage. Documents inside the embassy prove the US was working to Balkanize Iran by fomenting Kurdish and Arab separatist movements amid the revolutionary crisis. Patriotic anti-Iran rallies are mobilized across the United States, blaming Iran for rising gas prices, accusing Carter of being soft and weak, letting the US be humiliated.

November 13th, 1979 – Ronald Reagan announces he is running for President for the third time, citing rising energy prices and economic mismanagement by Carter. Reagan calls for higher military spending.

Nov. 14th, 1979 – Charges against RCP activists arrested at the "Death to Deng Xiaoping!" Rallies are dropped, but the decision is immediately appealed.

Nov. 17th, 1979 – RCP announces support for the Iranian Embassy Takeover at a Washington DC rally. RCP Chairman Bob Avakian proclaims "It's Not Our Embassy! Its not even our fucking country! We just live here!" RCP members begin attending right-wing anti-Iran rallies and burning US flags. This often results in the Communists being assaulted by mobs of right-wingers.

November 20th, 1979 – Saudi Shia Muslims inspired by the Islamic Revolution of Iran seize control of the Grand Mosque in Mecca. One of the most holy sites in Islam is subject to a two week siege in which hundreds are killed before the Saudi government ultimately retakes the Mosque and beheads the surviving revolutionaries.

December 24th, 1979 – Soviet troops arrive in Afghanistan to support the Democratic Republic against US-backed Islamist insurgents.

1980

February 2nd, 1980 – FBI launches "ABSCAM" sting operation, sending an FBI agent dressed as an Arab Sheikh to attempt to bribe elected officials. The target is "smokestack" democrats who support Nuclear

Power, have ties to Labor Unions, and don't support "the degrowth" policies of the Carter Administration.

February 10th, 1980 – New Hampshire Presidential Primary puts Ronald Reagan into the position of front runner for the Republican Nomination. Lyndon LaRouche put a very large effort into his Democratic Primary campaign with paid TV programs, radio ads, winning 2,400 votes. LaRouche and Reagan appear on the stage together at debate in January, seated next to each other and interact in a friendly way. Reagan praises LaRouche as one of the more serious minor candidates with good ideas.

March 8th, 1980 – The first ever Rock Music festival in the Soviet Union takes place in Georgia, near the birthplace of Stalin. The intent of local Communist Party leaders is to help placate the privileged urban youth who were enamored with western music and had been involved in nationalist anti-communist riots.

March 21st, 1980 – Jimmy Carter announces that the US will boycott the Summer Olympics to protest the Soviet Union's "invasion" of Afghanistan.

April 23, 1980 – Reagan has a debate with his largest opponent, George H.W. Bush. Eventually Reagan picks Bush as his Vice Presidential nominee in the name of unifying the party. Bush is seen as an "Eastern Establishment" "Rockefeller Republican" with ties to the Trilateral Commission, as opposed to Reagan's hard right-wing populism and direct ties to the military industrial complex.

July 25th, 1980 – David Duke resigns from the Ku Klux Klan and announces his intention to run for office. Rival Klansmen present the media with tapes in which he is heard offering to sell the list of KKK members names, and says derogatory things about those he has recruited.

April 23rd, 1980 – RCP member Damian Garcia is stabbed and killed in Los Angeles, several days after having ripped the US flag down from the Alamo in Texas and put up a Communist flag. Another RCP member, Hayden Fisher, is severely wounded in the attack.

May 1st, 1980 – The Revolutionary Communist Party calls a "General Strike" for May 1st. Street fighting takes place in a number of major cities with lots of arrests and injuries. RCP members burn US flags and provoke a number of street fights with working class Americans.

May 18th, 1980 – The Gwangju uprising breaks out in South Korea demanding democratic rights and an end to the military dictatorship. Underground Communist groups that support North Korea played a very significant role in the rebellion, but they were joined by many liberals who wanted an end to military rule. During the uprising 22 soldiers and 165 protesters were killed, and 76 more protesters were "disappeared" by the military and never heard from again.

July 1, 1980 – The Carter White House Publishes "Global 2000 Report" denouncing overpopulation and pushing forward the idea of "limited resources" being to blame for the energy crisis and global economic downturn.

June 27th, 1980 – Jimmy Carter announces that all US males aged 18 to 25 must register for the draft, citing the Soviet intervention in Afghanistan as a cause. This order remains in effect.

October 21st, 1980 – Bob Avakian and 78 other RCP members have criminal charges against them reinstated for the "Death to Deng Xiaoping" protests.

October 31st, 1980 – The Mariel Boatlifts from Cuba officially end with a total of 125,000 Cubans reaching Florida before the US government and the Cuban government formally agree on ending the rapid transfer of citizens. Cuba had utilized the "rescue" operation arranged with the Carter administration to empty out its prisons and mental hospitals and to deport known anti-Communists. US officials had been scrambling to handle the influx of Cubans that was far higher than expected.

November 4th, 1980 – Ronald Reagan wins the US Presidential Election in sweeping victory. During this election, Bernie Sanders is a registered elector for the Trotskyite Socialist Workers Party candidate Andrew Pulley.

November 20th, 1980 – The Gang of Four are placed on trial for Counter Revolutionary Crimes by the Chinese Communist Party. In televised trials the Chinese Communist Party repudiates the Cultural Revolution and makes clear it is transitioning away from the policies of the late-Mao era.

December 8th, 1980 – John Lennon is assassinated outside of his apartment building in New York City. The former Beatles rockstar had faced deportation proceedings during the 1970s and agreed to cease his political activism in exchange for being granted a permanent visa by the Nixon administration. Lennon had been associated with leftist politics donating thousands of dollars to the Black Panthers in the United States and Gerry Healy's Workers Revolutionary Party in Britain. Lennon had recently returned to the public-eye after years of silence, releasing his first new album in five years, *Double Fantasy.*

1981

January 20th, 1981 – Ronald Reagan is inaugurated as President. US embassy hostages in Iran are released on the same day. It was later revealed that Reagan negotiated with Ayatollah Khomeini to keep the hostages from being released until he had taken office.

March 1st, 1981 – Irish political prisoners, led by Bobby Sands, launch hunger strikes demanding they not be treated as criminals but as prisoners of war. After ten inmates die of starvation, the hunger strike is called off. The Hunger Strikes in Long Kesh Prison generate a wave of support for the Irish Freedom struggle.

March 17th, 1981 – Prosecutors in Italy unveil the existence of the P2 Masonic Lodge, a network of anti-Communist activists based in Rome who are tied in with US intelligence. The clandestine group had engaged in covert activities throughout the world. The Italian government resigned a few weeks later due to the massive scandalous revelations of illegal activities, manipulation of elections, weapons smuggling, terrorist attacks and much more.

March 30th, 1981 – John Hinkley shoots Ronald Reagan, failing to kill him. Hinkley is the son of an oil company executive with ties to the Bush family. Hinkley is later found "not guilty for reasons of insanity."

April 6th, 1981 – Bernie Sanders is sworn in as Mayor of Burlington, Vermont.

April 11th, 1981 – Brixton Riots take place in London. The unrest starts as a series of scuffles between Black youth of Caribbean descent and the police. There is widespread looting of stores and thousands of injuries and arrests. The event is pivotal to the Punk Rock movement and is blamed on rising unemployment and "stop and search" police policies.

May 3rd, 1981 – Workers World Party stages the People's Anti-War Mobilization protest in Washington DC with backing from surrendered Weather Underground leaders Bill Ayers and Bernadine Dohrn, the Communist Workers Party, and a large number of Maoist groups and former 1960s radicals. The crowd of roughly 100,000 people marches from downtown DC to the Pentagon chanting against Reagan and nuclear weapons and in support of various Marxist revolutionary groups around the world. Workers World Party inserts its hardline politics, giving the march a more radical character than the national protests of the previous decade. This is the first national anti-war protest with a Palestinian speaker, and the first national anti-war protest with a Gay Rights speaker. During the rally 300 followers of Rev. Sun Myung Moon disrupted by chanting "No More Cuba, No More War, Castro Out of El Salvador!" The scuffle between the Unification Church members and the Workers World Party team of marshals results in multiple injuries.

June 7th – Israel bombs Iraq's Nuclear Power facility, killing Iraqi scientists and a French citizen. The Nuclear Power facility in Iraq was being constructed in coordination with the French government nuclear power program. Israel justifies the attack arguing the Ba'athist government was dangerous and could have potentially developed nuclear weapons. Iraq was a signatory of the Nuclear Non-Proliferation Treaty, and no evidence of nuclear ambitions from the Iraqi government has ever been presented. At the time, the United States was actively backing Iraq in its war against Iran.

July 23rd, 1981 – John Africa, leader of the MOVE organization, is acquitted in Philadelphia on charges of owning illegal weapons and conspiracy. Despite having never completed high school and being illiterate, John Africa represents himself with no attorney and wins the jury over to acquitting him. Sam Marcy of Workers World Party sits in the courtroom during the trial, along with future US political prisoner Mumia Abu Jamal.

September 19th, 1981 – The AFL-CIO holds a massive Solidarity Day demonstration to protest against Reagan's use of the Taft-Hartley law to break the Air Traffic Controllers Strike. This is the first national protest called by labor unions in US history, and roughly half a million labor union members gather in Washington DC to denounce the Reagan administration.

October 15th, 1981 – Reverend Sun Myung Moon is indicted for filing a false tax return & criminal conspiracy. Despite all the innuendo in the press and accusations of much more serious crimes, the actual charges are quite mild. Moon is eventually convicted, given a much more harsh sentence than usual and imprisoned for 13 months.

November 23rd, 1981 – Ronald Reagan signs a secret order authorizing CIA to begin arming Contras in Nicaragua in their armed campaign to overthrow the socialist government.

Afterwards

June 4th, 1982 – Charges against Bob Avakian are dropped, in exchange for 10 other RCP members pleading guilty to felony charges. Avakian flees the US for France where he seeks political exile status, not returning to the USA until 2004.

March 23rd, 1983 – Ronald Reagan gives his "Star Wars" speech referencing LaRouche's "Strategic Defense Initiative" of ending the arms race with laser beam weapons.

May 13th, 1985 – In the infamous "MOVE House Bombing" 11 people, including John Africa are killed when the Philadelphia police department destroys a house with a firebomb dropped from a helicopter.

October 14th, 1988 – Lyndon LaRouche and six associates are indicted on "Mail Fraud and conspiracy to commit mail fraud" and eventually sent to prison.

Appendix 2: Three Socialist Movements and The Global Crisis We Now Face

This piece was originally published as an introduction to a new edition of Engel's classic pamphlet "Socialism: Utopian and Scientific" released by the Center for Political Innovation in 2023.

You are holding in your hands a new edition of one of the most important pieces of writing in the history of politics, economics, and arguably in the history of the world. The concepts were unoriginal. The author, Friedrich Engels simply articulated what Karl Marx had developed in decades of writing, and taught him over the course of years of collaboration. While Marx was a brilliant, innovative thinker, as he cut new ground and gave birth to a revolutionary new understanding of human events, his writing style was highly polemical and difficult for many in the mass audience to understand. Engels had the task of spelling out Marx's concepts in much plainer language.

Marx's work began in the field of philosophy when he became an outspoken interpreter and espouser of the teachings of Friedrich Hegel. Marx moved into political activism, composing the Communist Manifesto in 1848 and eventually forming the First International. Marx spent the final years of his life focusing on economics, utilizing the statistical information compiled by the British government in London. Friedrich Engels was a young radical and intellectual who met Marx and became his lifelong collaborator, ally, and patron.

Teaching Through Polemic

In 1877, socialism was very popular in Marx's home country of Germany. However, it was not the socialism of Karl Marx, but the socialism of a long forgotten intellectual mystic man named Eugen Duhring that dominated academia. With Marx's help, Engels composed a polemic against the socialism of Duhring, ripping it to shreds and explaining Marx's scientific understanding. Engel's magnum opus *Anti-Duhring* expanded from a simple polemic to a full history of socialist thought, philosophy and explanation of historical materialism. The title was in homage of Julius Caesar's book *Anticato*.

In 1880, as socialist movements and organizations influenced by Marx's ideas were popping up across Europe, aligning themselves with the emerging labor movement, Engels abridged and edited *Anti-Duhring* into a much shorter, three chapter pamphlet called *Socialism: Utopian and Scientific*. This short pamphlet educated millions of Germans, Britons, Frenchman, Belgians, and others as they became organized into the various Labor, Social-Democratic, and Workers Parties that made up the Socialist (Second) International.

The pamphlet's first chapter is dedicated to honoring the great Utopian socialist thinkers that predated Marx. Many confused readers misinterpret the opening chapter as criticism, but it's hardly that. Engels praises in glowing terms those who saw that the "brave new world" created by the French Revolution and the English Civil War was filled with injustice and inhumanity. Engels explains: "In a word, compared with the splendid promises of the philosophers, the social and political institutions born of the "triumph of reason" were bitterly disappointing caricatures. All that was wanting was the men to formulate this disappointment, and they came with the turn of the century."

Marx and Engels did not see Robert Owen and Saint-Simon as naive and primitive, but as heroic, moral people who wanted to correct the injustices they saw around them and were disappointed by the results of the revolutions that toppled feudalism. Engels describes the various idealistic communities created in Europe and America, similar to the Communes and Worker Cooperatives of today. He writes: "To the crude conditions of capitalistic production and the crude class conditions correspond crude theories. The solution of the social problems, which as yet lay hidden in undeveloped economic conditions, the Utopians attempted to evolve out of the human brain. Society presented nothing but wrongs; to remove these was the task of reason. It was necessary, then, to discover a new and more perfect system of social order and to impose this upon society from without by propaganda, and, wherever it was possible, by the example of model experiments."

Engels points out that even though these communities reorganized production on more egalitarian lines, they still operated within the context of a capitalist society. They could not overcome the society around them, and they could not overturn capitalism simply by example or logical arguments.

The second chapter of the pamphlet is dedicated to philosophy. Engels describes how thought is inseparable from matter that thinks, and that all that exists in the world is matter. He upholds the philosophical tradition called materialism in opposition to idealism, a debate that goes back to the classical era. Engels then points out that all the world is in a constant state of change and conflict. History is driven forward by contradiction, opposing social forces clashing into each other, driving civilization forward to higher ends. These concepts are called historical and dialectical materialism, and they comprise the Marxist philosophical understanding. Because the Utopians were not armed with this outlook, but stuck in religious idealism, they could not overcome capitalism.

The third and final chapter explains how history is moving forward constantly, from Hunter-Gathering civilization, to slavery, to feudalism and to capitalism. Human beings are in a constant drive to reach a higher plane of existence, a more advanced mode of production. Engels then explains that capitalism is holding back human progress. He describes the problem of poverty amid plenty, the crisis of overproduction, and why the irrational profit motive restricts the drive to create a more prosperous society. He then explains that the working class, the proletariat, has the historical duty of first winning the battle for democracy and seizing government power from the rich. From there, it must turn the means of production into public property and allow them to function on a rational basis. Liberating the economy from the irrationalism of the market will be the ultimate triumph of man over nature, and will lead to an egalitarian stateless, classless world.

This vision of socialism was contrary to the conservative, mystical and German nationalist socialism of Eugen Duhring. Duhring was an adherent of Henry Carey and Friedrich List and believed socialism would be achieved with a popular government balancing a "harmony of interests" and ruling for the good of society. Unlike his allies List and Carey, Duhring was anti-semitic and presented Jews as immoral, selfish outsiders who corrupted society. While Duhring was an atheist and critic of religion, presenting himself as scientific and modern, he saw socialism as a reassertion of morality and tradition and rejected class struggle. Marx and Engels saw the labor movement as the greatest expression of their ideas in practice, while Duhring saw his ideas put forward in German nationalism.

1. Marx, Engels and Internationalist Socialism

In order to give context to this important pamphlet, and explain why it is so vital in our times, it is important to go over how the ideas of Marx, Engels, and Duhring developed over the course of the 20th Century, and how they fit into the 21st Century. The socialism that exists in the world today is not the socialism of Marx and Engels, though it is heavily influenced by them and often claims their heritage. While it is not Marx and Engels socialism, it is certainly not the socialism of Duhring either. There have in reality been three distinct socialist movements in modern history, and only one of them has ever created non-capitalist societies. Understanding the three socialist movements and their impact will lay the basis for understanding why this very old pamphlet is so important in our times, and why the Center for Political Innovation has chosen to republish it now.

Marx spent his life promoting the teachings summarized by Engels in *Socialism: Utopian and Scientific.* Marx was not an armchair revolutionary or ivory tower intellectual by any means. He built the International Workingmen's Association, or the First International. He fought on the barricades and organized strikes. He served as the London correspondent for Horace Greeley's *New York Tribune*, the Republican Party-aligned newspaper of New York City during the US Civil War. Marx organized textile workers in London to refuse to work with cotton picked by slaves, and gave political guidance to August Willich and Joseph Weydemeyer, members of the First International who served as high ranking members of the US Army during the Civil War. Marx's followers joined with other socialists in 1871 to seize control of France's capital and establish the short-lived Paris Commune. This was a revolutionary working class government which Marx described as the first historical example of the Dictatorship of the Proletariat in which the workers were "storming heaven."

The portrayal of Marx in recent films and the widespread misconception that he was some kind of socially isolated academic is poppycock. Marx spent his life as an activist and organizer, and his work was intended to give guidance to real organizations of people, aligned with real social forces, to bring about real change in the world. Marx's primary political opponents within the First International were Anarchists, and ultimately the international organization Marx built collapsed due to political disagreements between Marx and the Anarchists.

When Marx died in 1883, he left behind a huge body of work published after a lifetime of organizing and writing composed as he and his family lived in poverty and fled from country to country. It was due to Marx's valuable insight and understanding of how human events developed, and the effectiveness of the methods of thought he promoted, that the emerging labor movement became dominated by adherents of Marxism. By the late 1880s and into the 1890s, Marxism had exploded across Europe. Millions of German workers joined labor unions and voted for the Social-Democratic Party. The labor movement of workers on the job in France, Britain, Austria and many other countries gave birth to a political expression in the form of parties that sought to establish the Dictatorship of the Proletariat and Socialism. Members of parliament were elected, trade unions were formed, and popular reforms were won.

Stabilizing the West, Setting the Stage for Imperialism

The socialism of Marx and Engels was internationalist. It said "Workers of the world, Unite!" It rejected nationalism, and said that the working people of Europe and the entire world shared a common destiny. The socialist movement favored free trade, because it would lead to bringing workers together, expanding the global economy, bringing the advancements of the west to the colonized world, and laying the basis for the global revolution. The socialist movement wanted votes for women, the separation of church and state, the abolition of monarchies, and the further battering down of any remnants of feudalism.

By the time the 20th Century rolled around, it became clear that the Second International and the Socialism of Marx and Engels was not going to create a revolution in Europe. In fact, it had largely contributed to enabling European capitalism to dominate the planet. Socialists won universal male suffrage, 12 hour work days, and union representation on the job. In Germany they won the creation of a national healthcare service and government daycare programs. In all the major western countries, the Marxist led labor movement had created a layer of well-paid skilled workers who saw their living standards go up as their capitalist bosses expanded across the planet. Though the benefits and higher wages these "skilled" workers received had been won on the picket line, their higher living standards cemented their loyalty to the western capitalist governments. The fact that "socialists" were elected and had roles at the highest level of government also helped embed the aristocracy of labor into the western capitalists government apparatus. As western capitalist banks and corporations began dominating the planet with "the export of capital" i.e. looting the third world and holding back development, the higher paid workers were loyal and obedient, and their labor unions and socialist parties were necessary to pull them along in the process.

As capitalism entered the phase Lenin would later call *Imperialism: The Highest Stage of Capitalism*, it could not be disputed that the internationalist socialist movement of Marx and Engels had been essential for making it happen. The Marxists had forced industrial capitalists to pay higher wages and create the "aristocracy of labor" among the workers that would be comfortable and loyal to the empire. The Marxists had forced the state to adopt social programs that made life more livable for the working class. The Marxists had championed free trade, enabling western corporations to spread their tentacles across the planet.

Lenin's angry polemics from Russia fumed with rage against the Second International, which he declared to be a stinking corpse. While all the Marxist parties of Europe had pledged never to support a war, never to vote to send working people to kill their class brothers, when the Guns of August roared in 1914 they all betrayed their pledge. The rage of Vladimir Lenin and Rosa Luxemburg in their heated polemics comes from their knowledge of the fact that the "socialist" movement had devolved into an essential part of the western capitalist power structure. It was only because of the collaboration of various "socialists" that the horrific event known as World War One could have taken place. 20 million workers were sent to their deaths as the colonial powers and ultra-monopolies of Europe fought over control of Asia, Africa, and South America.

The bulk of the socialist movement had largely turned its back on Eugene Debs, Rosa Luxemburg, Frank Little, and other heroic working class organizers who refused to be "social-imperialists" and support the war. Lenin's Bolshevik organization in Russia, formed in 1903 as a "party of new type" had long been rejected by the Second International. Its methods of "democratic centralism," "agitprop," and demanding a dedicated cadre who gave "the whole of their lives" drew heavily from Russia's tradition of secret societies and clandestine organizing, such as the Decembrists and the Old Believers. Its methods seemed authoritarian and cultish to the European intellectuals who favored transparency and widespread debate. Its methods for seizing power, which ultimately succeeded, were dismissed as coup plotting and conspiracy rather than the "mass strike" methods pursued by the western labor movement.

Communists around the world recognized that Bolshevism succeeded in Russia, taking power in 1917, because it was a distinct political movement that had broken with many of the major beliefs of Marx and Engel's scientific, internationalist socialist movement. Lenin embraced nationalism, and said the colonized world would be the primary battlefield against capitalism in the 20th Century. Lenin had even taken funding from German intelligence when he returned to Russia in April of 1917. He had changed the official name of the Bolshevik party to the "Communist" party, rejecting the label of "social-democratic" in order to differentiate himself from the European labor parties who had become mere appendages of imperialism.

As Bolshevism and the Communist International emerged following the Russian Revolution, the remnants of the International Socialism started by Marx and Engels have become more and more integrated into the western imperialist power structure, and less and less revolutionary in their content.

The push for liberal reforms came from various think-tanks and policy making entities like the Round Table Group established by the estate of British colonialist Cecil Rhodes, of which today's Council on Foreign Relations is a descendent. The voices who pushed for reforms were the likes of H.G. Wells, Bertrand Russell, and the Fabian Society, intellectuals cultivated by the ultra-rich to craft a "managerial" agenda to ensure the dominance of western capitalism over the planet. It was the Rockefeller oil monopolists in the United States who backed Roosevelt while Henry Morgan, Henry Ford and the National Association of Manufacturers sought his ouster. These ultra-rich monopolists had a more "globalist" outlook, and saw stabilizing reforms as a necessary method of securing social peace. The labor movement and social democracy enabled them to help make it happen, despite having a very different stated goal.

The United Nations, the World Economic Forum, and so many of the institutions that express the will of western capitalism and its platitudes about "human rights" in our time are staffed with "socialists" of the non-revolutionary, internationalist variety. Tony Blair, Francois Hollande, Alexandria Ocasio-Cortez, all see socialism as nothing more than the sum of reforms. Socialism is free healthcare, free college, transgender bathrooms, and Rock Stars performing John Lennon's "Imagine" on New Year's Eve in Times Square.

The first socialist movement ultimately failed because capitalism moved into its imperialist, monopoly stage with western finance capitalists making super profits, dominating the entire planet. In order to do it they needed to integrate the economy more closely with the state, and they needed a limited welfare state to stabilize society at home. The movement of Marx and Engels largely turned into its opposite.

2. The Legacy of Duhring: Right-Wing, National Socialism

But what of Eugen Duhring, and his non-materialist, moralistic socialism that condemned Jews and glorified the German nation state? In the late years of the 19th century it certainly faded into the background as the labor movement and social-democracy took center stage. One can see elements of a more Duhring-ist socialism in the work of Edward Bellamy, the popular American socialist who wrote the science fiction novel *Looking Backward* in 1888 and built "nationalist clubs" to promote socialism in the United States. One can also hear echoes of Duhring-ism in the words of some of the religious fanatics who built up the bulk of the radical abolitionist current that opposed slavery. The Communist Manifesto of 1848 gave special attention to "reactionary socialism" and various forms of right-wing anti-capitalism.

It wasn't really until after the First World War that right-wing anti-capitalism began suddenly to expand in popularity. The German Social-Democratic Party more or less took power following the First World War, and at the constitutional convention held in Weimar they refused to establish a socialist government. When Rosa Luxemburg and Karl Leibknecht continued fighting for a socialist republic, they were ruthlessly murdered. While the new Bolshevik brand of Marxism had taken power in Russia, the Marxism and leftism of Europe seemed stale. Its moment had come following the First World War and it had failed. Its mass parties became less and less revolutionary in their rhetoric.

But in Italy, Benito Mussolini seized power in his 1922 March on Rome. The Italian strongman had been a member of the Socialist Party, but had been an enthusiastic supporter of the First World War, and was heavily influenced by the teachings of the French Syndicalist, Georges Sorel. Mussolini had formed the Blackshirts as a group of street fighting strike breakers who espoused an ideology that mixed Italian nationalism, mystical admiration for ancient Rome, along with both anti-communism and anti-capitalism. Mussolini wrote that "the wheels of history are turned through blood." He ridiculed the Italian Socialists for failing to seize power in a revolution, and condemned the more radical Bolshevik groups as a foreign conspiracy from Russia. He put forward a model of a "corporate state" in which the government and private industrialists coordinated their actions in order to manage the economy. Fascism was "super capitalism" according to Mussolini. His government created an authoritarian state that crushed the labor movement, and stimulated the economy by spending huge amounts of money on weapons manufacturing, and maintaining a very large police force and apparatus of repression.

In Germany, various right-wing anti-capitalist thinkers emerged. The most prominent was Oswald Spengler who wrote *The Decline of the West - Form and Actuality.* Spenglerian thought argued that Capitalism and Socialism are two sides of the human spirit. Capitalism represents individualism and the drive to make money, while socialism represents obedience to authority and loyalty to one's tribe. Spengler argued that Europe was in decline due to weakness and lack of authoritarianism as well as radical individualism.

Ernst Junger, a fanatical German militarist, drew heavily from Spengler's work, coining his own concept of Prussian Socialism. This was a highly militarized state in which loyalty to the nation and religion overrode profits and individualism.

Factory Owners & De-Growth

The Nazis who seized power in 1933 drew heavily from Spengler and Junker, though they ultimately disagreed with many of their ideas. The Nazis were populists, who put forward the notion of a "people's revolution" to re-ignite the flame of German greatness that had been extinguished after the First World War. The right-wing anti-capitalism of Spengler and Junger rejected the very concept of popular movements. It argued that people should be subservient and aspiring to do the will of their leaders, and that the notion of mass political movements or politicians who aspire to win the people's approval was at the heart of Europe's decline.

Friedrich Nietzsche was always firmly opposed to any type of socialism, declaring socialism to be a modernized version of Christianity, the cry of vengeance from the poor and oppressed against the strong. The Nazis drew from Nietzsche and his worship of strength, and his belief that modern society was becoming soft and restraining the *ubermenschen* from ruling over their supposed natural inferiors. The writer William Preston points out interestingly that Nietzsche never studied the work of Marx and Engels, but based his critique of socialism solely on the work of Duhring, who focused much more on envy and moral indignation: "For in Duhring Nietzsche sees the scabrous, festering wound of a man who comes to the fore in every socialist society. The case of the "arrogant, immoderate and anti-Semitic" Berlin professor affords the psychologist a clear view of the sediment in the base of the depths of soul of the rabble. Duhring discloses the ugly psychological truth of socialism… For Nietzsche's anti-socialism stems not from Nietzsche's reaction to the specific ideas of this or that prophet of resentment, but from Nietzsche's joyous affirmation that exploitation is essential to life."

However, just as the internationalist socialism of Marx and Engels eventually deteriorated into the ideology of bankers, stabilizing western societies so capitalism could expand into its monopoly stage of imperialism, the right-wing "National Socialism" of Junker, Spengler, the Nazis, and others also never led to the creation of a non-capitalist society. Nazi Germany and Fascist Italy were bonapartist regimes in which factory owners and the government teamed up to heavily regulate the economy. Hitler was brought to power primarily because of Hjalmar Schacht, the economist and financier who resented the power of British and American banks, but also feared a working class revolution.

Fascism in the 1930s was the ideology of factory owners in their rivalry with oil monopolists and financiers, and their desperate drive to crush labor unions. In America, Charles Coughlin and the Black Legion condemned capitalism as un-Christian and immoral as they mobilized against the Sit Down Strike wave of 1937. They continued the work of those who had conspired in the 1933 "Business Plot" for a military coup against Roosevelt. The Silver Legion of America, led by William Dudley Pelley, functioned as strikebreakers, preaching religious and esoteric anti-communism while condemning capitalism. They put forward a vision of a "Christian Commonwealth" where religious principles would govern the economy and a supposed Jewish conspiracy against America would be eradicated.

The primary way the Nazis were able to reboot their economy in 1933 was with forced de-growth. The Nazis broke the labor movement and created a network of prison camps for Social-Democrats and Communists. This took hundreds of thousands of workers out of the job market and solved unemployment. They then stimulated the economy by supplying the concentration camp inmates as slave labor for Germany's wealthy corporations. The Nazis also relaunched military spending and began pouring huge amounts of money into building a huge military apparatus. The Nazis created the world's first prison industrial complex and then the first military industrial complex.

Like Social-Democracy, "national socialism" ultimately became a vehicle for attempting to stabilize western capitalism. The Nazis launched the Second World War in an attempt to re-seize the colonies German imperialism had lost at the Treaty of Versailles, and assert domination over the European mainland of which the German imperialists had long contended with the British in geopolitical intrigue.

One fascist thinker of Italian origin, Julius Evola, expressed the essence of right-wing anti-capitalism in his book *Man Among The Ruins: Post-War Reflections of a Radical Traditionalist* published shortly after the Second World War. Evola wrote about "the demonic nature of the economy." He argued that the problem with capitalism was not that it was holding back growth and progress, but rather that it necessitated it. Evola wrote glowingly about the Dalia Lama's feudal society in Tibet and the Indian Caste system, arguing that capitalism should be abolished and replaced with a strictly hierarchical society in which people do not want more than they already have, and the Buddhist ideal of "all things in balance" is realized by tradition.

During the Second World War, the horrors of "de-growth" as a mechanism for attempting to stabilize capitalism were revealed to the world. The Nazis "final solution" of exterminating millions of people and their demented and cruel eugenics experiments, shocked humanity. The rejection of any sense of morality, as called for by Nietzsche, seemed to be enacted. The utter inhuman cruelty of the "blonde beast" birthed by capitalism entering its imperialist, monopoly stage was largely revealed by forces who operated in the name of "National Socialism."

3. The Russian & Chinese Revolutions: Continental, Constructive Socialism

Unlike the internationalist socialism of Marx and Engels that gave birth to modern leftism and social-democracy, and the right-wing anti-capitalism of Duhring that laid the ideological basis for fascism, the type of socialism that has actually come into existence and created a non-capitalist society is of a third, distinct category. It certainly draws heavily from Marx and Engels.

Prior to the Russian Revolution, both the Bolsheviks and the western Marxist movement understood their ideas were not the same. The differences became even more acute after the revolution, when Karl Kautsky began attacking the Bolsheviks and Vladimir Lenin responded with his pamphlet *Proletarian Revolution and the Renegade Kautsky*. Lenin accused Kautsky of glossing over how violent and un-democratic western liberal capitalist societies were in his outrage that the Bolsheviks had not complied with democratic norms and did as he did in Germany by joining a constituent assembly. The mainstream of western Marxism objected to the fact that Bolsheviks and their ideological adherents were a minority of Russian society, but yet they took it upon themselves to seize the reins of power and direct the population. This was deemed "undemocratic."

However, the Bolsheviks saw themselves as morally justified and much of the Russian population agreed with them. When society enters a state of chaos and unrest, there is a feeling that some faction needs to take responsibility and step up to lead, bringing order out of the chaos. Waiting around for a semi-consensus or the articulation of approval from a clear majority of the population would be irresponsible. The chaos following Czar Nicholas abdication and deep divisions in Russian society regarding the First World War and the economic crisis necessitated someone stepping in to declare themselves the new boss. Lenin did it and was able to mobilize an army and political machine behind him. This alone made him worthy to lead in the eyes of much of the population. Order and stability was valued over a democratic mandate. The strength to get the job done and bring order was deemed more important than any ideological qualifications.

The ideology of the Bolsheviks was complex. It was a unique interpretation and application of Marxist theories that had been developed from 1903 to 1917. It strayed from classical Marxism in several key areas. The Bolsheviks did not expect for the majority of the population to understand their ideas or even be won over to them. They rather expected the population to see them as effective leaders who could get the job done and deliver the goods. Just as average people do not understand all the intricacies of biology in the way a trained biologist might, the average citizen was not expected to understand all the intricacies of statecraft and political economy. This was the field of work that the members of the ruling party had taken on, and it was their job to understand its complexities and methods. This approach is very Confucian, and more or less non-western. The Bolshevik revolution was the first step in the socialist movement leaving Europe and becoming a vehicle for the previously colonized world to express its independence and desire for independent economic development.

"Asiatic" Socialism

The break between Leon Trotsky and Joseph Stalin is even more telling. Trotsky held onto the Euro-centrism of Marx and Engels. He believed the only hope for Soviet Russia was to serve as a base area to spread the revolution to the industrialized west. His theory of Permanent Revolution argued that countries in the developing world were too backward to have socialism, and that socialism could really only emerge in the western imperialist homelands. Stalin argued that the USSR could have "Socialism in one country" and with Five Year Economic Plans, it could build itself into a modern industrial country.

In his biography *Stalin: An Appraisal of the Man and His Influence*, Trotsky refers to Stalin as "Asiatic," saying this refers to "blending of grit, shrewdness, craftiness and cruelty which has been considered characteristic of the statesmen of Asia." He quotes Nikolai Bukharin referring to Stalin as "Genghis Khan." The political and economic model that Stalin pioneered was certainly not western, and synthesized a number of competing tendencies. It involved the conservatism and patriotism of the peasantry, the nationalism of countries kept impoverished by the domination of foreign capital, the passionate drive for reform, science and modernization found among third world intellectuals, the ritual and semi-religious personality worship of traditional monarchies, the rage of entire nations at centuries of oppression and humiliation, and most of all the desire for historical progress and advancement.

The model of a one-party state that built up state-run industries, wiped out illiteracy, electrified countries and constructed collective farm systems has been labeled "Stalinism" by western academics. This model made Russia into a superpower that invented space travel, defeated the Nazis, electrified vast swaths of the planet, and constructed the largest power plants and steel mills the world had ever seen. This model was applied in China after the 1949 revolution, across Eastern Europe following the Second World War, and in many countries that broke free from western domination in the post-war years.

The Chinese Revolution was not simply the exporting of Bolshevism to China. Mao Zedong Thought had unique organizing methods that were China specific. The strategy of focusing on the peasantry had been rejected by the Bolsheviks and taken up by the Narodniks, their ideological rivals. But this was the road to power for the Communists who were able to transform China into a prosperous superpower.

In the second half of the 20th Century, Socialism became more and more ideologically divergent. African Socialism was pioneered by leaders like Ghana's Kwame Nkrumah and Tanzania's Julius Nyerere. Baathist Arab Socialism emerged as a mass movement after Michel Alflaq broke with the Syrian Communist Party in the 1930s. This movement took roots among the military and eventually gave political leadership to Iraq and Syria. Libya's Islamic Socialism was unique, and the 1979 revolution in Nicaragua brought to power a group of radical Christians called the Sandinistas.

The Islamic Revolution of Iran officially rejected Marxism, but instead pushed for 'Not Capitalism But Islam.' After taking power, Ruhollah Khomeini took a page from Stalin and launched a "construction jihad," a mass mobilization of the population for rapid industrialization much like the 5-year plans the defined the "Stalinist" economic model.

This new socialism was not about "class struggle" in the same way that Marx and Engels had spoken of it. The new governments spoke in the name of the proletariat and peasantry, but their goal was not to tear down some for the benefit of the others. The focus was on utilizing rational central planning to raise up the entire country. This new socialism was not "nationalist" or conservative in the same way fascism had been. It was not reinforcing social hierarchies, holding caste systems and authoritarian structures together as Spengler and Junger had called for. It was not about rebooting the economy with de-growth and destruction, marching closer to war as the Nazis had done. It was the opposite. The socialist governments empowered women, pushed forward youth, and mobilized all of society around a vision of economic growth and expansion.

The Cultural Revolution in China and the "Yezhovshchina" (The Great Terror) episode of mass fear and political repression in the USSR were seen as dark moments, that stained the overall optimism the governments pushed forward. As the socialist countries faced the problem of being surrounded and locked out of the western economies, Deng Xiaoping reinvented their economic model to utilize foreign investment and build up a domestic private sector, all while maintaining the hegemony of the Communist Party and its central planners over the economy. The success of "Socialism with Chinese Characteristics" in lifting people out of poverty, raising living standards and pushing a huge country forward is something that cannot be denied. With state run banks, five year economic plans, and a ruling Communist party, China has surged to amazing heights.

While the Soviet Union and Eastern Europe were unable to adjust, the Socialist Oriented Market Economy of Vietnam and micro-entrepreneurship programs of Nicaragua have been highly successful. The 21st Century model of an economy where state planning gets priority, with credit and natural resources under state control, along with a market sector that is subsidized to enact the state's overall vision has been highly successful, even more successful than the mass industrialization and modernization socialism carried out in the 20th Century.

The Political Re-Shuffling

While this new form of socialism speeds forward across the formerly colonized world, the old socialisms continued to just function as a defense of the old order. Social-Democracy was usurped by the cultural movement called the New Left, a response to the expansions in information technology. Zbigniew Brzezinski argued in his book *Between Two Ages: America Enters the Technetronic Era* that rather than suppressing the New Left, the US government should hijack it and utilize its destabilizing influence to work against the Soviet Union. This strategy seems to have dominated US intelligence circles in the late Cold War and largely helped the USA manipulate the Eastern bloc culminating in the events of 1989-1991.

In the new economic conditions of the post-WW2 years, most of the fascists and far-right elements embraced capitalism, and declared that the ultra-rich bankers and monopolists were somehow Communists. The declared goal became to defend the "real capitalism" of industrialists and small business owners from the "corporatism" of big monopolies. While right-wing anti-capitalist demagogy prevailed among the various military juntas of the third world that had US backing against the Soviet Union, in the west right-wing anti-capitalism became almost completely forgotten.

In the world of today, there is a block of resistance to western capitalism. In Russia it is led by Vladimir Putin who rebooted Russia's economy by centralizing it around two state controlled energy corporations. Putin's economic reforms, asserting state control and repudiating the neoliberal policies of Yeltsin, rescued Russia and restored its industrial base. The Soviet ideology is a big influence on contemporary Russia, but so are the thousands of years of Russian civilization that predate it. The "New Russian Patriotism" that honors the Czars and the Soviet Red Army together, compliments the ideological orientation of Chinese Communism where today Mao and Confucius walk hand in hand as part of China's unique history and non-western identity.

The Islamic Revolution of Iran, the Bolivarian countries of Latin America, the Houthis in Yemen, leaders of Zimbabwe, Angola, and Eritrea, all espouse their own brand of anti-capitalism rooted in their unique historical experience and circumstances. While they are all different, they are all neither purely Marxian or Duhring-ist. They are also all focused on the importance of economic growth and optimism, in the face of pessimistic confusion and economic neoliberalism coming from the west.

Russian academic Alexander Dugin wrote of the Fourth Political Theory, arguing that after liberal democracy (the first political theory) failed to be defeated by Communism and Fascism (the second and third political theories) that a new, fourth political theory was emerging in Russia and other centers of resistance to western capitalism. Dugin gave voice to this understanding that the wave of resistance to western capitalism that was spawned by the Bolshevik revolution in 1917 has moved beyond western political categories in the 21st Century. As Dugin observed, it draws from the Marxist critique of capitalism and imperialism, but also from the nationalism and traditionalism of the right-wing. It rejects western free markets and impoverishment, as well as western post-modernism and cultural decay.

Atlanticism vs. The City-Building Tendency

What is called 21st Century Socialism in Latin America and the Axis of Resistance in the Middle East is the political expression of a new economic order that stands in opposition to the western capitalist system.

Lenin's book *Imperialism, the Highest Stage of Capitalism* described how capitalism was becoming dominated by finance, and trusts, cartels and syndicates based in western countries that were actively holding back economic development. The western capitalist system evolved into "imperialism," in which western capitalists became the middle men in global trade.

When one looks at the work of Henry Carey and his critique of the British empire and its economic relationship with the world, the roots of this set up become clear. Henry Carey, the chief economic advisor to U.S. President Abraham Lincoln, wrote: "Two systems are before the world; the one looks to increasing the proportion of persons and of capital engaged in trade and transportation, and therefore to diminishing the proportion engaged in producing commodities with which for trade, with necessarily diminished return to the labor of all; while the other looks to increasing the proportion engaged in the work of production, and diminishing that engaged in trade and transportation, with increased return to all, giving to the laborer good wages, and to the owner of capital good profits. One looks to increasing the quantity of raw materials to be exported, and diminishing the inducements to the import of men, thus impoverishing both farmer and planter by throwing on them the burden of freight; while the other looks to increasing the import of men, and diminishing the export of raw materials, thereby enriching both planter and farmer by relieving them from the payment of freight. One looks to give the products of millions of acres of land and of the labour of millions of men for the service of hundreds of thousands of distant men; the other to bring the distant men to consume on the land the products of the land, exchanging day's labour for day's labour. One looks to compelling the farmers and planters of the

Union to continue their contributions for the support of the fleets and the armies, the paupers, the nobles, and the sovereigns of Europe; the other to enabling ourselves to apply the same means to the moral and intellectual improvement of the sovereigns of America. One looks to the continuance of that has fared freedom of trade which denies the principle of protection, yet doles it out as revenue duties; the other to extending the area of ultimate free trade by the establishment of perfect protection, allowed by the annexation of individuals and communities, and ultimately by the abolition of custom-houses. One looks to exporting men to occupy desert tracts, the sovereignty of which is obtained by aid of diplomacy or war; the other to increasing the value of an immense extent of vacant land by importing men by millions for their occupation. One looks to the concentration of wealth and power in a great commercial city that shall rival the great cities of modern times, which have been and are being supported by aid of contributions which have exhausted every nation subjected to them; the other to concentration, by aid of which a market shall be made upon the land for the products of the land, and the farmer and planter be enriched. One looks to increasing the necessity for commerce; the other to increasing the power to maintain it. One looks to underworking the Hindoo, and sinking the rest of the world to his level; the other to raising the standard of man throughout the world to our level. One looks to pauperism, ignorance, de-population, and barbarism; the other to increasing wealth, comfort, intelligence, combination of action, and civilization. One looks towards universal war; the other towards universal peace. One is the English system; the other we may be proud to call the American system, for it is the only one ever devised the tendency of which was that of elevating while equalizing the condition of man throughout the world."

This "English System" of ultra-monopolists dominating trade routes and grinding the world into poverty is also spelled out in the 1890 book written by US Naval Strategist, Alfred Thayer Mahan. His book *The Influence of Sea Power Upon History* was embraced by the British, American, and German governments. It argued that control of the trade routes could lead to the centralization of wealth in the hands of certain nations. It favored building up a military to serve to control international markets at the expense of investing in infrastructure and the physical economy on the mainland.

This was a model very similar to that of the Roman Empire. It was said "all roads lead to Rome" because the Romans, with their huge army and Navy served as the middle man in global trade, extracting tribute and slaves from every nation. Meanwhile, their ability to grow their own crops and produce their own products became diminished and weaker the larger their empire became, up until the point when the mighty city state could no longer even muster its own army and was forced to hire foreigners to fight its wars in its final years.

This model of global trade is rightly called *Atlanticism*, and it is not an outgrowth of some conspiracy but rather the natural result of capitalism moving to the stage of global monopolism. The roots of Atlanticism are not found in immoral thoughts, but in the natural workings of the capitalist economy. Atlanticism, like the Roman Empire in its final years, seeks to hold back historical progress and technological advancement. The rulers of the Atlanticist global order more or less feel that the human race must halt its historical advance, and not strive to a higher technological plane because this would lead to them being displaced. The world must stay poor so that they can stay rich.

Meanwhile, what Henry Charles Carey called the American System, what Marx observed in capitalism's early years as it industrialized the western nations, what Alexander Dugin calls "Eurasianism," what Stalin called "Socialism in One Country," what Deng Xiaoping called "Socialism with Chinese Characteristics," what Khomeini called "Not Capitalism But Islam," all represent the drive for human progress and growth. In our time, those who seek for society to become wealthier have come to realize that the market, left to its own devices, cannot achieve this. In our time, historical progress requires a strong state that directs a well organized population having hegemony over the economy. Growth in our time requires that the irrationality of the market be subordinated to a central plan. The means of production must be controlled by society, and operated according to a predetermined plan. This allows the "artificial restraints" of the market to be lifted and human progress to soar forward.

Is this the socialism of Friedrich Engels? Yes. The economic vision of Engels is for "production upon a predetermined plan" and overcoming the "anarchy of production." However, does it also contain elements of the Socialism of Eugen Duhring? Yes. It seeks stability, not chaos. It does not emphasize class struggle, but collective emancipation of entire nations, and ultimately the entire human race.

In its essence, the socialist movement that has come into existence from 1917 right up to today, is neither of the two previous strands of thought. It is the "City-Building Tendency" of human history. It is the organized political expression of the innate human drive to advance and reinvent our relationship with our environment. It is expressed in the form of governments that maintain a much more healthy, interactive and responsive relationship with their populations than those of the "democratic" west. Engels wrote "In short, the animal merely *uses* its environment, and brings about changes in it simply by its presence; man by his changes makes it serve his ends, *masters* it. This is the final, essential distinction between man and other animals, and once again it is labour that brings about this distinction."

The contradiction between sea-based civilizations and empires that seek to control trade routes, and land-based societies that focus on advancing technology and building up productive forces has been widely observed. Lyndon LaRouche promoted this understanding throughout his lifetime as an American political figure, writing about the "Eurasian future" in his text *Earth's Next Fifty Years* published in 2004. Many intellectuals and academics aligned with the governments of Russia and China promote this understanding as well.

We can call the form of socialism we see in the world today "continental socialism" or "constructive socialism." It is not focused on intensifying disagreement and antagonism in society in order to drive forward history through contradiction. It is also not focused on imposing authority and restraint while destroying productive forces in order to stabilize the economy. It is rather the expression of human beings and their unique-ness as the tool-making species. Human beings are constantly reinventing their relationship with the natural world, forcing it to serve them in more efficient ways, expanding their population and life expectancy. The socialism of our time is an expression of this inherent human drive, in the face of the crisis of outmoded western imperialism and the rule of profits. This really existing continental socialism is the only antidote to the *Atlanticist Pathology*, the decaying mode of civilization in the west as the internationalist financial system rots within its core.

The Confused Politics of Decaying Capitalism

The tragic irony is that while 21st Century Socialism has combined elements of the left and right to move toward more prosperity, the western capitalist system has pulled the worst elements from the left and the right in its all out drive to maintain power. Many Trump supporters and right-wingers believe that Joe Biden and Kamala Harris are "Marxists" and the "globalism" they espouse is somehow in league with Chinese Communists. This is, of course, incorrect. Even in many of the most radical sounding models espoused by Marxists and Democratic Socialists in America, profits still remain in command. The irrationality of the market and the problem of overproduction that Engels so poetically describes in this classic text is not overcome.

Engels described exactly the problems facing the western-centered economy in 21st Century writing: "It is the compelling force of anarchy in the production of society at large that more and more completely turns the great majority of men into proletarians; and it is the masses of the proletariat again who will finally put an end to anarchy in production. It is the compelling force of anarchy in social production that turns the limitless perfectibility of machinery under modern industry into a compulsory law by which every individual industrial capitalist must perfect his machinery more and more, under penalty of ruin. But the perfecting of machinery is making human labor superfluous. If the introduction and increase of machinery means the displacement of millions of manuals by a few machine-workers, improvement in machinery means the displacement of more and more of the machine-workers themselves."

The computer revolution, artificial intelligence and the huge technological leaps of our time have made capitalism more and more inefficient. Human labor creates value, not machines. The more the role of the worker in production is reduced, the less surplus value the capitalist can extract in profits. The fewer and fewer workers who are hired, the less spending power is in the hands of the consumer. Engels describes this problem in depth writing: "The whole mechanism of the capitalist mode of production breaks down under the pressure of the productive forces, its own creations. It is no longer able to turn all this mass of means of production into capital. They lie fallow, and for that very reason the industrial reserve army must also lie fallow. Means of production, means of subsistence, available laborers, all the elements of production and of general wealth, are present in abundance. But "abundance becomes the source of distress and want" (Fourier), because it is the very thing that prevents the transformation of the means of production and subsistence into capital. For in capitalistic society, the means of production can only function when they have undergone a preliminary transformation into capital, into the means of exploiting human labor-power. The necessity of this transformation into capital of the means of production and subsistence stands like a ghost between these and the workers. It alone prevents the coming together of the material and personal levers of production; it alone forbids the means of production to function, the workers to work and live."

None of these problems are resolved in the "worker cooperative" fantasies of BreadTube pseudo-Marxists. None of them would end production organized for profit. For them, socialism is nothing more than an employee stock ownership program, a system where workers receive a share of the profits rather than a set hourly wage. The antagonism between employer and employee, bourgeois and proletarian, is said to be resolved by making the worker a "co-owner" of his means of production. This is exactly the kind of utopian scheme that Engels explained could not overcome capitalism, as it does not address the fundamental problem of production organized for profit.

The solution isn't voluntary worker-cooperative enterprises, but rather a centrally planned economy. As Engels explains: "This point is now reached. Their political and intellectual bankruptcy is scarcely any longer a secret to the bourgeoisie themselves. Their economic bankruptcy recurs regularly every 10 years. In every crisis, society is suffocated beneath the weight of its own productive forces and products, which it cannot use, and stands helpless, face-to-face with the absurd contradiction that the producers have nothing to consume, because consumers are wanting. The expansive force of the means of production bursts the bonds that the capitalist mode of production had imposed upon them. Their deliverance from these bonds is the one precondition for an unbroken, constantly-accelerated development of the productive forces, and therefore for a practically unlimited increase of production itself. Nor is this all. The socialized appropriation of the means of production does away, not only with the present artificial restrictions upon production, but also with the positive waste and devastation of productive forces and products that are at the present time the inevitable concomitants of production, and that reach their height in the crises. Further, it sets free for the community at large a mass of means of production and of products, by doing away with the senseless extravagance of the ruling classes of today, and their political representatives. The possibility of securing for every member of society, by means of socialized production, an existence not only fully sufficient materially, and becoming day-by-day more full, but an existence guaranteeing to all the free development and exercise of their physical and mental faculties — this possibility is now, for the first time, here, but *it is here.*"

As Engels explains, this is a struggle for state power and control of government institutions. Engels writes: "The proletariat seizes the public power, and by means of this transforms the socialized means of production, slipping from the hands of the bourgeoisie, into public property. By this act, the proletariat frees the means of production from the character of capital they have thus far borne, and gives their socialized character complete freedom to work itself out. Socialized production upon a predetermined plan becomes henceforth possible. The development of production makes the existence of different classes of society thenceforth an anachronism. In proportion as anarchy in social production vanishes, the political authority of the State dies out. Man, at last the master of his own form of social organization, becomes at the same time the lord over Nature, his own master — free."

Yet, to the forces who dominate "leftist" thought in western countries, this concept is somehow inherently "fascist." The notion of mass popular movements seeking to reorganize the economy to serve public good by utilizing state power is labelled "fascist" and "Nazbol." Trump is said to be bad because he resembles Putin, Xi Jinping, Kim Jong Un and other leaders of societies in which the economy is organized in such a manner. The fact that he rallies working people against the power structure is seen as proof that he is evil and a fascist.

However, the essence of fascism is de-growth and rigid authoritarian destruction and restraint in the hopes of stabilizing capitalism. This sounds much closer to the ideas espoused by environmentalists and climate alarmists, who scream about the need for reducing the population and consumption. They repeat the claims of Neoliberal economists that capitalism is capable of endless growth, they just think this is an inherently bad thing. They see humanity as a dangerous force that must be contained in order to bring the world "back into balance" with nature, much like Julius Evola.

The forces dominating western society have combined the belief in contradiction and struggle, the drive for instability and chaos one finds in the philosophical side of Marxism, with the contempt for humanity and the desire to contain its creative power found in right-wing anti-capitalism. While 21st Century Socialism has combined the stronger elements of the left and the right, 21st Century Capitalism has hijacked the worst elements of Marxism and Fascism.

There is certainly a "dialectical" feeling throughout western civilization, as contradictions between people have never been greater. Families, social organizations, religions, and normal cultural institutions cannot stay together. Every disagreement is exacerbated and intensified by social media and information technology. People fear each other more than ever before. The rage of humans against each other and the lack of group identity and solidarity is more apparent than ever. If "struggle" was the way civilizations advanced and always led to a higher plane by resolving contradictions, we would be closer to Utopia than ever before.

The libidinal drive for sex and violence, along with the Oedipal drive for rebellion are no longer the property of the "left" as they were in the 19th and 20th Century. The most powerful forces in the world have taken hold of them. The forces of wealth and power based in Wall Street and London seek a society where all sense of collectivism and identity is broken down. Everyone is to be an atomized individual who stands alone before society with no religion, creed, identity or set of principles to adhere to or draw from. In their scheme each individual is a *tabula rasa* on which Facebook, Twitter, and Netflix can write whatever socially-engineered message they wish to deliver with the algorithm.

But what is their plan to stabilize society? It is not socialism and public ownership and planning of the economy. It is rather a rigidly controlled capitalism in which consumption is reduced, growth is restrained, and human beings are engineered like rats in a scientific experiment, fleeing pain and chasing pleasure without self-control or overall vision. They seek to bring the world economy and environment "back into balance" by reducing human beings to a more and more animalistic plain of existence, and reducing the population overall.

A Mission of Universal Emancipation

The liberal order employs the rebellion and struggle instincts of the past-era's "left" and the economic methods of the 20th Century Fascists, all in the hopes of saving an outmoded system of production organized for profit.

But Russia, China, Venezuela, Iran, Cuba, and many

other countries will not accept their vision. Meanwhile, many working people are being forced by material conditions to depend on each other and come together despite all the mechanisms intended to prevent their solidarity. The labor movement has become more essential than ever in the age of high tech exploitation in a service sector economy. In addition to that, the lower level capitalists of the western countries see the big monopolies as their competitors. Rather than seeking to collapse the US into an "open international system" the lower level capitalists want the domestic US economy to expand so they can enrich themselves. A growing layer of US society stands in contradiction to the de-growth models of the Great Reset, asserting their human drive to live and expand.

A global block of resistance, optimism and innovation exists and is becoming more solid each day. The US labor movement, the unemployed and hungry, the low level capitalists who want growth, and the rising anti-imperialist bloc around the world all share a common enemy and a common desire. In order to defeat the big monopolies and lift the artificial restraints on human innovation they will need to unleash popular power and mass movements. Populism is returning in a confused way, as the bulk of the working class sees the dark vision of the ultra-rich as intolerable.

At the center of the emerging forces of resistance will be the proletariat, those with nothing to sell but their labor power and nothing to lose but their chains. The class of wage workers is the overwhelming majority of the human population, and it is their labor that produces along with nature, all wealth in society. It will be the involvement of millions of workers in the process of breaking humanity free from the trap of pessimism and profiteering that will be decisive. As Engels wrote: "To accomplish this act of universal emancipation is the historical mission of the modern proletariat. To thoroughly comprehend the historical conditions and thus the very nature of this act, to impart to the now oppressed proletarian class a full knowledge of the conditions and of the meaning of the momentous act it is called upon to accomplish, this is the task of the theoretical expression of the proletarian movement, scientific Socialism."

BIBLIOGRAPHY

Adler, Solomon *The Chinese Economy*, 1957

Arendt, Hannah *Eichmann in Jerusalem: A Study in the Banality of Evil*, 1963

Billington, Mike *Reflections of an American Political Prisoner: The Repression and Promise of the LaRouche Movement*, 2000

Browder, Earl *The People's Front Against Fascism*, 1936

Brzezinski, Zbigniew *Between Two Ages: America's Role in the Technetronic Era*, 1970

Chang, Ha-Joon *Economics: The User's Guide*, 2014

Ciccariello-Maher, George *We Created Chavez: A People's History of the Venezuelan Revolution*, 2013

Coffin, Peter *Custom Reality and You*, 2018

——— *Woke Ouroboros: Segregation and Essentialism*, 2023

Copeland, Vince *Market Elections: How Democracy Serves The Rich*

Dimitrov, Georgi *The United Front Against Fascism*, 1935

Dugin, Alexander *The Fourth Political Theory*, 2009

Dutt, R. Palm *Fascism and Social Revolution*, 1934

Dyson, Michael Eric *Come Hell or High Water: Hurricane Katrina and the Color of Disaster*, 2007

Engels, Friedrich *Socialism: Utopian and Scientific*, 1877

Freud, Sigmund *Civilization and Its Discontents*, 1929

Foster, William Z. *Toward Soviet America*, 1932

——— *The History of the Three Internationals*, 1951

——— *The Twilight of World Capitalism*, 1948

——— *In Defense of the Communist Party and its Indicted Leaders*, 1948

Goldstein, Fred *Low-wage Capitalism: What the New Globalized, High-tech Imperialism Means for the Class Struggle in the U.S. 2008*

——— *Capitalism at a Dead End*, 2012

Gordon, Linda *The Second Coming of the Ku Klux Klan*, 2018

Huang Yibing *Ideological History of the Communist Party of China*, 2021

Han, Suyin *The Morning Deluge*, 1972

Johanningsmeier, Edward P. *Forging American Communism: The Life of William Z. Foster*, 1994

Kautsky, Karl *The Foundations of Christianity*, 1908

Kitson, Frank *Gangs and Counter Gangs*, 1960

Klien, Naomi *The Shock Doctrine: The Rise of Disaster Capitalism*, 2005

LaRouche, Lyndon *There Is No Limit To Growth*, 1983

Lenin, Vladimir *What Is To Be Done?*, 1903

——— *Imperialism and the Split in Socialism*, 1914

——— *Imperialism: The Highest Stage of Capitalism*, 1916

Lind, William S. *The Handbook of Fourth Generation Warfare*, 2016

Lukacs, George *The Destruction of Reason*, 1954

Luxemburg, Rosa *The Junius Pamphlet*, 1915

Parenti, Michael *The Assassination of Julius Caesar: A People's History of Ancient Rome*, 2003

Mao Zedong *Report on an Investigation of the Peasant Uprisings in Hunan Province*, 1926

Marcus, Lyn (Lyndon LaRouche) *Dialectical Economics*, 1974

Marcy, Sam *Generals Over The White House*, 1979

——— *Imperialism and the Crisis in the Socialist Camp*, 1979

——— *High Tech, Low Pay*, 1985

Marks, John D. *The Search for the "Manchurian Candidate": The CIA and Mind Control: The Secret History of the Behavioral Sciences*, 1991

Marx, Karl *The Eighteenth Brumaire of Louis Bonaparte*,

1852

――― *The Communist Manifesto*, 1848

――― *Theories of Surplus Value*, 1863

――― *Critique of the Gotha Program*, 1891

Montefiore, Simon Sebag *Young Stalin*, 2007

Morgan, Ted *A Covert Life: Jay Lovestone: Communist, Anti-Communist and Spymaster*, 1999

Morris, Kenneth E. *The Unfinished Revolution: Daniel Ortega and Nicaragua's Struggle for Liberation*, 2010

Ogelsby, Carl *The Yankee and Cowboy War*, 1978

O'Neill, Tom *Chaos: Charles Manson, the CIA and the Secret History of the Sixties*, 2020

Osbourne, R. *Freud and Marx: A Dialectical Study*, 1937

Peery, Nelson *The Future is Up To Us*, 2003

――― *Black Fire: The Making of An American Revolutionary*, 1994

――― *Black Radical: The Education of an American Revolutionary*, 2007

Quigley, Carroll *The Anglo-American Establishment*, 1981

Saunders, Frances Stone *The Cultural Cold War: The CIA in the World of Arts and Letters*, 1999

Schwartz, Benjamin *Chinese Communism and the Rise of Mao*, 1951

Sherwood, Carlton *Inquisition: The Persecution and Prosecution of the Reverend Sun Myung Moon*, 1991

Starobin, Joseph Robert *American Communism in Crisis 1943-1957*, 1975

Stalin, J.V. *History of the Communist Party of the Soviet Union (Short Course)*, 1939

Strauss, Leo *Persecution and the Art of Writing*, 1952

Strong, Anna Louise *The Stalin Era*, 1956

Sorel, George *Reflections on Violence*, 1912

Therr, Phillip *Europe Since 1989*, 2016

Vaisse, Justin *Zbigniew Brzezniski: America's Grand Strategist*, 2018

Wald, Alan M. *The New York Intellectuals: The Rise and Decline of the Anti-Stalinist Left From the 1930s to the 1980s*, 1987

Weitz, John *Hitler's Banker: Hjalmar Horace Greely Schacht*, 1997

Whitney, Joel *Finks: How the CIA Tricked The World's Best Writers*, 2017

Made in the USA
Middletown, DE
07 March 2023

26289512R00235